France and the United States

France and the United States

The United States in the World:
Foreign Perspectives
Akira Iriye, Series Editor

Jean-Baptiste Duroselle

France and the United States

From the Beginnings to the Present

Translated by Derek Coltman

The University of Chicago Press
Chicago and London

*Jean-Baptiste Duroselle is professor of the history
of international relations at the Faculté des Lettres
de Paris and director of the Center for the Study of
International Relations. His publications include*
L'Idée d'Europe dans l'histoire *(1964),* Introduction
à l'histoire des relations internationales *(1965, with
Pierre Renouvin), and* Le Conflit de Trieste, 1943–
1954 *(1966).*

French edition published in 1976 by Editions du Seuil
with the permission of the University of Chicago Press

The University of Chicago Press, Chicago 60637
The University of Chicago Press, Ltd., London

© 1976, 1978, by The University of Chicago
All rights reserved. Published 1978

Printed in the United States of America
987654321   82 81 80 79 78

Library of Congress Cataloging in Publication Data

Duroselle, Jean Baptiste, 1917–
    France and the United States from the beginnings to
the present day.

    (The United States in the world, foreign
perspectives)
    Translation of La France et les États-Unis des
origines à nos jours
    Bibliography: p.
    Includes index
    1. United States—Foreign relations—France.
2. France—Foreign relations—United States. I. Title.
E183.8.F8D8713   327.73'044   78–1467
ISBN 0-226-17408-5

Contents

Foreword
by Akira Iriye   vii

Introduction:
The Hereditary Enemy   1

1   **American Revolution
and French Revolution
(1776–1814)**   12

2   **A Century of Distant
Relations (1815–1914)**   46

3   **From Neutrality to
Two Million American
Soldiers (1914–18)**   83

4   **Wilson and Clemen-
ceau (1918–20)**   102

5   **From Dissension to
Isolationism (1920–39)**   121

6   **The Liberators**   147

7   A Diminished France
     and an Unequal
     Alliance (1945–49)   169

8   The Recalcitrant
     Satellite (1950–58)   187

9   General de Gaulie and
     the United States
     (1958–69)   212

     Conclusion   240

     Selected Bibliography   255

     Index   264

Foreword

THIS BOOK IS A VOLUME in the series entitled The United States and the World: Foreign Perspectives. As the series title indicates, it aims at examining American relations with other countries from a perspective that lies outside the United States. International relations obviously involve more than one government and one people, and yet American foreign affairs have tended to be treated as functions of purely domestic politics, opinions, and interests. Such a uni-national outlook is not adequate for understanding the complex forces that have shaped the mutual interactions between Americans and other peoples. Today, more than ever before, it is imperative to recognize the elementary fact that other countries' traditions, aspirations, and interests have played an equally important role in determining where the United States stands in the world. As with individuals, a country's destiny is in part shaped by how other countries perceive it and react to it. And a good way to learn about how foreigners view and deal with the United States is to turn to a non-American scholar of distinction for a discussion of his country's relations with America.

Professor Duroselle, to be sure, is not simply a French author. His numerous writings on international relations and foreign policy have had wide impact upon historians of many countries, some of whom have been trained under his guidance at the Sorbonne. His careful research, novel interpretations, and graceful style, which is evident even in translation, have justly earned him a reputation as a diplomatic historian of major stature today. At the same time, it is also clear that to this account of French-American relations—cultural, economic, political—he brings a perspective which could have been attained only by a scholar born and educated in France. The reader follows the story of these relations through the eyes of a Revolutionary French general, a nineteenth-century French novelist, or a twentieth-century French statesman. Familiar episodes, as well as events not generally discussed in American diplomatic history, take on fresh meaning when they are put in the context of French perceptions and responses. This is a welcome addition to the literature, and, together with other volumes in this series, it serves as an important corrective to the too often uni-national accounts of the history of American foreign relations.

AKIRA IRIYE
Series Editor

I AM EMBARKING upon an almost impossible task: the reduction of the relations between two peoples, those of France and the United States, to a brief summary. These relations have existed for over four hundred years if we include the period of colonization, and for almost two hundred if we limit ourselves to the relations between two independent states.

In the colonial era there were no worse enemies than the French and British settlers in America, and one may even say that the long conflict between France and Britain, in which, between 1689 and 1815, they confronted each other in eight successive and ruthless wars, was in large part due to the feud between their respective "Americans." Indeed, this remained true for a while even after the Treaty of Paris of 1763, which confirmed the total victory of the British colonists over the French colonists and cut the latter off from metropolitan France, so that they found themselves relegated almost entirely to "Lower Canada"; there, kept in isolation by their British guardians, they nursed the knowledge that they had been abandoned by a country that was no longer their homeland, and of which they today retain nothing but the language.

After two centuries of war, however, there followed two centuries of peaceful relations. The British colonists had no sooner eliminated the threat of rivalry from the French colonists, and isolated them from France, than they in their turn cut themselves off from Britain, the symbolic date of that separation being the Fourth of July 1776. At that point, France—the France in Europe, not the France still trapped in introverted isolation on the banks of the Saint Lawrence—became their first and only ally. From that date there was never to be any

further war as such between France and the young United States—
quite the reverse, in fact, since once in the eighteenth and twice in the
twentieth century French and Americans were to fight side by side. As
Americans know, they owe their very independence partly to France.
Their army, bivouacked, after its retreat, at the famous site of Valley
Forge, not far from Philadelphia, would never have held out during
that hard winter—despite the presence at General George Washington's side of a prestigious French volunteer, the marquis de Lafayette—had it not been for the 1778 alliance. One can go further:
Britain, having grudgingly granted independence to its American
colonies in 1783, might possibly have attempted to destroy that
independence, and, moreover, could well have succeeded in such an
attempt, if she had not been forced to concentrate the greater part of
her energies for twenty years on countering the threat posed to her very
existence by revolutionary and imperial France. As a consequence,
when the last attempt was actually made, in 1812–14, it came too late
to succeed.

NORTH AMERICA IS SO VAST that the French and British settlers could
very well never have come into conflict at all, or at least might have
avoided it for another century or more, if geopolitical reasons had not
forced them into a rivalry that proved ineradicable. After all, two enormous nation-states of nine million or so square kilometers each, Canada
and the United States, separated by what is the longest frontier in the
world after that between China and the Soviet Union, have been
coexisting peacefully now for well over a century. But the explanation
of that coexistence lies precisely in the very direction taken by British
colonization, which from the beginning was always an advance from
east to west. It is significant that the creation of the Dominion of
Canada, in 1867, was promptly marked by the construction of the
celebrated Canadian Pacific Railway, an important instrument of
unification strangely parallel and similar to the great transcontinental
railroad lines already under construction in the United States.

The French, on the other hand, from the moment when Jacques
Cartier, and later Samuel Champlain, first sailed up the Saint
Lawrence, adopted a north-south axis for their expansion. Jacques
Cartier reached the site of Montreal in 1535. Champlain founded

Quebec in 1608. The earliest clashes with the English took place in the first third of the seventeenth century.

From Lake Ontario to the sea, the Saint Lawrence flows more or less parallel to the coast, which means that anyone sailing up it is traveling in a south-southwesterly direction. Having reached the first of the Great Lakes, Erie and Ontario, the French explorers, trappers, and missionaries who preceded the settlers were tempted to continue their advance along the southern shore, particularly since they found themselves hemmed in on the west by Lake Huron and then by Lake Michigan. Lake Huron was discovered as early as 1610, then Lake Michigan in 1634, one year before Champlain's death, by Jean Nicolet. Over on the southern shores the French made their way up the rivers that fed the Great Lakes. They discovered that these rivers are very short, and that by means of easily negotiated portages one could gain access to a whole network of vast watercourses, all converging upon a single tremendous river running north to south, the "Father of Waters," the Mississippi. Spurred on by Louis de Frontenac, governor of New France, Louis Joliet and the Jesuit Father Jacques Marquette reached the Mississippi in 1673.

Once it was reached, what a temptation to continue on down it! Such was the object of the famous journey made by Robert Cavelier de La Salle in 1681–82. He did in fact reach the mouth of the river, whereupon he annexed the whole of the Mississippi basin in the name of the king of France, thus founding "Louisiana," an area comprising the whole of the vast territory stretching from the Appalachians to the Rocky Mountains.

The immediate result was the founding of Fort Saint-Louis, which formed the one and only French point of defense along the whole of the immense arc intended, theoretically at least, to exclude the British settlers thenceforth from four-fifths of the country. Four years later, Cavelier de La Salle set out at the head of another expedition, intending this time to reach the mouth of the Mississippi by the sea route. This attempt failed, however, and it was not until 1698 that Le Moyne d'Iberville and his brother Jean-Baptiste Bienville rediscovered the lower course of the river. After several previous attempts to start settlements, in particular at Mobile, Bienville finally founded New Orleans in 1717, and a small French colony began to build up there.

In practice, however, despite the subsequent construction of a few scattered forts, the vast expanse of Louisiana was French in name only. New France, the Great Lakes, Montreal, Quebec, were all really too far away. Admittedly, a number of French explorers did make their way up the western tributaries of the Mississippi by canoe, and in 1742 the two La Vérendryes, father and son, reached the Rocky Mountains. But meanwhile the real threat, at first barely perceptible in this area, was to the east. That threat lay in the presence of British settlers, who were just as rugged as the French and much more numerous.

They were superior in numbers partly, perhaps, because the French national temperament has a deep repugnance for mass emigration. But it must also be said that in saddling New France, from Acadia to the Great Lakes, with an agrarian regime based on feudal rights just as intolerable as those in the home country, the court of Versailles was doing little to encourage colonization. Similarly, when Louis XIV revoked the Edict of Nantes in 1685, thereby abolishing toleration of Protestantism in France, there might perhaps have been a chance of all the uprooted Huguenots emigrating to America, had it not been for the fact that the religious intolerance of the Roman Catholic Church was even worse in Canada than in France.

To the British, on the contrary, America appeared both as a refuge from persecution and as a high road to wealth. The government in London, subjected, as we know, to constant upheavals throughout the seventeenth century, was wise enough to avoid exporting either the feudal system or religious intolerance to the Americas. In New England one could acquire freehold land upon payment of a minimal fee. Even more important, the successive groups of immigrants belonged to a great variety of religious sects—including Roman Catholics. Lastly, the climate on the East Coast, where they were settling, had the advantage of being more temperate than that in Canada. For several months of the year the Saint Lawrence was blocked by ice, whereas the Hudson remained navigable more or less the year round.

The British had not in fact been the first arrivals on the East Coast. The Florentine Giovanni da Verrazano, in a ship flying the French flag, had "taken possession" of it as early as 1524, though nothing ever came of his visit. The Spanish, to the south, had started more lasting settlements in Florida. The Dutch had founded New Amster-

dam; but the fall of that town—the future New York—and the Treaty
of Breda in 1667 eliminated the Dutch from the race. From that
moment on, the entire coast, between French Acadia in the north (the
present Canadian Maritime Provinces) and Spanish Florida in the
south, was in British hands.

It had all begun, of course, in 1585, when Sir Walter Raleigh, with
a few buccaneering companions, founded Virginia. In 1606, with
admirable generosity, James I granted to the Virginia Company the
whole of those territories stretching from the Atlantic to the Pacific
oceans. In 1607 Jamestown was founded on Chesapeake Bay.

Following on the heels of this "trading" colonization—which
before long led to the importation of African slaves—we find the
beginnings of "refugee" colonization. In 1620 came the arrival on the
Massachusetts coast of a hundred or so "separatist" Puritans, the
Mayflower Pilgrims. Further groups of nonconformist Puritans joined
them in 1629, then 1630, and founded Boston. The religious
intolerance prevalent in Massachusetts then led to the foundation of
further settlements in Rhode Island, New Hampshire, and
Connecticut.

In 1633–34, religious refugees of a quite different persuasion—
Roman Catholics, albeit accompanied by a few Protestants—arrived to
found the future colony of Maryland. Between 1653 and 1670 it was
the turn of Carolina. Then came the annihilation of Dutch power,
resulting in the creation of the colonies of New York, New Jersey, and
Delaware. Finally, in 1681, the famous Quaker William Penn received
from Charles II a concession for the huge territory that became
Pennsylvania.

From the East Coast, cut into by its broad estuaries, the coastal plain
led westward to the Appalachian foothills, then to the parallel ranges
of the Appalachians proper, beyond which lay the Appalachian plain
and the descent into the Mississippi valley.

Even before the end of the seventeenth century the situation was
ripe for a confrontation between the east-west axis and the north-south
axis, especially since a considerable numerical imbalance had by then
begun to appear between the few thousand French settlers and the
tens of thousands of British (in 1760 the figures were 65,000 as against
1,200,000). Naturally neither group of colonists knew anything
whatever about geopolitics. They were simply aware that in certain

areas they were coming into contact with other whites who spoke a
different language, whose religious practices were distasteful, who, far
from practicing solidarity of white with white, had begun entering
into alliances with the Indians (the French with the Hurons, for
example, and the British with the Iroquois), and who were savagely
contesting, not actual possession of the land as yet, but certainly the
fur trade, fishing rights (off the Acadian and New England coasts),
and communication routes (especially those in the magnificent Ohio
basin).

The state of war between the two groups became more or less
continuous and wholly ineradicable. Sometimes it lay dormant,
carried on by the Indians as proxies. Sometimes, between specific
dates, it became an extension of the Franco-British wars at home.

Before French America finally ceased to exist there were four
"official" wars, to which the French and British gave different names:

1689–97	War of the League of Augsburg, or King William's War
1701–13	War of the Spanish Succession, or Queen Anne's War
1743–48	War of the Austrian Succession, or King George's War
1754–63	The Seven Years' War, or the French and Indian War

I don't need to recount here the events of all these wars in detail, but
will merely indicate their essential characteristics.

First, the French, despite their numerical inferiority, were by no
means in a bad position at the outset. The "Canadian shield," with
its vast Laurentian forest, provided them with an extremely deep
natural line of defense. Within that forest, the myriad opportunities
for ambushes and the use of guerrilla tactics, greatly facilitated by the
skills of their Indian allies, put them at an advantage. Of the Indians,
only the vast Iroquois Confederation was in alliance with the British.
The Iroquois had traditionally served as middlemen in the west-east fur
trade, and they objected strongly to seeing themselves supplanted in
that role by the French.

The second characteristic was the enormous responsibility in the
wars borne by the two homelands. The presence of a few thousand
disciplined and experienced professional soldiers was sufficient to
reverse the situation at any given moment. In this respect the British
government enjoyed an advantage almost wholly explicable in geographical terms: since it was an island (despite its monarchs' personal

possession of Hanover since 1714), Britain could concentrate all its
efforts at sea. France, with half its national frontiers on land, found
itself burdened by costly continental wars in which England was
playing no more than an external role. This situation, together with
Louis XIV's indifference to his navy after Colbert's death in 1683,
enabled England to dominate the Atlantic. This fact had two
important consequences: (1) it was easier for England to send regular
troops over to America as reinforcements for the colonists; and (2) the
British were in a position to sail up the Saint Lawrence and threaten
Quebec, in other words, to strike at the very heart of the enemy's
possessions.

The first of the four wars produced little in the way of results. The
British raid on Quebec failed. They succeeded in taking only Port-
Royal (Annapolis) in south Acadia, and even then the town was
restored to the French in 1697 by the Treaty of Ryswick.

The second was much more successful as far as Britain was
concerned, not so much because of any American gains, but because
France, opposed by a vast coalition, was reduced to a state of general
exhaustion. By the Treaty of Utrecht, signed in 1713, France ceded to
Britain not only Acadia and Newfoundland (except for fishing rights
along several hundred miles of its coastline, from then on known as
the "French Shore") but also a huge area of the Hudson Bay
hinterland in the far North.

It looked as though the British, having acquired Newfoundland,
now had complete control of the Saint Lawrence estuary and would
thus be able to cut the lifeline of all of France's Canadian settlements.
However, just before his death Louis XIV decided to fortify Louisbourg
on Cape Breton Island, at the very mouth of the great river. From
then on, as far as the British colonists were concerned, Louisbourg
became the key to the whole problem. To take it once and for all
would mean definitive victory.

As a result, the thirty years after the Utrecht treaty, although fairly
calm ones in Europe, were certainly not a time of real peace in
America. Rivalry became even more acute in the Ohio region, where,
thanks to the Ohio Company (founded in 1715), settlers from
Pennsylvania and Virginia were advanced as far as Lake Ontario, while
the French were founding Fort Vincennes on the Wabash. At the same
time, colonists from Carolina were crossing the Appalachians, moving

down the Tennessee valley, and, with support from the local Indian
tribes, were starting to threaten the tiny French forts scattered along
the Mississippi.

The third war brought what seemed to be a decisive British success:
the taking of Louisbourg in 1745. But then, to their fury, the British
settlers heard that at the Treaty of Aix-la-Chapelle, which ended the
war in 1748, the British government had made an empire-building
deal which involved handing Louisbourg back to France in exchange for
the Indian city of Madras, which the French had recently captured.
The British colonists, caring not one iota about Madras, were utterly
unable to accept the exchange. The next phase of the conflict was
spearheaded by colonists from Virginia, who began settling the
Allegheny and Monongahela valleys, which the French considered to
be integral parts of Louisiana. In 1754, delegates from seven colonies
met in Albany—a foretaste of independent organization inspired by
Benjamin Franklin—and threatened England with secession if it did
not resume the struggle against France.

The colonists then plunged into the fourth war even before it had
been declared in Europe. Its main theater was at first the Ohio basin
and western Acadia. In 1753 the British colonists built a fort at the
confluence of the Allegheny and Monongahela rivers, on the site of
what is now Pittsburgh. The Canadians then seized it and renamed it
Fort Duquesne. A detachment sent out by the Ohio Company under
the command of one of its principal shareholders, George Washington,
clashed with a French detachment commanded by Jumonville, and the
latter was killed as he was about to parley with his opponents. The
Virginians then built Fort Necessity nearby, but were forced to
capitulate on 2 July 1754.

When informed of this event, and of the Albany Congress, the
British government decided in October 1754 to levy two colonial
regiments in America, to send over two additional regiments from
Ireland, and to put the fleet on a wartime footing. Admiral Edward
Boscawen was sent to the mouth of the Saint Lawrence, and General
Edward Braddock set out to recapture Fort Duquesne, but both
expeditions were unsuccessful. Only the Boston militia had any
success: they captured western Acadia, and those of its inhabitants who
refused to swear an oath of loyalty to George II, or hadn't already left
of their own volition, were deported to New Orleans. Braddock was

defeated and killed on the Monongahela, and Boscawen achieved nothing.

These French successes were temporary only. With an army engaged in Europe since 1756 against Frederick II of Prussia, France sent scarcely any reinforcements over to Canada, where the command of the French troops was held by the marquis de Montcalm, an astute and courageous soldier. Meanwhile, also since late 1756, the British government had been led, except for one brief interruption, by the energetic and passionate William Pitt the elder.

By 1758 Pitt's influence was being felt. He shipped over reinforcements, and on 26 July Boscawen seized Louisbourg, thus closing the Saint Lawrence. Fort Duquesne was taken in the fall, as were all the other French outposts along the Ohio. Braddock's defeat had been avenged.

From that point the end was in sight. A British fleet sailed up the Saint Lawrence carrying an expeditionary force commanded by the young and brilliant General James Wolfe. On 13 September 1759 a decisive battle took place on the Plains of Abraham outside Quebec. The British won. Wolfe was killed and Montcalm was mortally wounded. Quebec surrendered on 18 October. Montreal was unable to hold out much longer and surrendered in its turn on 8 September 1760. It was the end. The French colonists in Canada were forced to bow to British authority.

The Treaty of Paris, signed in February 1763, merely confirmed this military outcome. France ceded Canada to England, together with all its possessions east of the Mississippi, which thus became the western boundary of the British colonies. As for the western section of Louisiana, between the west bank of the Mississippi and the Rocky Mountains, that was ceded to Spain in compensation for its having belatedly entered the war on the French side.

It was not the end of the French in America—there still remained those in Canada and the small group in Louisiana—but it was certainly the end of French political power there. The French colonists became subjects of the king of England. The break with France was definitive. France had ceased forever to be a North American power.

This outcome, it should be added, was a logical one. The British—and Pitt more than anyone—were passionately concerned about North America. After all, they had almost one and a half million active, enterprising colonists over there, all chafing at the thought of their irresistible westward expansion's being blocked by a few tens of thousands of Frenchmen. By contrast, France had never shown much real interest in Canada, which, apart from its furs (dearer, incidentally, than British furs), produced nothing that couldn't be found in Europe. As far as France was concerned, it had retained the most important thing: the majority of its colonies in the Antilles. However tiny these islands were beside the immensities of Canada and Louisiana, the French considered them far more valuable. Compared with those "acres of snow" that Voltaire was so contemptuous of, the Antilles, with their sugar and spices, were a hundred times more profitable to the homeland. What was the good of vast territories to a country so disinclined to emigration? Even later on, in 1800, when France recovered Louisiana west of the Mississippi from Spain, Bonaparte still saw that reannexation purely as a means of establishing a base that would enable him to reconquer the "riches" of Haiti, whose black population had revolted. As soon as he realized that such a reconquest was impossible, he sold off the entire vast tract of Louisiana to the United States (1803).

Pitt, however, although no longer prime minister, was still far from satisfied with the 1763 peace, and with good reason. Despite illness, he had himself carried into the House of Commons and conducted a vigorous attack on the Treaty of Paris. His complaint was that it still left France with the French Shore, its fishing rights along the Newfoundland coast. In those days, when ships were still made of wood and building them presented few problems, the possession of a powerful war fleet depended above all else on the training of large numbers of crews. Only the possession of distant fishing grounds, those off Newfoundland, could automatically provide the long and difficult apprenticeship essential to produce the crews needed for any future war fleet. Without the French Shore, France would become incapable of manning a navy worth the name. Pitt was right, as the War of Independence was to prove.

THE CURTAIN HAD FALLEN. After a century of strife between "hereditary enemies," one of them had completely triumphed. From then on, for almost two centuries, the remnants of the vanquished were to find themselves relegated to the wings of the world stage. While the

---

old conflict continued between France and England, completely new relations were to be established between France and England's American colonists. So great was the change, in fact, that one sometimes wonders with a certain bemusement whether the George Washington who commanded the troops responsible for the death of Jumonville can actually have been the same person as the great leader who was a close friend of Lafayette, admired throughout France, and later the first president of the United States.

What remains of those past struggles now? Records, documents, eyewitness accounts providing material for the labors of innumerable historians. A closeknit group of six million French-speaking Canadians in Quebec, New Brunswick, Nova Scotia, and the far North; another million scattered across the prairie provinces; a tiny nucleus of French-speakers in Louisiana, where an intense interest in the French language has recently begun to develop. And place names: Louisiana itself (named after Louis XIV), New Orleans (named after the French regent Philippe d'Orléans), the towns of Marquette and Joliet, Lake Champlain, Lake Pontchartrain, and the great city of Detroit; Des Moines and Baton Rouge, both with populations of over 100,000; and countless other places: Eau Claire, Fond du Lac, Seul Choix Point, Charlevoix, Gouverneur, Bellefontaine, Terre Haute, Du Bois, and so on. Finally, throughout the Middle West, there are innumerable La Salle, Joliet, and Marquette streets or avenues, vestiges of an epic whose traces, scattered across that vast tract of the globe's surface, still persist.

WHEN, AFTER A LONG STRUGGLE with England, the representatives of the thirteen colonies met in Philadelphia to proclaim the independence of the United States of America, on the Fourth of July 1776, it was by no means certain that France would intervene in the affair. Having lost its white colony in Canada, and with no overseas possessions except the mouth of the Senegal, a number of islands in the Antilles, and five cities in India, it had nothing to fear, as Spain had, from the disturbing example of colonists rebelling against their mother country. But it was itself prey to the most serious internal difficulties, which the French king, Louis XVI, like his grandfather Louis XV, who had died in 1774, was showing himself far from capable of resolving. There was a financial crisis—a trade deficit and a vast internal debt—that was made even more difficult by the fact that the burden of national taxation fell mainly on the peasants, since the privileged classes, the nobles and the priests, were largely exempt. There was also a crisis of royal authority, with more than one resemblance to recent developments in Britain. The French *parlements*, pointing out that they were empowered to register all laws, and also to make "remonstrances" prior to such registration, were struggling to acquire a power analogous to that of the British Parliament. But despite the use of the same word (*parlement*, parliament) in both countries, the French *parlements* were really no more than courts of law, membership in which was confined to nobles and was in practice hereditary. They enjoyed great popularity, because they openly resisted royal power; but that popularity was scarcely justified, since they also energetically defended the right of the privileged classes not to pay taxes. Louis XV had attempted to destroy their power by dissolving them. Louis XVI, in an ill-advised act of demagogy, had reconvened them.

Given such troubles, was this the time for France to enter into another war? Would it be wise, moreover, for an absolute monarch to defend the rebellious subjects of another monarch or to encourage the setting-up of a republic, however distant? It might prove a dangerous example.

Furthermore, those who most admired the Declaration of Independence in France were precisely those inimical to its absolute monarchy: the *philosophes* and their disciples. The vague image of North America then prevalent in France was greatly influenced by two noteworthy concepts. First there was the idea of the "state of nature," so dear to the heart of Rousseau, closely linked with the time-honored myth of the "noble savage." Many Frenchmen sincerely believed that man in America—and this applied to Indians and colonists equally—was naturally good. The other concept was a result of the strongly Latin-based culture common to all intellectuals of the time. They saw the rebellious colonies as akin to the early Roman Republic, and a republic, Montesquieu had said, must be founded upon "virtue." In consequence the insurgent colonists were viewed as plain-living worthies, and George Washington—the erstwhile enemy—as a new Cincinnatus, the peasant general ready to go back to his plow once the victory had been won. The fact that Washington was in fact the owner of Mount Vernon, a huge and prosperous plantation, along with a great many slaves, tended to be ignored.

All these ideas are to be found in many books, the most famous of which was the one by the Abbé Raynal published in 1770: *Histoire philosophique et politique des établissements et du commerce des Européens dans les deux Indes*. This was written in reply to an anti-American book, *Recherches sur les Américains*, written by the Abbé Cornelius de Pauw and published in Berlin in 1768. It is worth recording that the most celebrated French writer of the day, Voltaire, after initially admiring Pauw, later became a supporter of the ideas put forward by Raynal, one of which went as follows: "As our own peoples grow weaker and all succumb one to another, so the population and agriculture of America will grow; the arts will take root there swiftly, having been transplanted by us; this country, sprung from nothing, is impatient to take its place on the face of the globe and in the history of the world." In the year of his death, 1778, Voltaire left his retreat at Ferney to pay a visit to Paris. There he met Franklin, who was a regular visitor to the salons frequented by the *philosophes*, a friend of Mme Du Deffand, Mme Helvétius, the Abbé Morellet, the physician Pierre Cabanis, the encyclopedists Jean d'Alembert and Denis Diderot, the philosopher Anne Robert Turgot, and "everyone to be found in Paris of any note, either in literature or government" (Mignet, *Vie de Franklin*, p. 124). Voltaire uttered a few words in English and spoke the phrase "God and Liberty" over his spiritual grandson by way of a blessing. If I add that one of the principal agents in the secret negotiations with America was the famous playwright Pierre-Augustin Caron de Beaumarchais—author of those celebrated and disturbing satires on the nobility, *The Barber of Seville* (1775) and *The Marriage of Figaro* (written in 1776 and performed in 1783)— then it becomes only too clear what mistrust the royal court may well have felt toward the Americans.

1. French intervention (1778–83)

There were two men who played a decisive part in the French decision to help the young United States: the comte de Vergennes and Franklin.

When Louis XVI formed his cabinet, he chose not to recall the duc de Choiseul, who until 1770 had been laboring to reconstruct the French fleet. Instead, he selected as his prime minister—albeit without that title—the comte de Maurepas, a courtier and former secretary of state for the navy. As his finance minister he named the economist Turgot. And as minister for foreign affairs he settled on Charles Gravier, comte de Vergennes, a career diplomat who had for several years been French ambassador to Sweden. "He was a man of quiet sense, lacking any true genius. He had a taste for work, and the daily labors he imposed upon himself made him one of the world's best-informed men" (Castries, *La France et l'indépendance américaine*, p. 105).

There was in France a pro-English party, led by the ambassador in London, the comte de Guines, and encouraged by the queen, Marie-Antoinette. Turgot, though not a member of this group, was nevertheless also hostile to war—for quite different reasons.

"We ought to avoid war," he said, "as the very greatest of misfortunes, since it would render impossible, for a long time and
perhaps forever, a reform that is absolutely necessary to the prosperity
of the state and the relief of our peoples."

Vergennes was not of the same opinion. Kept well informed by the
secret missions carried out by Beaumarchais in England and Achard
Bonvouloir in the United States, he aimed at the restoration of French
power, so humiliated by the 1763 Paris treaty. In 1775 he wrote his
"Réflexions" (a secret report) for the king, in which he concluded that
the Americans had taken an irrevocable decision and that England
would oppose them with all its strength. "The inveterate enmity of
that power imposes upon us the duty to lose no occasion of weakening
it, so that we cannot but gain by seizing the one now being offered; we
must, therefore, give support to the independence of the insurgent
colonies." Another argument put forward, by Beaumarchais this
time, was that an alliance with the insurgents was the only way of
preserving the French Antilles. Failing such an alliance, the British
and Americans would enter into a reconciliation and seize the French
islands.

Turgot agreed that the Americans should be given a million pounds
in aid but continued to oppose war. The king, apprehensive of
Turgot's reformist tendency, decided to dismiss him in May 1776.
Vergennes's hands had been untied. He undertook to add consignments of arms to the gift of money. Thus, even before the Declaration
of Independence, France had already agreed to aid the colonists
indirectly.

The Declaration enabled Vergennes to go even further. During a
council meeting on 31 August 1776 at Versailles, he read the king a
memorandum in which he advocated an alliance with the United
States, not with a view to regaining the lost colony of Canada, but as a
means of weakening the British. He predicted that such an alliance
"would not be one of those ephemeral bonds brought into existence,
then broken again by the need of the moment. Since no interests can
divide two peoples whose communication is across vast tracts of ocean,
the inevitable trade relations established between them must form a
link, if not eternal, then at least of very long duration" (quoted in
Castries, *La France et l'indépendance américaine*, p. 139). Despite this
exhortation, Louis XVI contented himself for the moment with

dispatching a naval squadron to the Antilles and increasing his financial aid and arms consignments. Another eighteen months had to pass before Vergennes's project could be realized.

One does not enter into alliances with the defeated. Both French public opinion and the French government waited with passionate interest for news of the war. After the loss of New York and other setbacks that caused the insurgents' commander-in-chief George Washington grave concern, the latter at last achieved two notable successes in late 1776 and early 1777, at Trenton and Princeton.

It was just before these successes that Versailles saw the arrival of the man who, along with Vergennes, was to be the great artisan of the Franco-American alliance, Benjamin Franklin. This printer, publisher, businessman, scientist, and philanthropist had spent much time in England and had already visited France before, in 1768. And of course he had helped Thomas Jefferson in drafting the famous Declaration of Independence. It was thus hardly surprising that Congress's secret Committee of Correspondence should have decided to supplement its representatives in France—the Connecticut merchant Silas Deane and Richard Henry Lee, formerly an American agent in London—with the prestigious Franklin. The three men had been directed not only to negotiate for subsidies and arms but also to achieve an alliance with the French and Spanish Bourbons, linked at that time by the "Family Compact." Deane was a hesitant man, while Lee was quarrelsome; so Franklin assumed leadership of the delegation from the outset. True, he spoke very bad French, but he was very famous as a scientist and *philosophe*, and, what is more, he was a Freemason. His misleadingly ingenuous manner and his bourgeois clothes delighted the French at a time when Marie Antoinette herself was playing the shepherdess in her Petit-Trianon farmyard. Although not officially accredited, Franklin was regarded very highly by the French government. Even more important, he already possessed, or knew how to win, the admiration of the various groups of influential men and women who created public opinion in France.

He landed on the southern coast of Brittany, at the little port of Auray on the Gulf of Morbihan, on 6 December 1776. He traveled to Paris via Nantes and took up residence at Passy. The French government was unable to receive him as an ambassador as long as it continued not to recognize the United States—which would automatically have entailed war with England—but Vergennes had a secret meeting with him on 28 December 1776, then a more official one on 5 January.

Once more it was clear that the conclusion of the alliance was dependent on the fortunes of war, and during much of 1777 these were running against the Americans. Besides the British navy, Washington was having to fight two armies for every inch of ground in New Jersey and outside Philadelphia. On 25 September, Philadelphia was in fact taken, by the marquis of Cornwallis's second-in-command, Admiral Richard Howe. Meanwhile, General John Burgoyne, setting out from Canada in command of the northern army, moved south around the Great Lakes, in July took Fort Ticonderoga, and was dangerously close to Albany on the Hudson. But his lines were overextended, the Americans harassed him relentlessly, and on 17 October he was forced to surrender at Saratoga. It was the first great American victory, and it set the seal on the French alliance.

For one thing, when the news of it reached Vergennes on 4 December, it convinced him that total victory for the insurgents was now a possibility. In addition, he had apparently learned that a British agent named Wentworth had crossed the English Channel with the intention of entering into peace negotiations with Silas Deane. If he did not seize this opportunity to act, he might never have another. On 17 December, without even the certainty that Spain would support him, he promised the American envoys imminent recognition of the United States. On 7 January 1778, Louis XVI gave the royal consent. Two treaties were speedily drafted, then signed on 6 February. By the terms of the "treaty of friendship and trade," France recognized the United States of America, and both countries promised to develop their trade with each other—a clause that was no mere formal flourish, since in the eighteenth century all homelands customarily retained a monopoly over trade with their colonies, and it was only in 1776 that the United States had repudiated that monopoly. The treaty of alliance further laid down that if hostilities should break out between France and England, neither of the allies would lay down arms separately before independence had been "officially or tacitly achieved." So France had pledged herself to the cause of United States independence, and in return the United States guaranteed France's American possessions, including any of the British-held Antilles she might conquer. At the same time, France renounced all claims to any territories east of the Mississippi and in the Burmudas.

While the approval of Congress was still pending, France began preparations for war. On 13 March, Britain was informed that France had recognized the United States. Hostilities began at sea on 17 June 1778. Congress received the two treaties on 2 May and ratified them two days later.

GENERAL WASHINGTON had waited all winter for this great news. Since the British under General William Howe were occupying Philadelphia, he had taken up position at Valley Forge, about twenty miles outside the city, in a camp consisting at first simply of tents, then later of log cabins. It was cold. There was a shortage of both food and clothing. And there was also an intrigue afoot to oust Washington in favor of Horatio Gates, the victor of Saratoga.

During the long wait for the news from France—which arrived in the form of a letter from Franklin that reached Valley Forge in April 1778—Washington had drawn strength from a celebrated friendship, that with Gilbert Du Motier, marquis de Lafayette, a young man scarcely twenty years old and therefore twenty-five years his junior.

Several European officers, mostly French, had already offered themselves as volunteers on the side of the insurgents. The first, in 1776, had been the chevalier de Kermorvan. If Lafayette has become the symbol of Franco-American friendship, it is because he belonged to the very highest ranks of the aristocracy, because he had already attracted a great deal of attention to himself, because his departure for the United States had provoked incidents, and lastly because, almost as soon as he arrived, Congress conferred on him the rank of major general in the United States army.

At seventeen Lafayette had married a fifteen-year-old daughter of the duc d'Ayen. His wife's grandfathers were both famous men, the Maréchal de Noailles and the chancellor d'Aguesseau. Lafayette had inherited a vast fortune and set about using it to lead an extremely licentious life, whereupon his father-in-law had him posted to the garrison at Metz. While there, he heard about the American colonists' cause from the visiting duke of Gloucester, brother of George III and a supporter of American independence. Lafayette, who hated the English—his father having been killed in a battle against them—made up his mind to fight for the Americans. It meant he would be able to exchange the dismal life of a French garrison officer for one of high adventure that would bring him military glory. Through a secret agent, the baron de Kalb, he was put in touch with Silas Deane. Then he secured leave of absence from the French army and set about trying to leave the country on a ship, *La Victoire*, that he had bought in Bordeaux. Louis XVI disapproved. The ship was unable to sail, and Lafayette learned that he was about to be arrested. However, on 20 April 1777 he did finally manage to weigh anchor and in due course arrived with de Kalb and a number of other officers at South Inlet in South Carolina. On 27 July he arrived in Philadelphia, where he promptly appeared before Congress, presented letters of recommendation from Deane and Franklin, announced that he wished to serve the United States without pay and at his own expense—a gesture made possible by his private fortune—and was thereupon commissioned as major general. On 1 August 1777, at a dinner for members of Congress, he met Washington for the first time. The latter "decided to take this young officer under his wing as a flesh-and-blood symbol of French support for the American cause" (Castries, *La France et l'indépendance américaine*, p. 157). "I came over here to learn, not to teach," Lafayette told Washington in the course of a review. During the whole of that winter of 1777–78, Lafayette remained beside Washington at Valley Forge. When news of the alliance arrived, the American army was reformed. On 18 May 1778 Lafayette took up his first command and went into action against the British. On 18 June Admiral Howe ordered General Henry Clinton to evacuate Philadelphia and fall back on New York.

THE REOCCUPATION OF PHILADELPHIA by the Americans was the first indirect consequence of French intervention. It was fear of the imminent arrival of a French fleet and French troops that had led Howe to abandon the city. According to the British historian Marcus Cunliffe, in his biography of Washington, Valley Forge marked the low point of the American war effort. On the other hand, he points out, historical hindsight now makes it clear that the French alliance provided the turning point of the war. As soon as the British were once again grappling with their old enemy, and with Spain, their naval supremacy was in doubt. From then on, as long as the French kept their word, victory and independence for the United States were already in sight. For Vergennes was meanwhile using his diplomatic skills to such good effect that he eventually persuaded Spain, and later Holland, to intervene as well, and in 1780 fostered the formation of the League of Armed Neutrality, which was extremely disadvantageous to the British.

THE ASSISTANCE PROVIDED BY FRANCE in the War of Independence was both complex and decisive. I shall give no more than a general summary of it here; but it is clear that many individual episodes have acquired great emotional value in the psychological history of the two peoples. On 17 June 1778, for example, the British frigate *Arethusa* attacked the French frigate *La Belle Poule*, which the next day evaded further attacks from two British ships and managed to regain Brest. Admiral Louis d'Orvilliers promptly left Brest at the head of thirty-two ships of the line and eleven frigates, determined to avenge the incident. On 27 July he came upon a British fleet under Admiral Augustus Keppel in the open sea off the Ile d'Ouessant: 2,282 British cannon against 1,944 French. With the wind set against him, Keppel elected to fall back to Portsmouth. Louis XVI congratulated d'Orvilliers, and Keppel was courtmartialed. Militarily the incident had little significance, but it was the herald of much more important ones.

It was the Toulon fleet, commanded by Admiral Jean Baptiste, comte d'Estaing, that was to undertake the first major operation. With twelve ships of the line and fourteen frigates, carrying the first French ambassador to the United States, Gérard, comte de Munster, as passenger, together with Silas Deane, who had been recalled by Congress, d'Estaing dropped anchor in the mouth of the Delaware on 7 July 1778. Lafayette made contact with him without delay. Both were from the Auvergne, Lafayette having been born at the Château de Chavaniac near Brioude, d'Estaing at the Château de Ravel not far from Clermont-Ferrand. D'Estaing speedily succeeded in having Louis XVI's order to arrest Lafayette rescinded. But the combined French and American operations suffered a setback at Newport. D'Estaing withdrew with his fleet to Boston, and some sourness became apparent in Franco-American relations (one must remember that the two had been enemies, inveterate enemies, until less than twenty years before). Washington held d'Estaing in high regard, however, and it was decided that Lafayette should sail back to France to ask for reinforcements. He was given a triumphal welcome in Brest, where he arrived on 6 February 1779, while d'Estaing was sailing south to carry the war into the Antilles.

The year 1779 saw the beginning of Spanish intervention, but also the failure of a plan to invade England, for a very specific and unpredictable reason: the French fleet commanded by d'Orvilliers—a good sailor but too old and insufficiently decisive—was prevented from sailing because of an epidemic of scurvy and smallpox. As for d'Estaing, who had been summoned to the Antilles to beat back a British attack on Georgia from Florida, he too suffered a setback off Savannah and was forced to sail back to Brest.

Faced with these reversals, and under pressure from Lafayette, the French government rather hesitantly adopted a new strategy. Since it was impossible to make a landing in England, why not send an expeditionary force to the United States? The decision to do so was taken on 2 February 1780. Lafayette had hoped to be given the command, but he was still only twenty-three and had served very little in the French army. He was passed over for a man of fifty-five, Lieutenant General Jean Baptiste Donatien de Vimeur, comte de Rochambeau. "He was a brave soldier, an excellent strategist, and what is more a man of great soul and noble character. His appointment contributed decisively to the American victory" (Castries, *La France et l'indépendence américaine*, p. 236). The expeditionary force was to consist initially of six thousand men. Lafayette sailed ahead of it, landed at Boston on 28 April 1780, and set off immediately to rejoin Washington and inform him of Rochambeau's imminent arrival.

On 2 May 1780, Rochambeau's force left Brest. It dropped anchor at Newport, Rhode Island, on 11 July and set about preparing for the campaign. But it was forced to wait for the arms and ammunition still on their way from Brest, and the British meanwhile succeeded in blockading Newport. On 20 September Washington and Lafayette met Rochambeau at Hartford, Connecticut. Their joint plan of campaign was finalized, Washington requested troops and credit from Congress, and Rochambeau sent for reinforcements from France. Liaison between the French and Americans was to be effected through the post at West Point.

Then came the notorious treachery of General Benedict Arnold, the commander of West Point, who sold himself to the English for thirty thousand pounds and almost brought about the capture of Washington and LaFayette. The arrest of Major John André, the British officer who had been acting as Arnold's go-between, caused the plan to misfire. Nevertheless, no decisive operations could now be undertaken in 1780.

Marquis Charles-Eugène Gabriel de Castries, the new French minister for the navy, decided to send out a powerful fleet under Admiral François Joseph comte de Grasse, who was to assume command of all the French warships on the American coast, with Louis Antoine de Bougainville and Barras under him, while bailli Pierre-André de Suffren was dispatched on an expedition to India. Two other able admirals, the comte Luc-Urbain de Guichen and comte Toussaint de La Motte-Picquet, were sent to the Antilles. There, as well as off Gibraltar, Majorca, and Minorca, numerous operations were carried out that contributed to keeping large numbers of British warships away from the coast of the United States. Their outcomes varied a great deal, and in April 1782, in a naval battle off Dominica, de Grasse was to be defeated and taken prisoner by the British admiral George Rodney.

It was in 1781, however, that the crucial point was reached. It was decided that the French naval forces should be concentrated down near Chesapeake Bay, so that they could operate off Virginia, where Lafayette was engaged at the head of an American army. Barras's squadron sailed down from Newport, while de Grasse returned from the Antilles, bringing thirty-two hundred French troops. Rochambeau, with four thousand more French troops from Rhode Island, joined forces with Washington on land, and together they marched through Philadelphia amid tremendous popular acclamation. All this meant that the French and Americans were converging from three different directions on the British base at Yorktown. De Grasse, with the support of Bougainville, attacked the British fleet under admirals Thomas Graves, Samuel Hood, and Sir Francis Samuel Drake, early in

September 1781. The British ships were forced to withdraw. By 28
September Yorktown was under siege, and despite all the efforts of
Cornwallis, the British general, it was forced to surrender on 19
October 1781. Eight thousand British troops were taken prisoner and
214 guns captured. The concentrating maneuver of the two allies had
meant that Yorktown was finally surrounded by nine thousand French
and seven thousand American troops, not to mention the twenty
thousand French manning the fleets of de Grasse and Barras.

Enthusiasm in the United States ran high. Congress voted to erect
statues in honor of de Grasse and Rochambeau. In France too, there
was a similar explosion of enthusiasm at the news of the victory. Not
only did Yorktown set the seal on Franco-American friendship, it also
meant that the war was to all intents and purposes won. However, as
Cunliffe points out, after this triumphant apogee the war did in fact
drag on for two more long and wearisome years, in a mixed
atmosphere of exuberance, doubt, and recriminations. There were no
more important battles after Yorktown. De Grasse set off back to the
Antilles, where he was to experience defeat and captivity. The French
troops left Virginia in 1782. But most important of all, the British
were evacuating all their forts one by one and had stopped sending
over reinforcements. Peace was assured; but there still remained the
problem of its terms.

2. The first disagreements: The peace of 1783 and the war debts

In the course of the first peace negotiations in their history, the
Americans had the opportunity to make certain not uninstructive
observations: first, that members of a coalition, however apparently
united by shared dangers and the thrill of victory during the course of
the actual war, may stumble across many subjects for disagreement if
their interests differ; second, that negotiations conducted by one able
man are more valuable than complex diplomatic parleyings in which
delegates of different temperaments and opinions are all working in
isolation from one another; and third—and this remained true until
the invention of the telegraph—that distant plenipotentiaries have
only too many opportunities to exceed their instructions.

As a result, the peace signed at Versailles on 3 September 1783, far

from ushering in a Franco-American alliance and the beginning of
lasting relations, was accompanied by wrangles, or at least by recriminations, between the two countries.

As was customary under *l'ancien régime*, peace negotiations had
been started while the war was still being fought, even though they
did not reach a stage of any importance until 1782. At that point, with
the fall of Yorktown, it became clear that Britain was not going to
succeed in regaining its colonies. But it was equally clear that despite
its financial difficulties, as well as the troubles in Ireland and a
political crisis at home, it was countering the French and Spanish
offensives in the Mediterranean and the Antilles very successfully
indeed. The one great obstacle was the determination of George III
himself not to yield to the insurgents. But George III, as it happened,
was also a symbol of the monarchy's attempts to regain supreme
power, and in that respect he was viewed as an opponent by the
Whigs. His prime minister, Lord North, who knew perfectly well that
the struggle was over, had made approaches to France in March 1782.
The failure of the resulting meetings had brought about his fall, and
he was replaced by Lord Rockingham, a Whig, with Charles James Fox
at the Foreign Office and the earl of Shelburne as minister for home
affairs. Together, they speeded up the peace negotiations. The death
of Rockingham on 1 July 1782, and the appointment of Shelburne as
prime minister after Fox's departure, made it possible to overcome the
king's last efforts at resistance.

Clearly England had no choice but to accept the independence of
the insurgents. But at least the damage could be lessened by
attempting to drive a wedge between France and the United States.
Such a course might at least enable Britain to retain the trade
monopoly with the new state which it had automatically enjoyed while
the United States was still a colony.

Spain, which had still not recognized the independence of the
British American colonies, had ambitions in America embarrassing to
Vergennes, who somehow had to cope with the divergent wishes of his
two principal allies. Having acquired sovereignty over Louisiana in
1763, Spain now wished to extend that sovereignty, south of the
thirty-first parallel at any rate, over the whole of western Florida, as
well as over all the territories between the Mississippi and the
Appalachians. It also wished to ban American shipping on the lower

Mississippi, though it was prepared to recognize the whole of the Ohio region south of the Great Lakes as British. Thus the Americans, having been blocked to the west before 1763 by the French, would now continue to be so, on the north by the British and on the south by the Spanish.

The insurgents naturally rejected such a solution. What they wanted first and foremost was independence, but they also had economic preoccupations very much on their minds: they meant to have access to the Mississippi and navigation rights on it. They also wanted their fishing rights extended northward to New England and Newfoundland. Two of their negotiating team—John Jay, ambitious but muddleheaded, and John Adams, whose hostility to France sprang from national pride and resentment that the United States hadn't been left to liberate themselves—allowed the British negotiator Richard Oswald to convince them in August 1782 that France was betraying them. She had already sent a representative, Joseph-Mathias Gérard de Rayneval, to London. Might she not attempt to support the Spanish claims? Might she not be seeking to recover Louisiana from the Spanish, to whom it had been ceded in 1763 in compensation for their support? Might she not attempt to regain Canada, despite the treaty of 1778? Any of those three outcomes would mean a halt to western expansion, a return to the same situation that had prevailed in the seventeenth century and in the eighteenth until 1763. The Americans were not going to accept that at any price. As Jay wrote on 27 November 1782, referring to the French: "They are interested in separating us from Great Britain, and on that point we may, I believe, depend upon them; but it is not their interest that we should become a great and formidable people, and therefore they will not help us to become so" (quoted by Stourzh, *Benjamin Franklin*, p. 174). The third American negotiator, Franklin, understood Vergennes and the French position infinitely better. But he was extremely ill with gout. As a result, Jay and Adams were negotiating with Oswald without informing Vergennes—or even Franklin, to a large extent—of what they were about. Such secrecy was strictly contrary to the formal instructions of Congress, which had laid down that no negotiations were to be carried out except with the knowledge of the French.

The bargaining between the Americans and the British centered on recognition of independence and the status of the eastern bank of the

Mississippi. In lieu of total recognition the Americans accepted a compromise: Oswald was accredited to negotiate with "the delegates of the committee appointed by the colonies designated as the Thirteen United States." In exchange for this, the frontier was to run down the center of the Mississippi—with navigation and trade rights for both countries—and a northern frontier was agreed upon that left England with Canada and certain other territories between the Saint Lawrence and New England. The agreement was signed on 30 November 1782.

Was France really harboring the dark designs imputed to her by Jay and Adams? It is indisputable that she wished to keep the young United States under her tutelage, as it were, and to obtain the trading advantages laid down in the treaty of 1778. She had also promised Spain in the 1779 Treaty of Aranjuez not to end the war until Gibraltar was once more under Spanish rule. But the siege of Gibraltar had failed. Compensations therefore had to be found for Spain. The American negotiators were in error, however, when they credited France with territorial ambitions of her own. When Franklin passed the text of the treaty on to Vergennes, he found himself in a very embarrassing position. He was almost prepared to think that the American delegates had acted dishonestly. That was naturally the opinion of Vergennes, since a separate peace between Britain and the United States must appreciably weaken France's position in her own negotiations. Moreover, the United States was in desperate need of money. It took all Franklin's diplomatic skills to obtain a fresh loan of six million pounds on 21 December 1782. He publicly exposed the errors of the American delegation, spoke inspiringly of Franco-American friendship, and reestablished in France the confidence that the activities of Jay and Adams had so severely undermined. Up until his death in 1790 Franklin continued to proclaim to his compatriots the necessity for maintaining friendship with France: "If we were to break our faith with this nation . . . England would again trample on us and every other nation despise us" (quoted by Stourzh, *Benjamin Franklin*, p. 179).

Franklin reassured Vergennes by convincing him that the agreement of 30 November 1782 would be applied only within the framework of the general peace treaty. Moreover, with the consent of Spain, Vergennes was able to sign a preliminary treaty of his own with

England on 20 January 1783. The final treaty, embodying essentially all the preliminary agreements unchanged, was signed at Versailles on 3 September 1783, and despite the political agitation across the Atlantic that year—many soldiers were urging the setting up of a monarchy, an idea that General Washington himself, a republican by conviction despite his aristocratic temperament, would have none of— Congress ratified this important agreement in early 1784. As the American historian John Richard Alden rightly claims, with their independence already recognized by France (since 1778) and Holland (since 1782), the United States was never again to find itself refused full participation in "the concert of nations" (quoted by Alden, *The American Revolution*, French ed., p. 386).

IF FRANKLIN is the American who best symbolizes the American attitude toward France between 1777 and 1783, it may confidently be claimed that during the next thirty years that role was played by Thomas Jefferson. In turn minister to France from 1784 to 1789, secretary of state from January 1790 to December 1793, leader of the Republican opposition to the Federalists, vice-president from 1797 to 1801, and finally president of the United States from 1801 to 1809, his role was a considerable one. He represents neither the very francophile attitude of Franklin nor the francophobe tendency of John Adams. His position was much more balanced and merits analysis, since it may fairly be said that many Americans to this day display an attitude toward France inspired by the same principles and the same feelings. There have been many admirable studies of the man, in particular that by an eminent French historian, Gilbert Chinard, who from 1908 until his death in 1971 pursued his profession in the United States. His very situation led Chinard to take a passionate interest in the psychological relations between the two peoples, and to him Jefferson was first and foremost "a unique spectator of his age."

Like Washington, Thomas Jefferson was a Virginian and a great landowner; but he was born in 1743 and was thus younger by eleven years. His plantation, Monticello, about a hundred miles from Williamsburg (one of the most historic towns in the United States and still meticulously preserved today) consisted of ten thousand acres, and he took an active interest in its management. He was also a lawyer. Exceptionally well educated, he could read Greek and Latin at sight and was thus never at a disadvantage with the French intellectuals he met in Paris. His curiosity led him to take an interest in the sciences and jurisprudence, and he was the principal author of the Declaration of Independence. Whereas Washington's greatness was that of a military leader, Jefferson appears above all in the light of a philosopher and a legislator. His friend the marquis de Chastellux described him as "an American who without ever having quitted his own country is at once a musician, skilled in drawing, a geometrician, an astronomer, a natural philosopher, legislator, and statesman" (quoted by Saul K. Padover, *Jefferson*, p. 106). It should also be added that, unlike Washington, he was not in favor of slavery.

In 1782 his wife died, and he accepted the post of plenipotentiary in Europe alongside Franklin, Jay, and Adams. But the winter ice, then an English expedition, prevented his departure, so that news of the preliminary peace talks reached him while he was still in America. On 27 May 1784, Congress appointed him minister with full powers to negotiate trade treaties with foreign nations alongside John Adams and Dr. Franklin.

> Jefferson was then forty-one years old. He knew life and men and had no illusions. . . . But neither his disappointments nor his sorrows had made him a misanthrope. . . . The tall spare man in black was no longer able to feel his heart moved by the early emotions of his youth. Next to Washington, who remained in America, and to Doctor Franklin, a debonair patriarch, he was the most famous national figure of America. None was better qualified . . . to represent America and to speak for his country.
> . . . He felt also that he had a certain mission and intended to fulfill it: it was to convey to the European statesmen whose wiles he distrusted the impression that the United States existed as a country, that they did not form a loose and temporary confederation of States, but a nation to be reckoned with and respected (Chinard, *Thomas Jefferson*, pp. 153–55).

This time the weather smiled on his crossing. Jefferson arrived at Portsmouth nineteen days after leaving Boston, and reached Paris on 6 August 1784.

After remaining subordinate to Franklin for some months, he became sole minister, or in other words ambassador of the United States to the court of Versailles (where Vergennes was to die in 1787).

He was thus a spectator of the years immediately preceding the French Revolution and of its beginnings, since he did not leave France for good until 8 October 1789, two days after Louis XVI had been forced to return to Paris.

Before studying Jefferson the observer, however, we must look at Jefferson the active participant. Everything was to hinge on economic problems, although Jefferson was also to remain extremely vigilant with regard to possible territorial ambitions on France's part and was in particular mistrustful of various "explorations" being made by French subjects west of the Mississippi. The situation was a foreshadowing of the one we shall meet during the years directly after World War I, only on a smaller scale with the roles reversed. French finances were in a disastrous state, which the War of Independence had done nothing to improve. This economic situation, together with the aspiration to liberty, was to prove one of the major causes of the Revolution, since the main motive behind the convening of the Estates-General in 1789 was the hope of finding solutions to the financial crisis. The United States owed a great deal of money to the French crown (not to mention debts to private individuals like Beaumarchais and to the *fermiers-généraux* [tax-farmers], plus the repayment of the much less substantial loans granted by Holland and Spain). In 1783, the debt—including the 4 percent interest on it—amounted to twenty-eight million francs, plus the extra six million Franklin had obtained early in that year, making thirty-four milllion in all. France had also made gifts amounting to twelve million francs not included in that figure. Added to all this was the back pay still owing to a large number of French volunteers, less wealthy than Lafayette. Finally, the United States also owed considerable sums to British subjects, on debts incurred before the war.

But the United States was itself in the worst possible financial situation. Congress and individual states had prodigally been issuing paper currency and now had no idea how to pay the interest, other than by fresh loans.

The only way of paying off so huge a debt was by trade. The Americans would simply have to export more to France than they imported from her. But that course was made difficult both by the disparity in the two countries' technological development and also by the inveteracy of old habits, themselves linked to self-interest. For example, it was very difficult to persuade the *fermiers-généraux* administering the French tobacco monopoly to take their supplies directly from Maryland or Virginia rather than via London. In just the same way, a hundred and thirty years later, the United States was to insist on France repaying her debts while at the same time raising its own tariff barriers to an extent that made such repayment impossible.

Jefferson, influenced like Franklin and many other Americans by the French physiocrats and Adam Smith, believed in the benefits of free trade, a term that in those days implied the abolition of colonial monopolies. (It is worth noting that France gave the Americans permission to trade with her possessions in the Antilles, whereas England, despite its desire for a reconciliation, remained firmly opposed to any such trade with the British "Sugar Islands"). This was already a foreshadowing of the "new diplomacy"—the term was first used in 1793—based on the theory that trade, when shorn of all privileges and monopolies, would encourage peace by replacing violence and the henceforth pointless hunger for territorial possessions. Thus, in Franklin's words, the "general good of mankind" would join with "the national interest," and foreign policy would become a moral activity (Stourzh, *Benjamin Franklin*, p. 254). True, other, noneconomic factors still played their part in the external policies of monarchies. "A war, to acquire that territory and to retain it, will cost both parties much more, perhaps ten times more, than such sum of purchase money. *But the hope of glory and the ambitions of princes are not subject to arithmetical calculations*" (quoted by Stourzh, p. 241). A republic, free from such hankerings after prestige, could have much more "moral" policies than any monarchy. Already we see appearing the notion of "moral superiority," a "missionary" aspect in American foreign policy, together with that particular brand of unconscious nationalism, widespread ever since, that makes so many Americans believe, in all sincerity, that "what is good for America is good for the world." This belief was to increase steadily during the next two hundred years, and in the 1950s was even to lead to a "great debate" between such celebrated writers as George Kennan and Hans Morgenthau, both advocating the abandonment of moralizing attitudes and illusions— Morgenthau's book was entitled *In Defense of the National Interest*— and others, such as Dexter Perkins and Frank Tannenbaum, who continued to defend the notion that American policy really is "more moral" than the policies of other countries.

International morality, according to Jefferson, must be maintained. He asserted energetically that the United States, even though it could not repay its debts just at the moment, nevertheless considered them sacred and would pay them one day. Apart from the moral advantage of this position, it also paid psychological dividends. It strengthened the financial as well as the moral credit of the United States at a time when new loans were needed to pay off the interest on the old, or at least on that made by the Dutch, since the French government did not seem unduly concerned over the matter.

Apart from establishing this principle, however, Jefferson did not achieve any spectacular results. He was deeply humiliated by his country's inability to repay its debts, and he also felt himself to be at a disadvantage in his negotiations. The ten thousand dollars his government had allocated him for his embassy was insufficient to provide the sumptuous receptions that, as a great Virginia landowner, he had been accustomed to. This humiliation reached its nadir when the former French volunteers staged a demonstration in order to secure the back pay still owed to them, and Jefferson had great difficulty in persuading them not to bring suit. He was also wounded by the criticisms of his government expressed by the Assembly of Notables of 1787. In the end, he attempted to solve the problem by two successive methods, both of which proved unavailing. First, he tried to convert the "political" (state to state) debt into a "commercial" debt: certain Dutch bankers proposed to set up a company that would lend the United States the millions of francs then due to France in interest; the sum would from then on be owed by the United States to the banks, and not to any state. Toward the end of 1787, to Jefferson's great despair, Congress rejected this proposal. He then devised another plan: to pay the debts with some of the assets that would accrue to his government from the sale of several million acres of land west of the Appalachians. But this procedure proved much too slow, and by the end of his term as minister Jefferson had still not settled the problem. It is noteworthy, by the way, how modest the French were in their demands during the whole of this affair. Was this discretion perhaps the result of political worries at home—the increasingly overt opposition to royal power—distracting the court's attention from the

American problem? The yawning hole in the royal finances was certainly such that even immediate repayment of the debt in full—which was materially impossible—would not even have begun to solve France's financial problems, since the annual national budget at that time was somewhere in the region of eight hundred million francs.

As Jefferson himself said, trade was the only way the United States could repay its debts, and during the whole of his five years in France he labored to increase the volume of Franco-American commerce. He had some successes, in particular the lowering of French duties on such American products as whale oil, pearl ash, furs, leather, and timber. In addition, since France was going through a period of famine at the time, he managed to persuade the French to buy American salted meat and fish, as well as wheat and rice. In 1789 the United States exported $3.3 million worth of goods to the French Antilles and $1.4 million worth to France (the dollar then being worth approximately four francs). At the same time, the marked American preference for British products kept French exports to the United States down to $155,000 worth from France itself and $1.9 million worth from the French Antilles. The resulting trade surplus could therefore be employed—in the future—for repayment of the American debts.

JEFFERSON'S ATTITUDE toward the French nation was less wholehearted than that of Franklin, and very typical of Americans in all ages. He was attracted by the peculiar charm of the French life-style, by the French *douceur de vivre*, and like many Americans worked assiduously at becoming a connoisseur of French wines and cooking. He appreciated French fashions and French skill in the luxury trades. Above all he loved their books. The society he moved in was more or less that of Franklin's friends: Mme Helvétius, Destutt de Tracy, the Abbé Morellet. He had his female admirers, Mme de Houdetot, Mme de Tessé, a cousin of Lafayette, and Mme de Corny—with whom he was in love—as well as a number of very good men friends, in particular Lafayette, who assisted him in all his diplomatic endeavors, and the marquis de Chastellux. He had many meetings with Vergennes and with his successor comte Armand-Marc de Montmorin. He made journeys to England, to various other European countries, and also through France: the Côte d'Azur, Avignon, Nîmes, Montpellier, Frontignan, Carcassonne, Bordeaux, Rennes, Angers, Tours. Wherever he went, he was an assiduous observer and investigator of both agriculture and industry. "Were I to proceed to tell you how much I enjoy their architecture, sculpture, painting, music, I should want words. It is in these arts they shine" (letter to Bellini, quoted by Chinard, *Thomas Jefferson*, p. 174). Yet, despite the charm of French manners, he never lost his preference for the American way of life. For one thing, it was only a tiny French elite that enjoyed the charm: "the great mass of the people suffer under physical and moral oppression; but the condition of the great if more closely observed cannot compare with the degree of happiness which is enjoyed in America. Among them there is no family life, no conjugal love, no domestic happiness; intrigues of love occupy the young and those of ambition, the elder part of the great" (*ibid.*, p. 173).

Such was the image of France, clearly a stereotype, that he brought home with him. But he also brought a conviction that absolute monarchy alone was responsible for those ills. As Chinard summarizes it:

> A well-meaning king, not by any means a tyrant, unable to prevent the dissolution of the nation, a corrupt hereditary aristocracy, in the main narrow and selfish, a State religion, monopolies, a standing army, *lettres de cachet*, no freedom of the press, everywhere ignorance and misery: such was the picture of France that presented itself to his eyes; and conditions were such that they could not be remedied effectively except through a bloody revolution (*ibid.*, p. 202).

3. The United States and the French Revolution

The French Revolution may be said to have begun with the meeting of the elected Estates-General on 5 May 1789. Originally divided into three estates—clergy, nobility, and third estate—this body, despite the king's opposition, transformed itself into the National Constituent Assembly. The storming of the Bastille on 14 July was a symbolic expression of resistance to royal reaction. On the night of 4 August all privileges were abolished. At the end of that month a Declaration of the Rights of Man and of the Citizen was adopted—a document on which Lafayette had consulted Jefferson. On 6 October, two days before Jefferson left and was replaced by Gouverneur Morris, the king was forcibly brought back to Paris. There he was obliged to remain, to all intents and purposes a prisoner, his Roman Catholic faith outraged by the reforms in the status of the church passed by the Constituent Assembly. The king's attempted flight in June 1791, culminating in his arrest at Varennes on the eastern border, meant that he was viewed by the most extreme "clubs" (Jacobins and Cordeliers) as a traitor. Under the Legislative Assembly (October 1791–September 1792) the declaration of war against Austria raised tension to the explosion point. On 10 August 1792 the mob stormed the Tuileries palace. The Constitution was annulled. A National Convention was elected, and it proclaimed the Republic on 20 September 1792. On that same day, at Valmy, the revolutionary armies won their first great victory.

The dangers inherent in the war were to lead to the trial and then the execution of the king (21 January 1793), to the victory of the extreme "hard-liners," the Montagnards, and finally to the creation of a Committee of Public Safety, of which the leading figure was Maximilien Robespierre. Along with Lazare Carnot, Robespierre succeeded in achieving victory against a vast coalition of European sovereigns, but he also ushered in the Reign of Terror.

The revolutionary tide first showed signs of ebbing when Robespierre and his friends were arrested and guillotined on 9 Thermidor (27 July 1794). The Thermidorian Convention survived until October 1795, practicing more moderate policies. The constitution it voted on and adopted, that of the Directory, preserved the Republic (with five directors presiding over it), but it was a regime characterized by poverty among the masses, *coups d'état*, corruption, and a mixed succession of military defeats and victories. One of the victorious generals, Napoleon Bonaparte, brought the Directory to an end with his *coup d'état* on 18 Brumaire Year VIII (9 November 1799), and it was Bonaparte who was to govern France until April 1814, first as consul, then from 1804 onward as emperor of the French.

Viewed from America, all these events seemed a long way away. Yet those violent upheavals were to have profound effects on Franco-American relations.

First, it must be remembered that events in America since 1776 had made the United States very popular with French liberal opinion. But the image that had grown up of the new nation was vague in the extreme. Happily there existed the group referred to as *les Américains*, meaning those who had firsthand knowledge of the New World— for the most part former volunteers or officers who had fought in the War of Independence. The most famous of these was of course Lafayette, who also played a very important part in the early days of the French Revolution, first in 1789 and then, to an even greater degree, in 1790, which one of the great historians of the Revolution, Georges Lefebvre, has termed "the year of Lafayette." On 14 July, when the people of Paris were seeking weapons to use against the royal troops—and it was in order to seize supplies of arms that they stormed the Bastille—they formed militias that took the name "National Guard." Lafayette was immediately named commander-in-chief of this National Guard, an appointment that invested him with enormous power.

> The "hero of two worlds" with his chivalry and magnanimity dazzled the bourgeoisie, who were thrilled to have such a leader. A great lord, at once magnificent and liberal in his ideas, he was likewise an enormously impressive figure to the populace. . . . His dream was to become France's Washington, to rally the king to the cause of the Revolution and the Assembly to the idea of a powerful and active executive. Filled with naïve optimism, and also quite certain of his own genius, he set out to walk this high wire while his friend Jefferson trembled for him and Gouverneur Morris sarcastically foretold his fall (LeFebvre, *La Révolution française*, p. 42).

Thus, just before he left France, Jefferson was able to write to James Madison assuring him that it would be impossible to wish for a more friendly attitude toward the United States than that expressed by the Constituent Assembly. At every turn, he said, the Assembly was actually adopting actions taken in America as its models (see Chinard, *Thomas Jefferson*, p. 240). Indeed, when Franklin died in 1790, the Assembly went into mourning.

Lafayette himself also had a great many connections in the United States. He had personally urged George Washington, in a letter written in January 1788, to accept nomination as first president of the United States, "in the name of America, of all mankind, and of your own fame."

Lafayette was no republican, however. Despite the hatred he felt for the queen and his bafflement at the king's attempted escape, he still sought to shore up the latter's power. As a result, after the "second French Revolution"—the fall of the monarchy on 10 August 1792— he left the army he was commanding and, accompanied by a number of fellow officers, went over to the Austrian camp, where he was made a prisoner. It is worth recording that Washington provided Madame de Lafayette with financial assistance during that time.

On the American side, francophile feelings remained lively. Jefferson, by then secretary of state, wrote to Lafayette, "Wherever I am, or ever shall be, I shall be sincere in my friendship to you and to your nation" (quoted by Chinard, *Thomas Jefferson*, p. 274). In February 1791 Jefferson was expressing hopes that a republic would be set up in France. When the Republic was declared, a large section of American opinion applauded the move and greeted the victory at Valmy with enthusiasm. Jefferson did not recognize the new government immediately, but he made no protest at the execution of Louis XVI. The opponents of the new French Republic in the United States were all on the side of the party in power, the Federalists; mostly they were great admirers of England and were markedly aristocratic by temperament. Washington himself belonged to this group. The precipitating agent of their hostility was to be the ill-judged behavior of the new ambassador sent over by the National Convention, Citizen Edmond Genêt.

The Convention was under the impression that it had made a good choice when it appointed Genêt on 19 November 1792, since he was both a friend of Jefferson and an admirer of the United States. But Genêt entertained the most erroneous notions about the possibilities presented by the solidarity between the two republics. Moreover, he had a positive genius for diplomatic blunders. He had no sooner landed, on 8 April 1793 at Charleston, than—before even presenting his credentials or consulting the American government—he launched an eloquent appeal to the citizens of the United States to come to the aid of France, which had recently become embroiled in yet another war with England. Yet the fact was that this latest war had no "American" motives behind it at all, having been caused by the invasion of Belgium by French troops and the Convention's decision, unacceptable in London, to reopen the port of Anvers, which had been closed since the early seventeenth century. Genêt soon followed words with actions. He began arming privateer vessels in American ports—fourteen of them between July and October—and enrolling volunteers. Then he set out for Philadelphia, though not before learning that on 22 April President Washington had proclaimed United States neutrality.

From Charleston, where he had landed, to Philadelphia, his march had been a triumph. The citizens of Philadelphia, hearing that the President might refuse to receive him, had even decided to give him an ovation and to meet him at Gray's Ferry. He delivered his credentials on May 18, and at once communicated the object of his mission in a style which now appears grandiloquent, but simply reflected that enthusiasm for America which was running so high in France at the time (Chinard, *Thomas Jefferson*, p. 291).

In the event, Washington, who viewed the disorder and Terror then reigning in France with great distaste, received Genêt very coolly. But it was mainly the excessive zeal displayed by "Citizen Genêt" himself that, before many weeks were out, had exasperated not only most of American public opinion but even the leader of the francophiles, Jefferson himself. Genêt behaved as though the United States were a country he had conquered, and thus deeply wounded American pride. By late summer the Americans had decided to ask the Convention for Genêt's recall. On 31 December 1793, the very day on which he handed in his resignation as secretary of state—partly for internal reasons, because as leader of the Republicans he was totally at variance with the Federalist Hamilton—Jefferson wrote Genêt a letter of reprimand. The Convention did in fact recall Genêt, though it is worth noting that in order to avoid the guillotine he in fact remained in the United States and eventually became an American citizen!

In addition to the Genêt affair, and simultaneous with it, there were two other episodes, both connected with the war and both much more serious. So serious were they, in fact, that they put an end to the 1778 Franco-American alliance.

Since Britain had by now regained its naval superiority, France, in order to continue the struggle at sea, was making use of "privateers"—armed ships of various sorts issued with "letters of marque" to distinguish them from pirates, who were of course bandits in common law. The British riposted by vigorously upholding their right to board any ship, search it, and then—if a prize court so directed—seize both vessel and cargo if they were intended for the enemy. The French privateers adopted the same procedure.

The 1778 treaty had included two important clauses, however: (1) The French recognized freedom of neutral trade for United States vessels in times of war. Therefore French warships and privateers were not permitted to seize American ships. (2) France was to enjoy not only most-favored-nation treatment in American ports but also what were termed "exclusive rights": her privateers were entitled to sail freely into American ports with their prizes, then freely leave again without payment of any toll or duty. Access to American ports was to be forbidden, on the other hand, to all enemy warships and privateers—which in this instance meant British vessels.

In May 1793, yielding to the necessities of trade and war, the National Convention violated the first of these clauses by ordering the seizure of any neutral vessel (in other words, including American ships) with an enemy port as its destination. In October 1794 there were three hundred American ships being held in French ports as a result of this decision. Ulane Bonnel, an American historian, has established that in the period prior to 1800 there were 834 such seizures. In consequence, there were thousands of American sailors being held virtually prisoner in French ports—although it is only fair to add that a great many of them solved their predicament by signing on with French privateer vessels! (Bonnel, *La France, les Etats-Unis, et la guerre de course*, p. 115).

The Americans then violated the 1778 treaty in their turn, and even more seriously, by concluding a trade treaty on 19 November 1794 with Britain (the Jay Treaty). This came as a particularly disagreeable surprise to the French, because since 1 August 1794 the United States minister to France was no longer Gouverneur Morris—who was not only as big a blunderer as Genêt but led a scandalous private life to boot—but James Monroe, the future president of the United States, who was a friend of Jefferson's, a Republican, and an avowed francophile. Monroe (who was to remain in Paris until 30 December 1796) had in all good faith been categorically denying the rumors that had begun to circulate about the possibility of just such an Anglo-American treaty. Hence the shock when it was learned in Paris not only that the treaty had been signed but that it gave England rights as most favored nation—which meant that France's "exclusive rights" had been abolished—and granted British privateers access to American ports. Worse still, England made no recognition whatever of freedom for neutral shipping, and loftily announced the maintenance of its right to board and search. The treaty was not actually a formal repudiation of the 1778 alliance, but it was only a hair's-breadth away.

It does seem paradoxical to find the hitherto excellent relations between France and the United States deteriorating in this way just at the moment when France became a republic. The cause lay in the war and in American trade interests. Despite the risks of seizure, the Americans were sending a great many ships over to France and England, since the profit on such ventures was well over 200 percent. But the volume of trade with England was much greater. Bonnel has set out the consequences of these facts on American public opinion with great lucidity.

> The Federalists (Washington, Adams, Marshall), northern govern-
> ers and magistrates, businessmen, sailors, inheritors of the country's
> government from the English, preached hatred of the French
> Revolution and its leaders and wanted to make common cause with
> England; the Republicans, on the other hand (Jefferson, Madison,
> Monroe), southern landowners, intellectuals, still looked to France
> as the source of their republican faith, even while deploring the
> excesses of the Revolution, and strove to prove that the damage
> caused to American trade by England was considerably greater than
> that caused by the French. Every episode of the struggle between
> France and England was to find an echo, in the United States, in
> the political struggle between the two parties (Bonnel, *La France,
> les Etats-Unis, et la guerre de Course*, pp. 54–55).

Accurate though it is, this stark antithesis does need some qualification. Beyond doubt, Washington was pro-British. But he had no wish for war or even for an alliance with England. His hostility to alliance with any European power was made very clear in his celebrated Farewell Address of December 1796 and was to become the golden rule of American foreign policy for the next one hundred fifty years. Jefferson, despite the accusations of his enemies, was no Jacobin and wanted neither war nor an alliance with France. It was he, not Washington, who coined the term "nonentanglement." What he advocated, in Chinard's phrase, was "total Americanism." The United States, its trade now expanding at a remarkable rate, was already what we would term "isolationist." But it was having great difficulty convincing the two greatest powers of the day that it was no longer dependent on them and that it must be treated as an equal.

It was under the presidency of the Federalist John Adams (1797–1801), with the Republican Thomas Jefferson as vice-president—in accordance with the electoral system then in force—that the crisis with France was to reach its height, in the form of the "Quasi War," the "Undeclared War," or, as Adams himself referred to it, the "Half War." It was this episode which (apart from the days immediately after the North African landings on 8 November 1942) was to provide the only example in history of bloodshed between France and the United States.

The Undeclared War was simply a worsening of the situation already existing since 1794. In 1795 the Convention had been replaced in France by the Directory, and in 1796 exchanges between the two countries had already begun to turn sour. Protests on both sides became more vigorous, and by early 1797 Monroe had been forced to leave France. On 16 May 1797, John Adams convened an extraordinary session of Congress to request the institution of measures for the nation's defense. Then, in October 1797, he sent three delegates, John Marshall, Charles Cotesworth Pinckney, and Elbridge Gerry, to Paris. Talleyrand accorded them a brief interview, then negotiated with them through three emissaries. But then their negotiations were complicated by the XYZ Affair, so called because in the ensuing debates in Congress Talleyrand's three delegates were referred to by those letters. It was a complicated and shady business. It appears that as a precondition of any negotiation Talleyrand wanted a "bribe" of $250,000, in return for which he would arrange for France to request from the United States a large loan and a new treaty to replace that of 1778. Naturally nothing came of all this, but a number of documents relating to the negotiations were published. The result, in the United States, was a scandal leading to a triumph for the pro-British Federalists. Jefferson was insulted, caricatured, lampooned, and accused of having sold himself to France.

Adams did not declare war, but a state of "quasi war" was to exist from 1798 to 1800. Adams ordered the capture of all French ships wherever they were encountered. American trading vessels were armed and authorized to resist any French attempt to board and search by

force. He placed an embargo on all French products, including those
from the Antilles, and supported the rebels of Saint-Domingue, the
present Republic of Haiti. The Directory instituted similar measures,
with the result that there were a great many incidents, seizures of
shipping, and minor skirmishes.

Very soon, however, one becomes aware on both sides of what the
best historian of this Undeclared War, Alexander De Conde, calls the
"decline of the martial spirit." Talleyrand made overtures and
announced that he would welcome a new American minister to Paris.
Adams jumped at the opportunity and in early 1799 appointed the
former American minister to the Netherlands, William Vans Murray,
to the post. In October he sent over two more delegates to assist Vans
Murray in negotiating a new treaty with France. Upon disembarking at
Lisbon on 27 November 1799, the two representatives received news
of the *coup d'état* in France, on 18 Brumaire, that had brought the
thirty-year-old General Bonaparte to supreme power. They did not
arrive in Paris until 2 March 1800. Bonaparte promptly received them
at the Tuileries palace and appointed a French delegation to be
headed by his brother Joseph Bonaparte. After arduous negotiations,
during which Bonaparte defeated the Austrians in Italy at Marengo, a
treaty was signed on 3 October at Mortefontaine, Joseph's estate,
eighteen miles north of Paris, where he subsequently gave a magnificent entertainment to celebrate the event.

The terms of this new agreement included the reciprocal restitution
of all captured property, the payment by the French state of debts due
to American citizens, free trade between the parties in accordance with
the principle of most favored nation—which represented a demotion
for France from her former "exclusive rights"—and freedom of
neutral trade other than war contraband. This treaty, finally ratified
by the Senate in 1802, brought the Undeclared War to an end. It fell
far short of resolving all the problems; but it did mean, as article two
stipulated, that the 1778 alliance was no longer operative.

4. The United States and Napoleon Bonaparte (1800–1814)

The Undeclared War partly explains the subsequent success of the
Republicans and Jefferson's election to the presidency in 1800. Not
only did it present them in the light of moderates in comparison with

the Federalist "war hawks," but it also left the Federalist party divided, since Hamilton, an advocate of explicit war, had parted company with the more moderate and cautious Adams. As Alexander De Conde has pointed out, the agreement signed at Mortefontaine "helped secure the goodwill of Bonaparte, and thus laid the ground-work for the acquisition of Louisiana two years later" (*The Quasi War*, p. 338).

Louisiana, in 1803, comprised not only the lower Mississippi basin but the entire territory between the Mississippi River and the Rocky Mountains, so that its acquisition, which doubled the surface area of the United States at a stroke, is inevitably seen as the most important event in Franco-American relations during the era when the United States was governed by Jefferson and France by Bonaparte, two men as different from each other as it is possible to imagine.

Yet that acquisition should not make us forget another funda-mental factor: the constant struggle between the world's two largest sea powers, France and England. This struggle, which had been going on since 1793 and was broken off only for one brief period by the Peace of Amiens in 1802, certainly led to a great many irritating incidents between the neutral Americans and the two belligerents. But it also had the immense advantage, as far as the young United States was concerned, of neutralizing not only any desires for revenge harbored by England (still regretting the loss of its colonies) but also any possible ambitions on the part of Napoleon.

Pierre-Louis Roederer, one of the French negotiators of the Morte-fontaine agreement, had grasped this fact clearly: "The United States are too near our colonies for it not to be useful to us to have them as friends." The United States, he went on, could not really isolate itself from Europe, since it had "a powerful interest in the liberty of the seas" and in "the equilibrium of the Powers of Europe" (quoted by De Conde, *Quasi War*, p. 337).

In this context, Jefferson appears as an isolationist, in theory at least, and consequently as indifferent to the balance of power in Europe and a champion of American moral superiority. In his inaugural address of 1801 he declared, in a "prophetic and inspired" tone, that America had become

> a standing monument and example for the aim and imitation of the people of other countries; and I join with you in the hope and belief

that they will see, from our example, that a free government is of all others the most energetic; that the inquiry which has been excited among the mass of mankind by our revolution and its consequences, will ameliorate the condition of man over a great portion of the globe (quoted by Chinard, *Thomas Jefferson*, p. 397).

He was not, of course, advocating any kind of proselytism: it was by example alone that the United States was to act. But, as Chinard suggests (p. 398), there was a "naïve and almost unconscious imperialism" involved. On 31 October 1801 Jefferson wrote to a friend, assuring him, "The day is within my time as well as yours [that we shall] say by what laws other nations shall treat us on the sea. And we will say it" (quoted by Chinard, p. 399).

It was in October 1800, by the terms of the Treaty of Saint Ildefonso, that France obtained the retrocession of Louisiana from the Spanish, to whom it had been ceded in 1763. The treaty was a secret one, since France was unable to occupy the territory there and then; and it was not until March 1801 that Rufus King, the American ambassador in London, was informed of the transfer. For Jefferson and his isolationist policy the news was a genuine disaster. As Saul K. Padover points out, it brought all his hopes of remaining aloof from European affairs crashing to the ground at a single blow. After all, Spain was so weak that no one in the United States was particularly concerned over the thought of huge areas of the American continent being under her domination. Eventually a way would be found to take Florida and Louisiana away from her. But the France of Napoleon was quite a different matter.

Jefferson faced the bleak prospect of having to ally with England, the nation he most distrusted, against France, the nation he most liked. It was a bitter choice. The day, Jefferson said grimly, that Napoleon's troops set foot on the soil of New Orleans, that day "we must marry ourselves to the British fleet and nation" (letter to Robert Livingston in Paris, quoted in Padover, *Jefferson*, p. 315).

American public opinion was on the whole in agreement.

Jefferson had absolutely no knowledge of Bonaparte's intentions. It does seem, however, that the latter never felt any strong desire to start an empire on the American continent. What he did want was to use New Orleans as a base for the reconquest of Saint-Domingue, in those days regarded as much more important than Louisiana itself for reasons of trade. But the insurrection in Saint-Domingue proved victorious. General Charles Leclerc, husband of Napoleon's sister Pauline Bonaparte, had met his death there, and in France the *idéologues*, who were friendly toward America, particularly the *philosophe* Comte de Volney, were favoring a peaceful transfer of the territory to the United States.

Negotiations over this cession began under the leadership of the American minister, Livingston. Jefferson then decided to employ the additional services of an old friend, the economist Pierre Du Pont de Nemours, who had been living in the United States but in April 1802 was preparing for a visit to France. As a preparatory measure, the president persuaded Congress to vote a credit of two million dollars to be used as seemed fit. Finally, in March 1803, Jefferson decided to send James Monroe over to France to assist Livingston in the purchase of a section of Louisiana and, if possible, of western Florida as well. Secretly, he had authorized him to go as high as fifty million francs (about twelve million dollars) without consulting Congress.

To his great surprise, Monroe found the situation in France much more favorable than he had expected. Bonaparte had already decided, on 10 April, to give up Louisiana. By the time Monroe arrived in Paris, Livingston had already signed a preliminary agreement, and the treaty was concluded on 2 May 1803. Whereas Livingston had asked only for New Orleans and had discussed Florida, Talleyrand had in fact offered him the whole of the French territory. Only the price remained to be haggled over. Bonaparte wanted a hundred million francs. Livingston and Monroe offered fifty. Finally both parties settled for sixty million francs (fifteen million dollars), which was in excess of the limits set not only by Congress but even by the president. It is true, however, that the new price was for the *whole* of the territory. "It was a phenomenal bargain," Saul K. Padover writes. "After Livingston had signed his name to the treaty, he exclaimed prophetically: 'From this day the United States take their place among the powers of the first rank' " (Padover, *Jefferson*, p. 320). The Senate eagerly ratified the Louisiana Purchase by twenty-four votes to seven.

Once this transaction had been completed—a magnificent one for the United States and a reasonable one for France, albeit without any direct profit—relations between the two countries became dominated entirely by the savage struggle for world leadership between France and England. Jefferson's policy consisted in a defense of American foreign trade against both Napoleon's Continental System and the British blockade of France. Despite innumerable incidents with the French, it was against England that American grievances were most bitter. On pretext of recovering deserters from their own ships, the British were practicing "impressment," in other words, seizing American vessels and press-ganging their crews. Since the accents were still indistinguishable in those days, they were forcibly signing on sailors of both nationalities. The Embargo Act of December 1807, banning British products, did not succeed in stopping this form of recruitment, so odious to the Americans.

Even without entering into a formal alliance with either France or England, the United States still found it very difficult to avoid being drawn into the struggle. There were in fact several occasions when open hostilities were only just averted before Congress finally did declare war on England, on 18 June 1812, for two very specific reasons: first, on account of the British impressment and blockade, and second on account of the danger represented by Britain's Indian allies in the Great Lakes area. France had nothing to do with it. From 1812 onward she was far too preoccupied with the European coalition already threatening to crush her. June 1812, which saw the start of what has been called the "Second War of Independence," was also the month when Napoleon's army, to its great misfortune, marched into the vastnesses of Russia. The American people were divided, and the antiwar Federalists accused President Madison and his party of having wanted to help Napoleon. It need hardly be said that the argument was purely polemical. The American military operations, the Treaty of Ghent in December 1814, and Andrew Jackson's victories had nothing whatever to do with the abdication of Napoleon in April 1814, the restoration of the Bourbons, the return of Napoleon, the Hundred Days, or the battle fought on 18 June 1815 at Waterloo.

THE TREATY OF GHENT freed the United States from all British threat. Henceforward, London was to make no further attempts to reestablish sovereignty over the lost colonies, and any territorial differences were always settled by friendly negotiation (the northwest frontier, Oregon). Post-Waterloo France was meanwhile once more under the rule of the Bourbons, who were unpopular, it must be admitted, but at least not given to expansionism. In 1825 they even officially accepted the independence, acquired in practice in 1794, of the former colony of Saint-Domingue, now Haiti.

On the *political* plane, therefore, relations between the two countries were to remain both secondary and desultory. Any crises or difficulties were always to prove susceptible to settlement by peaceful means.

On the *psychological and intellectual* plane, however, things were otherwise. Although the interest felt on the American side with regard to France remained limited, other than in certain well-defined sectors of public opinion, the French were passionately interested in the achievements of the distant United States. It is in France, rather than in Britain or Germany, that we find the most remarkable analysts of the American reality. Even apart from such writers, however, the French public as a whole took a lively interest in the distant republic.

Most important of all, however, was the slow but inevitable change taking place in the power relations between the two countries. The word "power" is ambiguous. If it is to refer solely to available military strength, then the disproportion between French and American resources may be viewed as changing hardly at all. In 1815, even in defeat, France remained a great military power. In 1914, its army on a peacetime footing numbered 750,000, whereas that of the United States consisted of a mere 75,000, plus a militia of 120,000. The American navy had by that time outstripped its French counterpart but was in turn still outclassed by both the British and the German fleets. On the other hand, if we are talking about *potential* power rather than actual numbers, a strength essentially economic and demographic in nature, then the reversal is total. In 1814 the United States had a population of about nine million, France of twenty-eight million. By 1914, France still had less than forty million, whereas the American figure was almost a hundred million. Admittedly, that figure can almost be matched if we count in French colonial possessions; and since the colonies provided troops, they did, indisputably, increase France's effective strength. But all the same, a million or so white colonists apart, almost all of them in North Africa, none of the inhabitants of the colonies were actually French citizens with full rights, sharing the life-style of France itself. Resistance to French domination was as yet very limited, but nationalism was nevertheless already a rising force in some places, and the day was to come when the colonies would be a drain on French power rather than a contribution to it.

If we consider the land surfaces involved, we find that France plus its colonies occupied a slightly larger area than the United States. But if we restrict ourselves to the two states themselves, then the France of 1914 occupied less territory than the France of 1815—it had annexed Nice and Savoy but had lost Alsace and Lorraine—and its area was fourteen times smaller than that of the United States (excluding Alaska, Hawaii, Puerto Rico, and the Philippines).

Without going into detailed statistics, it is equally clear that the economic potential of the United States had increased vastly and that in this respect it had become by 1914 the world's foremost power, outstripping both Britain and Germany, with France occupying only fourth place.

Lastly, as a result of continuing immigration from Europe, a profound change had taken place in the composition of the American population. In 1815, the whites in the United States were exclusively British in origin, and this British preponderance, boosted by a high British immigration rate during the rest of the nineteenth century, was to be maintained. Nevertheless, by 1914 we already find closeknit groups of German-Americans, Irish-Americans, Italian-Americans, and others originating from Scandinavia, Greece, the Slavic countries, and so on. What we do not find, however, is any such group of French-Americans. Let us be quite clear about this: it is true that several tens of thousands of French people settled in the United States, but they had all come over as individuals. Nowhere was there any specifically French community capable of carrying political weight as a voting body or psychological weight as a result of bonds maintained with its country of origin. As a result, every European country eventually developed such links with the United States *with the single exception of France*. This situation developed only slowly, but it was bound to have an influence on the future of Franco-American relations.

1. Political relations: The main phases

Since France had relinquished all the territories it had possessed in North America (apart from the two tiny islands of Saint Pierre and Miquelon and two small islands of the Antilles group, Martinique and Guadeloupe) in 1763, 1803, and finally 1815, relations between the two countries could not be direct ones. In addition, Britain had now ceased to be a threat to the United States, so that the new nation's security was absolute, and Washington's advice in his Farewell Address—not to become involved in European affairs, not to conclude any alliance in Europe—could be faithfully adhered to. This meant that there could no longer be any question, where France was concerned, either of alliances or of territorial problems. That being so, there remained only the problems connected with trade or the liquidation of certain debts, and those involving Latin America. It is therefore hardly surprising that the word ''France'' appears scarcely at all in the indexes to general histories of the United States covering the period we have now reached.

On the political level relations were intermittent and correct. The most important dates involved were 1823, 1861–65, and 1898.

After the Congress of Verona (1822), at which the conservative powers banded together to stifle the liberal movements in Europe, the France of Louis XVIII conducted a brief military operation in Spain that successfully restored the Spanish monarch to the position of

absolute power that he had lost, in 1821, as the result of an army
rebellion. This was of no interest whatever to the United States (which
had bought Florida from Spain in 1819) as long as Latin America did
not appear to be involved. For Latin America was then in open
rebellion against Spanish domination, and the independence movement was victorious everywhere, with the full support of the United
States and encouragement from England. Yet it was those very
Spanish troops instrumental in bringing the liberals to power in 1821
who were about to reestablish Spanish domination in America. There
was good reason to fear that, with the return of absolutism, a new
expedition might be organized and sent across from Spain, and
President Monroe believed that the "Holy Alliance"—a somewhat
inappropriate term used to denote the reactionary European states—
might send troops as well, Russia and France in particular. George
Canning, then the British foreign secretary, also became disturbed at
this possibility, and suggested to Monroe a common declaration of
Latin American independence. These fears did not last. On 9 October
1823, the comte de Polignac, the French ambassador in London, gave
formal assurance that his country had not the slightest intention of
sending troops to the Western Hemisphere. This partly explains why
the president of the United States chose to express unilaterally, and
without any previous agreement with Canning, what soon came to be
known as the Monroe Doctrine (2 December 1823). Any European
intervention in Latin America, any expansion of the European colonies
in America, would be "dangerous to our peace and safety." Con-
versely, the Americans affirmed that they would eschew all involvement in European affairs.

   After this one brief instant during which credence was given to the
existence of a French "threat," France vanished almost totally from
American foreign policy. A period began, lasting until at least 1862,
when the Americans came to view their two former partners in
increasingly different lights. With Britain there was the long frontier
with the future Dominion of Canada to be settled, a task that made
close and continuous relations a necessity. With France no such
relations were required, since Franco-American trade still remained of
secondary importance; thus she soon began to fade away, as it were,
into a misty distance. At most there was recognition and approval of
the July Revolution of 1830, when the reactionary Bourbons were

deposed in favor of the duc d'Orléans, Louis Philippe. For one thing the new king had actually lived in America during the French Revolution—in a house that may still be seen in Boston—and, in addition, the now elderly Lafayette, who had made a triumphal visit to the United States in 1824 and was now a member of the Chamber of Deputies, played an important political role in the 1830 upheaval. It was his support, in fact, that ensured success for the political maneuver that successfully prevented the proclamation of a republic by offering the throne to Louis Philippe. At the age of seventy-three, Lafayette was once more named commander-in-chief of the National Guard, as he had been at thirty-two. However, he was obliged to resign the post several months later, and it is odd to find Lafayette, so great a figure in the history of the United States, appearing in French history in the role (as Mirabeau put it in 1790) of the "champion of indecision."

It was not these events, however, difficult as they were to follow from the other side of the Atlantic, that held the attention of President Andrew Jackson (1829–37), but rather the thorny problem of the still unpaid French debts, dating back to the Napoleonic era. Not that the worries this matter caused the forceful Jackson were more than minor. It is noteworthy that many general histories of the United States do not breathe so much as a single word on the matter, and even Paul Thureau-Dangin, in his seven-volume *Histoire de la monarchie de juillet*, fails to mention it. So let us simply set down for the record that, on 4 July 1831, William C. Rives signed a treaty with the French government by which the latter agreed to pay twenty-five million francs to cover the losses inflicted by French warships on American property under Napoleon, while the United States agreed in return to pay one and a half million francs in compensation for infractions of the trade agreement incorporated into the Louisiana Purchase of 1803. The American Senate ratified this treaty, but the French Chamber of Deputies, after letting the affair drag on for two years, refused to do so, on the pretext that twenty-five million was a greatly exaggerated sum. Although the treaty's opponents in the Chamber claimed they had no wish to jeopardize Franco-American friendship, their action staggered the French government. Jackson, for his part, was furious. His natural preference was for brutal methods (according to René

Rémond, *Les Etats-Unis devant l'opinion française*). In his dispatch of
2 December he accused the French of bad faith and threatened to seize
French property in the United States. In 1835 indignation erupted in
the French press. There was talk of war. The French minister to
Washington was recalled. However, the negotiations were resumed,
under pressure from the business community, which was vitally
opposed to the conflict. In April 1835 the Chamber revoked its earlier
decision, mollified, if not by apologies from Jackson, at least by
explanations from him. In the event, this wrangle, so typical of the
mutual incomprehension between the two countries, dragged on until
1836, when France at last began to make payments.

The War of Secession, a result of fifty years of mounting internal
conflict among the states, set the North (the Union) against the South
(the Confederacy) in a bloody four-year struggle (1861–65) that had
the side effect of suddenly intensifying relations between France and
the United States. The news of the secession declared by South
Carolina reached Paris on 7 January 1861. The French were of course
expecting some such event, and they had gleaned at least some
emotional inkling of slavery and its problems from Harriet Beecher
Stowe's *Uncle Tom's Cabin*, which had been translated into French
and enjoyed enormous sales during the 1850s. But no one was in a
position to predict all the repercussions this grave conflict was to have
on the interests of France and the lives of French people.

The first reaction of the emperor Napoleon III and his foreign
minister, Edouard Thouvenel, was to issue a statement favoring the
preservation of the Union. As Thouvenel said to Henry Sanford, the
American minister, on 24 April 1861: "We consider ourselves to be
interested in the integral maintenance of the North American Union,
and we sincerely desire to see reestablished the harmony which has
unfortunately been disturbed" (quoted by Case and Spencer, *United
States and France*, p. 30). As for French public opinion, that was
largely favorable to the North, simply because the South was opposed
to the abolition of slavery. This attitude is even more plain from the
reports of provincial officials than from the press, the freedom of
which was too restricted for it to be reliable as evidence. However,
these pro-North feelings were stronger among the republicans, the
royalists, and the liberal Bonapartists, such as Prince Jerome

Napoleon, than among the conservative Bonapartists, whose newspapers, *Le Constitutionnel*, *Le Pays*, and *La Patrie*, took up a pro-South stance.

Three days after Thouvenel's statement, news of the attack on Fort Sumter, in other words, of open war, reached Paris. From that point onward the problems were to grow in number and gravity.

To what extent was France—which with rare exceptions was to follow a policy very similar to Britain's throughout the war—to recognize the Southern Confederates? Between nonrecognition and recognition of a government there lay a third formula that the United States had itself made use of earlier in the century during the war in Latin America. This was the "recognition of belligerence," enabling states to apply the rules of neutrality in the case of a civil war. What happened was that in April 1861 the South announced that it was going to employ privateer vessels in order to destroy trade with the North, while the North set up its own blockade of the Confederate ports. After consulting together, Britain and France (the first on 14 May 1861, the second on 10 June) declared "a strict neutrality . . . between the government of the Union and the States which claim to form a separate confederation" (Case and Spencer, *United States and France*, p. 59). There was no doubt that though this formula was not a recognition of the Confederacy's *government*, it was a recognition of it *as a belligerent*, since the two sides were being treated not as a legitimate power and a rebel force but simply as two adversaries. The indignant protests of William Seward, the American secretary of state, were unable to prevent this policy from being applied.

It was the blockade by the North that was to pose the most dramatic problem. The South—and this of course was its principal weakness—produced almost nothing but cotton. Indeed, it had become far and away the largest producer of that commodity in the world. France, possessing as she did a very large textile industry, was importing 93 percent of the cotton she needed in 1860 from the seceding states. Two hundred seventy-five thousand French workers were cotton-spinners or weavers (principally in the North, Normandy, and Alsace, but in other regions as well), and there were, in all, 700,000 people dependent on the cotton industry for their existence (Claude Fohlen, *L'Industrie textile en France au temps du Second Empire*, pp. 128 ff.). Moreover, the blockade of the South was effective, since only the

North had any real war fleet. True, there were "blockade-runners,"
who managed to slip through it quite often (it has been estimated that
there were 7,500 such runs, while 1,054 vessels were captured or
destroyed by the Northern forces). But the cargoes they brought out
were pitifully small compared to the prewar trade, so that the price of
cotton shot up dramatically, and the stocks held by French (and
British) dealers and manufacturers were soon exhausted. France had
imported 114,000 metric tons of American cotton in 1860, and
109,000 in 1861. This figure fell to 295 metric tons in 1862, 254 in
1863, 900 in 1864 (Fohlen, *L'Industrie textile*, pp. 284 ff.). When
existing stocks ran out, many factories cut back or completely halted
production. Unemployment in the Rouen cotton industry was running
at 55 percent by early 1862. Since in addition to this a great many
export industries were also affected, with the North buying less and
the South virtually inaccessible, the crisis in France soon spread far
beyond the cotton industry. All the efforts of Napoleon III and
Thouvenel to obtain preferential treatment for France or a relaxation
of the blockade were met with firm refusals by President Abraham
Lincoln and Secretary of State Seward.

The political consequences of such a social situation were potentially
very serious. Various chambers of commerce (those in the textile towns
of Lyons, Rouen, Mulhouse) demanded explicit recognition of the
Confederacy and measures that could well have brought France into
the war on the Southern side. The "cotton famine" was thus an
enormous potential danger. The capture of the British vessel *Trent*, on
8 November 1861, while carrying the two Confederate diplomats
James Mason and John Slidell on their way to England and France,
respectively, further increased the risk of war. Was Britain going to
tolerate such behavior? Would France be able to avoid following the
British example? War would provide a chance to break the blockade
by the North, thereby restoring access to the South and its steadily
accumulating piles of precious and sorely needed cotton. Thouvenel,
like the British, protested firmly, with the result that President Lincoln
decided to free Mason and Slidell. It is undeniable that the idea of a
Franco-British alliance with the slave states would almost certainly
have enraged all shades of liberal opinion in both Britain and France,
and this certainly carried great weight in Napoleon III's decisions. But
the fact nevertheless remains that Lincoln's decision was a wise one.

Slidell did eventually reach Paris, and set to work pleading the South's cause with Thouvenel.

The danger Lincoln had sensed receded only slowly. The Northern victories, and particularly the taking of New Orleans, contributed to this relaxation of tension, as did the Emancipation Proclamation made on 23 September 1862, announcing that slavery would be abolished in any state that had not rejoined the Union by 1 January 1863. Even so, the North's opponents pointed out that Lincoln was also implicitly guaranteeing the maintenance of slavery in any state that did return to the fold. Edouard Drouyn de Lhuys, who succeeded Thouvenel as foreign minister in October 1862, continued his predecessor's waiting game. He did attempt to persuade Britain and Russia to join France in a joint offer of mediation, but nothing came of it. Again in 1863 he made a unilateral mediation offer, but that too proved vain.

NAPOLEON III was favorably disposed toward the South for one very special reason: the French expedition to Mexico, one of the emperor's most opportunist and dubious initiatives. The leader of the Mexican democrats, Benito Juárez, had seized power there in January 1861. The policies he put into practice were antireligious and xenophobic (seven French citizens met violent deaths in early 1861), and on 17 June 1861 he passed a law suspending the country's European debts, including what was termed the "Jecker debt," in which Napoleon III's half-brother, the duc de Morny, had an interest. Despite warnings from the United States, an agreement was reached by France, England, and Spain, on 21 October 1861, to mount a joint naval and military show of power, intended to intimidate Juárez into paying these debts. But Napoleon III, influenced by certain conservative Mexican *émigrés*, decided to take advantage of the expedition to oust Juárez altogether and set up a Roman Catholic empire in Mexico, the throne of which was to be offered to the archduke Maximilian, brother of the Austrian emperor Franz-Josef. This idea was totally at odds with British views. The three contingents landed at Vera Cruz in January 1862. From there they advanced on and took Orizaba.

After the arrival of French reinforcements, however, both the Spanish and the British withdrew. Aware of the fact that the United States, embroiled in its own War of Secession, was powerless to apply the Monroe Doctrine, Napoleon had decided to pursue his plans for

Mexico. In May 1862 the French troops were defeated at Puebla; but in May 1863 they succeeded in capturing it. In June they also took Mexico City. Juárez fled and set to work organizing a very efficient guerrilla resistance movement. The Mexican conservatives proclaimed a monarchy, and on 27 November offered the throne to Maximilian. Having been promised money and troops by France, Maximilian accepted and entered Mexico City on 12 June 1864. Meanwhile, the French expeditionary force, commanded by General Achille-François Bazaine, was extending the area under its control, particularly toward the North.

The Mexican affair assumed great importance in the relations between France and the Union. In 1862–63, when the operation was still barely under way, Secretary of State Seward and the French foreign minister Drouyn de Lhuys were already working out a policy acceptable to both sides: France promised to abstain from all ambitions of conquest in Mexico and to evacuate its troops as soon as the regime she was advocating had been established; the United States was to maintain a policy of strict neutrality with regard to the two Mexican factions, Juárez and the French-backed conservatives. In other words, France remained neutral between North and South, while the United States was to be neutral between Mexican republicans and monarchists.

This prudent stance on the part of the Washington government— which was fearful of driving Napoleon III into recognition of the Confederate government—nevertheless did not entirely conceal their very real hostility to the French expedition. American public opinion and Congress itself were both much more outspoken. In February 1863, Senator James A. McDougall proposed a resolution in the Senate condemning the French intervention. In April 1864 it was the turn of the House of Representatives. Newspapers in the United States were quite open in proclaiming their sympathy with Juárez. Above all, French consuls were reporting that shipments of arms and men were being sent to Juárez from the United States. The American minister in London, Charles Francis Adams, was actually giving official encouragement to such ventures. Moreover, once New Orleans had been taken, the Union was in possession of a base from which it could provide Juárez with even more effective aid. In the spring of 1864 a secret club was formed for precisely that purpose. Michael Hahn, the governor of Louisiana, stated in a public speech that he "was not

afraid . . . to propose that Federal and Southern troops join together
to chase the French and Maximilian out of Mexico" (quoted by Case
and Spencer, *United States and France*, p. 521).

It is therefore understandable that Napoleon III should have been
attracted by the idea of recognizing the South and assisting its
survival, in order to provide a buffer state between the Union and
Maximilian's empire. According to the Bonapartist newspaper *La
France*, the Confederates were given to celebrating the French victories
in Mexico, although one is bound to be skeptical of such a claim, since
we know for a fact that Confederate troops were actually crossing the
border to fight in support of Juárez.

Napoleon III was cautious. The Northern victories, the appointment of Ulysses S. Grant as commander-in-chief of the Union army in
May 1864, General William Tecumseh Sherman's march through
Georgia (May–September 1864), and Lincoln's reelection to the
presidency combined to make him edge away from what was clearly a
lost cause. This is not to deny that right up to the summer of 1864—to
be precise, the moment when Maximilian was assuming power in
Mexico—he was frequently seized by sudden impulses to recognize the
South. At one point he had a dispute with the North because he was
allowing ships to be built in Bordeaux for Confederate use. Another
quarrel arose over an incident that brought the Civil War vividly home
to the French people: the hour-and-a-half battle off Cherbourg—
whose entire population climbed up onto the roofs to watch—between
the Southern privateer *Alabama*, which had destroyed 257 Union
vessels, and the Northern warship *Kearsarge*. The *Alabama* was sunk,
but Washington made an official protest because, prior to the
engagement, the *Alabama* had put into a French port for repairs. This
particular naval battle seems to have fired the French popular
imagination, and one can still see prints depicting it in some French
homes.

From the summer of 1864 onward, Napoleon III confined himself
to a stricter neutrality and attempted negotiations with the Union over
his Mexican adventure. His illusions were to be destroyed one after
another. Seward, who had earlier resigned himself to the policy of
neutrality between the two sides in Mexico, altered his opinion with
the arrival of Maximilian. After the fall of Richmond, the Southern
capital, speaking informally to the crowd that had gathered, he cried:

" 'What shall I say to the Emperor of the French?' The answer came immediately: 'To get out of Mexico!' " (Case and Spencer, *United States and France*, p. 543).

It was almost a year, however, before Napoleon III, in his speech from the throne on 21 January 1866, announced that he was withdrawing all French troops from Mexico, a withdrawal that was to be more or less complete by December 1866. Behind these events lay the fact that he had been unable to consolidate Maximilian's empire before the victory of the North. Juárez's guerrillas were becoming steadily stronger, the "emperor's" clerical regime more and more bungling, the French troops increasingly hated by the Mexican population, and, in addition to all this, Maximilian couldn't get on with General Bazaine. The time had come to improve relations with the North, especially since French public opinion was extremely favorable to them now that they had abolished slavery. The assassination of Lincoln was greeted with stupefaction, and for two days there was a constant stream of visitors at the Paris residence of the American minister John Bigelow. The seventy-four opposition deputies sent Bigelow a special message: "We desire to express ... our admiration for the great people who have destroyed the last vestiges of Slavery, and for Lincoln, the glorious martyr to duty" (quoted in Case and Spencer, *United States and France*, p. 573). On the Fourth of July 1865, when Bigelow celebrated Independence Day in the Bois de Boulogne with an entertainment that included dancing and a sumptuous buffet, Drouyn de Lhuys and Justin Chasseloup-Laubat, the minister for the navy, both attended it.

The Mexican adventure was to end in high drama. Having refused to leave with the French troops, Maximilian was captured by Juárez's partisans and shot by a firing squad on 19 June 1867 at Querétaro.

After these dramatic events, Franco-American relations were once more to sink into virtual nonexistence, although one may justifiably share the opinion expressed by Case and Spencer:

> One cannot but feel that the ordeal of the Civil War was in its totality beneficial to Franco-American relations. For the first time the common man in France became acquainted with America and its system of government. He also learned one of the early lessons of the industrial revolution—that the world was becoming economically interdependent. The Northern States, which for a time had

appeared as crass and power-hungry conquerors and oppressors, again became credibly the emancipators of a downtrodden race and the preservers of democratic ideals and institutions. There is a clear connection between the victory of Democracy in America in 1865 and the liberalization of the Empire between 1867 and 1870 (Case and Spencer, *United States and France*, p. 607).

In 1870, France finally became a republic once more, as it had been between 1792 and 1799, then again between 1848 and 1852. But in its early days, weakened by the French defeat in the ill-considered war that Napoleon III had declared on Germany, the Third Republic was reduced, in the words of its first president, Adolphe Thiers, to a "policy of inner recollection." After that it was to launch itself into the great colonial adventure, while never accepting the loss of Alsace and Lorraine, annexed by Germany against the wishes of the inhabitants. A certain number of Americans had, incidentally, fought in the 1870–71 war as volunteers on the French side, among them James Roosevelt, father of Franklin.

As things fell out, the United States, now preoccupied with its own national recovery and the tremendous industrial expansion that was making it into a great power, was to have only the most insignificant contacts with France during this time. Even during the brief period of their colonial expansion, the two countries had no geographical contacts. The result, taken all in all, was "cordial but superficial relations," in the words of Nouailhat (*La France et les Etats-Unis, août 1914–avril 1917*).

There was one crisis, however, in 1898. The French government found itself embarrassed by the war between the United States and Spain over Cuba. On the one hand, France was not only a Latin and Roman Catholic country like Spain, it was also the biggest investor in that country ($400 million). On the other hand, there could be no question of offending the United States. The French foreign minister of the day, Gabriel Hanotaux, urged the great European powers on 7 April 1898 to make a joint effort to avert the war—in vain. During the war, France proclaimed her neutrality but agreed to look after Spanish interests in the United States. French opinion was on the whole pro-Spanish, which irritated the Americans.

The United States government refused to accept any European diplomatic intervention after its victory but did "agree to any peace

proposals Spain might make being conveyed by France as intermediary'' (Nouailhat, p. 5). The peace conference was held in Paris,
and France did eventually play an appreciable role in the negotiations.
But the main consequence of the whole affair was to leave a
perceptible rancor on both sides. There were those in France who had
begun to speak of the "American peril," while Brooks Adams on his
side advised the French to resign themselves to a continuing decline.
The future, he told them, belonged to the Anglo-Saxons. The
excellent ambassadors France sent to Washington (Jules Cambon,
followed in 1903 by Jean-Jules Jusserand, who remained for more than
twenty years) had some difficulty clearing the air again.

The French did not intervene in Latin America, unlike the British
and the Germans, even though their investments in that area
increased between 1900 and 1914 from two to six billion francs. After
the bankruptcy in 1892 of the French Panama Canal Company, on 18
November 1903 France recognized the new Republic of Panama,
created under the aegis of the United States. In Haiti, she was
progressively supplanted by the United States in both the financial
and economic spheres. Over the Open Door policy in China (1900)
and later (1904-5), during the Russo-Japanese war, France and the
United States collaborated without significant disagreements. The
Americans on their side recognized France's colonial conquests without protest, while attempting at the same time to preserve equal
trading rights. Relations with Theodore Roosevelt were good. His
colleagues Elihu Root and Henry Cabot Lodge were both francophiles
and unfavorable to William II. France, Lodge said, is "our natural
ally," and he added that it would be a sad day for the United States if
Germany decided to crush France (quoted by Nouailhat, p. 15). At
the Algeciras Conference on Morocco, in 1906, the American delegate
supported the French point of view against Germany. Finally, in
accordance with its policy of concluding "arbitration treaties" with a
view to diminishing world tensions, the United States began in 1904
by signing such a treaty with France, the first in a series of twenty-five.

All these matters were superficial, and the same is true of economic
relations between the two countries. It is true that American products
represented about 10 percent of France's gross imports, and in 1913
the United States was the third largest exporter to France, after Great
Britain and Germany, but it was mainly raw materials that were

involved. French sales to the United States doubled from 1910 to 1913 and in the latter year represented 6 percent of all French exports. The United States was France's fourth largest customer, after Great Britain, Belgium, and Germany, and more or less on a par with Switzerland. The products involved were mainly luxury manufactured goods and comestibles, notably wine. Trade between the two countries was generally in balance. But since both imposed high protective tariffs, there was no appreciable expansion and disputes were legion.

Financial relations also remained at a low level. Although France was at that time second only to Great Britain as a world provider of capital (forty-five billion francs invested abroad in 1914), she had invested only a mere two billion francs (four hundred million dollars) in the United States compared with the four and a quarter billion dollars invested by Britain. American investment in France was also low.

Between 1815 and 1914, then, it is the distance between the two countries rather than their relations that strikes one most. In the spheres of politics, immigration, trade, and finance, there were few bonds between the French and the Americans. Was the same true in the intellectual and emotional spheres?

2. Famous French travelers in the United States

During the hundred-year period covered in this chapter, the French never ceased to feel a lively interest in the inhabitants of North America. Despite the diplomatic doldrums, despite the absence of any substantial immigration, despite the physical distance, which meant long and hazardous Atlantic crossings (at least until the last quarter of the nineteenth century), this curiosity on the part of the French resulted in visits by a number of travelers. As luck would have it, at least two of those travelers, Alexis de Tocqueville and Michel Chevalier, are to be counted among the best foreign observers the United States has known throughout its history.

However, there was a host of others, too, many of them very interesting characters. Réne Rémond, in his admirable book *Les Etats-Unis devant l'opinion française, 1815-52*, has made a study of forty or so such visitors during this period; during the second half of the century their numbers increased still further. What sort of people

made the journey to the United States? Well, to begin with we had
better exclude the diplomats, who were not always assiduous
observers. When Gustave de Beaumont—whom we shall meet again
later—landed at New York in May 1831, he was immediately invited
to the house of the French consul, the baron de Saint André. "They
are a very likable family," Beaumont wrote of his hosts, "but there is
nothing to be gained from their conversation; they know nothing
whatever about the country they are in and are totally lacking in the
spirit of observation" (*Lettres d'Amérique*, p. 39). Many of these
diplomats, it must be admitted, felt even more exiled than twentieth-
century diplomats in some underdeveloped country. "Coming from
Florence, from Munich, from London or Paris, they quite frankly
loathe it here; they are unanimous in deploring an utter lack of
conversation and society" (Rémond, *Les Etats-Unis devant l'opinion
française*, p. 328). But we mustn't overgeneralize. There were other
diplomats who were in fact penetrating observers, from Hyde de
Neuville, an ardent royalist who lived in exile in the United States
from 1807 to 1814 and later became France's minister in Washington
from 1816 to 1822, to Jean-Jules Jusserand, French ambassador from
1902 to 1924 (both countries' legations were raised to the rank of
embassies in 1893).

The Roman Catholic missionaries also form a category apart. In
what was a mainly Protestant country until the massive Irish immigration after 1846, a large section of the Roman Catholic clergy
consisted of French priests. Before 1860, "thirty-five French eccles-
iastics had ranked among the holders of episcopal office" (Rémond,
Les Etats-Unis devant l'opinion française, p. 124). These priests came
over in their hundreds, some of them secular, some members of
religious communities: Trappists, Sulpicians, Jesuits. In 1841, the
Fathers of Sainte-Croix du Mans (Holy Cross Fathers) set up a
community in Indiana, where they were to found the most famous of
the Catholic universities in America, Notre Dame, which still retains
its French name. In the other direction, the absolute freedom of
worship in America and the collaboration of Catholics with Protestants
of various sects elicited a lively interest in France, and toward the end
of the century a number of French priests, notably the Abbé Félix
Klein, who had earlier worked with Charles Cardinal Lavigerie,
attempted to introduce "Americanism" into France—in other words,

a democratic, liberal, social, and, as we would say today, "ecumenical" Catholicism as preached by the famous American prelates James Cardinal Gibbons and Archbishop John Ireland. The result was a dispute with conservative Catholics, and in 1899 Pope Leo XIII officially condemned "Americanism." It is nevertheless worth noting that this term was chosen in France to designate an audaciously modern and liberal form of Catholicism.

Other visitors who can also be set to one side were of course the businessmen, especially those merchants and dealers, really high-class salesmen, who went over to America to foster the sale of their products or to buy cotton. A number of the larger French concerns even kept a permanent agent in the New World, including the mirror-making firm of Saint-Gobain, which sent over the son of the chemist Joseph Gay-Lussac, or the Banque Laffitte. Such travelers have left little in the way of writings, their concerns being almost wholly unalloyed with intellectual curiosity. For example, Gustave de Beaumont describes a Saint-Malo wine merchant he sailed with as follows: "Apart from the wines of Burgundy, which are his party, and the *Marseillaise*, which is his favorite ballad, he recognizes no other path to salvation" (*Lettres d'Amérique*, p. 25).

The travelers we shall concentrate on belong to other categories. During the previous period there were the *émigrés*, refugees from the French Revolution, and it is beyond dispute that one of the greatest of all French writers, Vicomte François René de Chateaubriand, derived from his five-month visit in 1791 not only a moving tale, published in 1827, but, more important still, certain poetic and affecting strains that continue to haunt the memory of all cultured French people to this day. As a provider of accurate information about the New World, on the other hand, he ranks rather low. Diligent literary historians have had little difficulty proving that he in fact did not visit many of the regions he so magically described.

During the period we are considering now, however, political emigration became rare, though it was to revive to some extent during the Second World War. It was replaced by a different kind of immigration: that of the *utopian socialists*. These groups, inspired by the example of the Englishman Robert Owen, came over with the express intention of setting up model communities in America, thereby providing examples that they believed would eventually transform the world. In the event it was an abortive form of immigration, since all these experiments failed. The principal one was Cabet's "Icarie" in Texas. At one time there were about five hundred French disciples living there with him, but, like all the other similar enterprises at that time, it came to nothing in the end.

Another category was that of the *scientists*: geologists, geographers, and naturalists, such as the two botanists F. A. Michaux and his son, or Jacques Milbert, who sent back eight thousand specimens to the Paris Jardin des Plantes. Still others contributed to the exploration of coasts and ports on both the eastern and western seaboards.

But the most important category of all, the one that produced the most interesting and informative records, was that of the men sent over on *official missions* to study human, economic, or technical problems, as Alexis de Tocqueville and Gustave de Beaumont, for example, were sent to investigate American prisons, and Michel Chevalier the American railroads.

Thus we find that, in comparison to the exchanges of the twentieth century, certain categories of visitor are rare (pure tourists or press correspondents) or more or less silent (diplomats).

Let me list a few names, in chronological order, without going into any great detail except in the cases of the most famous, all of them already mentioned. We shall pass quickly over Achille Murat, the son of the king of Naples, who arrived in the United States in 1823, bought land in Florida to develop as a plantation, married a grand-niece of Washington, then sailed back to Europe to fight in the Revolution of 1830 before returning once more to the United States, where he died in 1847. He published several books on the United States, all deeply imbued with Southern anti-Yankee sentiments, but he counts far more as an immigrant than as a foreign visitor.

The situation is very different in the case of the two young French officials, Gustave de Beaumont and Alexis de Tocqueville. Their visit was a very brief one, lasting only the nine months from May 1831 to February 1832, yet in that time they managed to accumulate the material for some of the best studies ever produced of the United States. They were almost exact contemporaries. Beaumont was born in the Sarthe in 1802, Tocqueville at Verneuil, eighteen miles west of Paris, in 1805. Both belonged to the old nobility, both were royalists and supporters of the Restoration, Tocqueville's father having been an *émigré* and Beaumont's having refused to serve under the Empire. Neither family was commonplace, however. Both held cultivation of the intellect in the highest esteem, and both were sufficiently endowed with the liberal spirit to be converted later, after 1848, to support for a moderate republic. Lastly, both young men studied law and entered the magistracy, and it was while carrying out their official duties at the court of Versailles that they first met, shortly before 1830. Apart from all this, they were also distantly related.

The 1830 July Revolution, which removed the senior branch of the French Bourbons from power and brought Louis Philippe d'Orléans to the throne, put both Tocqueville and Beaumont in an uncomfortable position. They had neither of them cared overmuch for the part played in these events by Lafayette, "the hero of two worlds," and as an alternative to resigning they managed to persuade the minister of justice to send them on a mission to the United States, where they were to conduct an investigation into American prisons with a view to reforms in the French penal system. Their book, *Du Système pénitentiaire aux Etats-Unis et de son application en France*, actually written in the main by Beaumont, appeared in 1833. But their nine-month visit produced other and very much more important results. While in the United States they stayed mainly in New York, spent ten days inspecting the famous prison at Sing Sing, continued on up the Hudson toward Albany, in order to visit Auburn prison, traveled on to Utica, and then to Syracuse, where they encountered an Indian tribe for the first time. Next they wanted to see the Niagara Falls, but, once at Buffalo, "we felt a temptation we were unable to resist . . . that of reaching the furthest frontiers of civilization" (Beaumont, *Lettres d'Amérique*, p. 104). They therefore took ship across Lake Erie, passed through Detroit, and set off on horseback toward Saginaw, near Lake Huron. "During that ride we encountered many French Canadians and found them all animated with that national feeling never absent from the Frenchman's heart; they were all furious at being British; they cannot wait to throw off their yoke and become independent." If that were to happen, Beaumont added, "Canada will become one more province for the United States" (*Lettres d'Amérique*, p. 105). They also met a great many Indians and found them stern and honest. They made an excursion by boat on Lake Huron, near Sault Sainte Marie, and went to take a look at Lake

Superior. It was not until they were on their way back again that they visited Niagara and evoked the name of Chateaubriand. From there they continued on to Montreal and Quebec. From Quebec they went south to Boston (September 1831), Hartford, Connecticut (October), and Philadelphia (November). They next aimed to visit the South before Congress began its next session in January 1832. But having decided to go by way of Pittsburgh and Cincinnati, then on down the Ohio to the Mississippi, they discovered that, because of the exceptionally hard winter, the Mississippi was frozen. They were stranded for some time in Memphis. Eventually they arrived on 1 January in New Orleans, which they had to leave almost immediately in order to get back to Washington on schedule. They spent two weeks in the capital and were received by President Andrew Jackson, who enchanted them with his simplicity. In February they started back to France. They had been wonderfully well received everywhere, and they had extended their passionate observation far beyond America's prisons to its people—people rather than things, since neither of them was a scientist and economics held no attraction for them.

Nine months, and a very cursory visit, were sufficient to enable these two young men to produce important works. Let us begin with Beaumont. André Jardin, the excellent editor of both Tocqueville's and his friend's works, writes that Beaumont's tone

> is very different from Tocqueville's: where the latter analyzes as a political philosopher, the former pleads like an impassioned barrister. And the theme lying at the heart of Beaumont's works is never more than occasionally present in Tocqueville's; it is the very modern notion of men's fundamental equality, whatever their race, their creed, or their state of civilization. Throughout his active life, Beaumont's concern was always for the American Indians and Blacks, for the French Canadians, for the Irish, for the Algerian Arabs, in a word for all defeated and oppressed peoples (Jardin, Introduction to Beaumont, *Lettres d'Amérique*, pp. 18-19).

As early as 1835, Beaumont used his American experiences in a novel, *Marie, ou l'esclavage aux Etats-Unis*. It is the story of a lovely, cultivated, sweet-natured young woman who is ultimately excluded from society because she has traces of "impure" blood in her veins, the legacy of Negro ancestors. Although no work of genius, this book achieved considerable success, since it was "the first novel in any

language to treat a freeborn colored person as a tragic hero or heroine"
(Pierson, Foreword to Beaumont, p. 9). In our day, thanks to Pierson
and Jardin, we possess another work by Beaumont dealing with the
United States, his *Lettres d'Amérique 1831–32*, mentioned earlier.
These letters teem with the sort of human observations that Tocqueville provides only very sparingly. Let us merely quote his remarks on
the moral aspect of American life, which echo Jefferson's comments at
the time of his ministerial appointment in France. Beaumont admits
that the American people are "hard-bargaining," in other words,
grasping. "Everyone here has apparently only one thought, one goal,
that of achieving material success." The opposite side of the coin,
however, is that "their morals are extremely pure. . . . To tell the
truth, one meets with none but happy marriages. . . . The unmarried
men pay attention only to young ladies, while the latter, once
married, pay absolutely no attention to any man but their husbands."
Before marriage, girls were very free in their behavior and—something
that struck the young Frenchman forcibly—"one sees them out
walking alone, for example." What was the reason for this virtue?
Undoubtedly the religious spirit of the nation. "All religions here are
free and honored, but a man who belonged to no religion would be
regarded as a *brute beast*." However, there was more to it than that:
there is "only one class, that of the *merchants*, all absorbed by one
and the same interest and rivaling one another in the pursuit of a
single object, *wealth*. So that here there is no idle class; you do not
find as you do in France a certain number of individuals who if they
were not occupied in seducing women would have nothing to do"
(*Lettres d'Amérique*, p. 41). This picture, though of course exaggerated, is nonetheless interesting, and we shall meet it again.

In 1835, Tocqueville also published a book, his *Democracy in
America*. For a hundred and forty years now, in France and even more
in the United States, this work has continued to be read, in Rémond's
phrase, "with devotion," and to accumulate commentaries and
exegeses. Admirably prepared before his journey by extensive reading,
a talented observer and investigator, endowed with a mind both
analytic and synthetic, skilled in distinguishing the permanent from
the merely topical, animated by a constant concern for objectivity and
impartiality, Tocqueville directed his attention exclusively to one
aspect of the United States: the political democracy of the whites. He

simply disregarded slavery, social inequality, and violence. His book is
a work of such importance that we must restrict ourselves here to an
outline of its essential argument: "The salient point of the social state
of the Anglo-Americans is that it is essentially democratic." Starting
from this basic principle, Tocqueville wove a minutely detailed
description of American institutions. The powers of the president and
Congress were already fairly well known in Europe; Tocqueville also
gave due weight to federalism, the powers of the state governors, and
the powers of the judiciary.

Above all, he attempted to provide an explanation of the American
phenomenon, and he was later to expand that explanation in a second
volume of *Democracy in America*, originally published in 1840 under
the title *Démocratie et société*. Customs, traditions, and history had
created an egalitarian society, one in which there are rich and poor but
in which it is possible to move from one of those categories to the other.
Individualism had been replaced by association. "America is of all
countries the one where profit has been derived from association and
where that powerful tool of action has been applied to the greatest
diversity of aims." The result was a "patriotism exempt from fanati-
cism," respect for "rights," political activity in "a balanced social
body." The danger was "the omnipotence of the majority," which if
not counterbalanced could exercise a "collective tyranny." Liberty was
menaced by a formidable social pressure. "In America, the majority
draws a firm boundary around men's thought. Within those limits the
writer is free; but woe to the man who dares to cross them." Such a man
would experience this pressure in the form, not of violence, but of
constant daily reproach. The result was conformism. Only decentrali-
zation, education, and good sense would make it possible to fend off
this permanent threat.

This deeply considered and critical book produced a twofold
reaction in France. Some, the antidemocrats, used it as additional
ammunition against democracy. Others, on the contrary, found in it
fresh arguments for transforming France into a republic once more.
When the Revolution of 1848 did eventually create such a regime in
France, Tocqueville was elected to the Assembly and became a
member of the constitutional committee. Possibly it was he who
originated the notion of electing the president of the republic by
universal suffrage. Alas! the electors, victims of their inexperience,

promptly selected the candidate with the best-known name, Prince
Louis Napoleon Bonaparte. For a time, Tocqueville was to be his
foreign minister, but it was not long before he ceased his association
with the future dictator and emperor.

Selections from Michel Chevalier's *Lettres sur l'Amérique du Nord*
were published in the *Journal des Débats* between late 1833 and late
1835. Later, in 1837, with very generous additions, they appeared in
two-volume book form, two years after Tocqueville's and Beaumont's
books. Although the author is not so well known in America, these
letters of Chevalier's constitute a work quite the equal of Tocqueville's
in interest.

Michel Chevalier was born in 1806, only a few months after
Tocqueville, but he was a fundamentally different character altogether. He came from the lowest ranks of the petty *bourgeoisie*, his
father having been a flannel merchant in Limoges. He had been a
student not of law but of the sciences, and in 1823 he came in first in
the competitive entrance examinations of the celebrated Ecole Polytechnique, which was in those days the training establishment for
artillery officers and also—in the case of class leaders—for state
engineers. In 1829, when he was twenty-three, Chevalier was already
an engineer in the Corps des Mines, one of the most brilliant
appointments available at the time to young and exceptionally gifted
Frenchmen. It was at this point that a curious phenomenon occurred:
he was converted to the ''Saint-Simonian religion.'' After the death of
the great utopian reformer, the comte de Saint-Simon, in 1825, a
number of his disciples had attempted to start a new religion, one
based on a freer morality, the cult of the ''couple,'' and—an
important detail in this context—the industrialization of France.
Michel Chevalier rose in the hierarchy of this curious church until he
was second only to its leader, ''Father'' Barthélemy Enfantin; but this
explosion of youthful folly proved brief. The Saint-Simonians were
accused of immorality, and in December 1832 both Enfantin and
Chevalier were imprisoned in Sainte-Pélagie. At this point a further
change of heart occurred. While in prison Chevalier quarreled with
Enfantin, abandoned the ''religion,'' and decided to forget past
follies in order to devote himself to more realistic ambitions. After his
release from Sainte-Pélagie, he succeeded, with the help of influential
support, in persuading Thiers, then minister for home affairs, to send

him on an eight-month foreign mission for the purpose of studying
the North American railroads, then beginning their great expansion.
The order appointing Chevalier, signed on 9 September 1833,
stipulated that "upon his arrival in the United States, [he] shall
immediately proceed to gather full details of the methods of intervention employed by the federal government in public works, and of
its participation in the expenses and enterprises of the workers" (J. B.
Duroselle, "Michel Chevalier, Saint-Simonien," *Revue historique*
[April-June, 1956], p. 253).

Chevalier duly set out during October 1833, traveling via London
and taking ship in Liverpool. In January 1834 we find him already in
New York, then Philadelphia; by March he was in Baltimore, then
Richmond; by April in Washington; by May in Charleston. After a
tour of the South he returned northward to New England, visited the
textile town of Lowell, and spent some time in Boston. He was back in
New York again for the 1834 November elections, then visited
Pittsburgh, Cincinnati, Louisville, and Memphis during the remainder of that year. Like Tocqueville, he traveled by boat down the
Mississippi to New Orleans, though at a much more leisurely pace.
"However fine these boats, however great the services they render to
the American nation, one's initial curiosity once satisfied, a journey on
them offers but little attraction to the traveler with any cultivation of
mind and manners" (Chevalier, *Lettres*, vol. 2, no. 21, p. 16). He
then went on to spend a few days in Mexico, returned north, and
settled down for a large part of the summer of 1835 in Pennsylvania,
to study its canals. Finally, he went on a tour of the southeastern
states South Carolina and Georgia. After two years in America he set
off home again toward the end of 1835.

Michel Chevalier wrote an extensive technical report on the American railroad system. But what interests us here is the content of his
letters. Printed as they were in the *Journal des Débats* with its vast
readership, they enjoyed a notoriety in their day as great as that of
Democracy in America; and when published in book form they ran to
several editions.

It would be hard to imagine two more different temperaments than
those of Tocqueville and Chevalier. Tocqueville was a philosopher. He
enjoyed abstract reflection, had little interest in concrete examples,
paid no attention to statistics, dealt with political economy in only the

vaguest terms, and was entirely ignorant in technical matters. Chevalier was essentially concrete in outlook. Not only did he hunt down and accumulate statistics, he also described everything he saw in precise and abundant detail: towns, railroads, canals, the banking system, trade flows, electoral practices, slavery, the everyday life of the women textile workers of Lowell, the rights of individual states, the secession problem, and so on. It is fair to say that his letters, for all their discursive form, depict with wonderful accuracy all the material and social aspects of American life, although admittedly not the intellectual ones. Taken as a whole, despite a few concessions to local color, his book is an amazingly serious one.

As examples, I shall include here only two famous passages. First is the comparison he draws between the Yankee and the Virginian in letter ten. The Virginian

> is open, cordial, expansive; his manners display courtesy, his sentiments nobility, his ideas grandeur; he is a worthy descendant of the English gentleman. Surrounded from childhood by slaves who free him from all manual labor, he is physically not very active, he is even lazy. He is generous and spendthrift.... When his mind has been cultivated by study, and when his manners and imagination have acquired the grace and polish provided by a European tour, there is no place in the world where he may not figure with advantage.
>
> The Yankee on the contrary is reserved, inward-looking, mistrustful ... his bearing lacks grace yet is modest without being obsequious; ... his mind is narrow but practical.... He possesses not the slightest hint of chivalry in his disposition, and yet he is adventurous.... His house is a sanctuary he does not open to the profane.... He wields words without effort; yet he is not a brilliant orator, he is a close logician.... He is an able administrator and a prodigious businessman. Although he has small natural aptitude in the management of men he has no equal in dealing with things, in coordinating them, in extracting their full value from them. It is no slight advantage for a people to contain two such sharply characterized types of physiognomy when they coexist as harmoniously as these within the bosom of a common nationality.

Clearly Chevalier had no notion that the harmony he perceived would be insufficient to avoid a ruthless war between the two.

The other passage I shall quote (letter six) is also one of far-reaching importance. Aligning himself with Jefferson and the traditional ideas of the "New Diplomacy," Chevalier grasped that the nations of Europe would be well advised to take a leaf out of the Americans' book and rid their foreign policies of all emotional considerations. What happy chance had given to America might France not achieve by conscious effort?

> The word *politics* cannot have the same meaning in the United States as in Europe. The United States is not engaged, as the peoples of Europe are, in perpetual intrigues over territory and the balance of power. They require no treaties of Westphalia or Vienna to disentangle their affairs. They are quite free from all those difficulties that derive in Europe from differences of origin and religion, from the conflicts between rival claims. . . . They have no neighbor to give them offense. *Politics* in the United States means extension of their trade and expansion of their agriculture into the vast domain that nature has bestowed on them.

As a result, he contends, the real government of the country lies as much with the banks as with the Constitution. One might almost be reading the speech that President Calvin Coolidge made, in 1925, when he said that there were two forces in the nation, the government and business.

Tocqueville and Chevalier were both in many people's minds again after 1945, in the years when the world had become "bipolar," reduced to a mere two superpowers, the United States and the Soviet Union. For had they not predicted as much a century earlier? Here is what Tocqueville wrote: "Today there are two great peoples on earth which, starting from different points, seem to be advancing toward the same goal: The Russians and the Anglo-Americans. . . . Their points of departure differ, their paths are not the same; nevertheless, each seems summoned by a secret plan of Providence to hold in its hands one day the destinies of half the world" (*Democracy in America*, conclusion of book 1). And here is how Chevalier expresses it in his more exuberant and high-flown style:

> Who can say that the two great figures today rising at opposite sides of the horizon, the first in the east, with one foot in Moscow and the other about to descend on Constantinople, the second toward the setting sun, still half-hidden by the vast forests of the New World, its limbs lying as yet recumbent on the earth from the

mouth of the Saint Lawrence to that of the Mississippi; who can say
that these two young colossi, their gazes meeting across the Atlantic
and touching one another on the coasts of the Pacific Ocean, will
not soon share the domination of the Universe? (Letter nine, 24
April 1834)

In fact, although Tocqueville was the first great political analyst of
the United States and Chevalier its first great economic analyst, their
prediction of Europe's decline and a world dominated by the
Americans and the Russians is less original. Napoleon on Saint Helena
had already conjured up that same prospect. So had Stendhal. The
idea was in the air.

Back in France, Michel Chevalier continued to make a brilliant
career for himself. He was appointed professor of political economy at
the Collège de France, became a great champion of economic
liberalism, was made a councillor of state under the Second Empire—
of which, unlike Tocqueville, he approved. Along with Richard
Cobden he was the person chiefly responsible for the ephemeral
establishment of quasi-free trade in Europe. He was to achieve the
rank of senator under the Empire, and to oppose the Republic that
followed it.

After these two observers, the other visitors cut less imposing
figures. I shall begin by mentioning Georges Clemenceau, more on
account of his future role than because of any originality in his
contribution. Having concluded his medical studies in Paris in 1865,
at the age of twenty-four, and having become deeply involved in the
subversive activities of the young republicans against the Empire, he
followed his father's advice and decided to go abroad for a while. He
set out first for England, where he met the philosophers Herbert
Spencer and John Stuart Mill, then moved on to the United States,
arriving just after the end of the war and Lincoln's assassination. Just
as Michel Chevalier had become an occasional correspondent of the
Journal des Débats, so Clemenceau reached a similar agreement with
the newspaper *Le Temps* in order to earn himself a little money. In
addition, when his father attempted to force him home by withdrawing his allowance, he also turned to teaching French—and
horseback riding—at a college for young ladies at Stamford, Connecticut. He lived in New York, in a house in Greenwich Village that was
said to have been occupied during the 1840s by his archenemy Louis

Napoleon Bonaparte, later Napoleon III. He made a great many friends, notably Horace Greeley, editor of the *New York Tribune*. Toward the end of his stay, in 1869, he fell in love with one of his students, Mary Plummer. His hopes of marrying her were at first fruitless, since, being a staunch atheist, he insisted that there could be no religious ceremony. Back in France, however, he received a summons from Miss Plummer to return to America: she had decided to accept his stipulation. He married her and took her back to France just as the 1870 war was beginning. The couple were to have three children, but the marriage did not remain a happy one for long, and in 1884 they were divorced. In any case it is interesting that one of the principal figures of the Third Republic, the "Tiger," Wilson's partner at the Paris peace conference, knew the United States so well as the result of his five-year visit, and spoke English so perfectly.

His sixty-nine articles (which he never did collect into a book) bubble with wit and exuberance. Six of them are devoted to the attempts to impeach President Andrew Johnson, six to Ulysses S. Grant's election in 1868. He wrote about Reconstruction, about the Democrats' illusions, and about their antiegalitarian prejudices with regard to the blacks. It is noteworthy, however, that he was not won over to the idea of presidential democracy, and continued to prefer the British parliamentary system. Moreover, the low opinion he had of Grant led him to write: "American democracy, perhaps not without reason, is mistrustful of men of genius, of saviors guided by some mysterious inspiration and summoned by Providence to think and act on behalf of others" (*Le Temps*, 24 March 1869). In other words: no Napoleon III!

During the forty years separating the two Franco-German wars, the increasing ease of trans-Atlantic travel brought a proportionate increase in the flow of visitors. The building of the great trans-continental railroads resulted not only in an influx of American wheat into Europe; it also enabled a number of French writers to discover the whole of the continent and the Pacific coast. "Living six months over there is worth more than ten years of study anywhere else." Those were the words, written in 1869, of Edouard Portalis, grandson of one of Napoleon I's ministers, editor of a short-lived weekly *Le Courrier des deux mondes*, quoted by Simon Jeune in his *De Graindorge à Barnabooth* (p. 104), a book from which much of the information

that follows has been drawn. Another visitor during this period was
Louis Simonin, a mining engineer, born in 1830, who sailed over to
America in 1859 to work in the California and Colorado gold placer
mines and sent home articles that were printed in a number of French
magazines, picturesque pieces about the Indians and "frontier" life.
He later used them as material for several books, the principal one
being *Le Grand Ouest* (1869).

Curiosity was aroused in France by the staggering industrial
development in the United States as well as by the vast spaces of the
Far West. A cousin of Tocqueville's, the royalist baron de Mandat-
Grancey, has left evidence of this double interest in two books: *Dans
les montagnes Rocheuses* (1884) and *En visite chez l'oncle Sam,
New-York et Chicago* (1885). However insignificant in comparison to
those of his celebrated relation, these books, both illustrated, were still
being read as late as 1914.

One of the dominating features of the period was the number of
travelers drawn to the United States by an interest in various aspects of
American education. This was the case with Baron Pierre de
Coubertin, founder of the Olympic Games, who paid a visit in 1889.
Similarly with Paul de Rousiers, whose book *Universités transatlanti-
ques*, full of admiration for its subject, appeared in 1890. His friend
Edmond Demolins, though he did not himself visit the United States,
drew a number of sensational conclusions from Rousiers's work in a
best-selling book of his own, *A quoi tient la supériorité des Anglo-
Saxons?* (1897):

> If the Americans, like the English, have a tendency to world
> domination . . . it is because the Anglo-Saxon, by nature an
> individualist, is enterprising, active, daring and persevering on his
> own, or in only temporary association with his peers, whereas the
> Latin, home-loving and sheeplike, likes to feel himself fenced in
> and protected, even at the cost of sacrificing all freedom; but it is
> also because the Anglo-Saxon, both at home and at school, receives
> an education at once concrete and complete: full development of
> his physical energy, respect for independence, awakening of a sense
> of responsibility, teaching oriented toward the necessities of con-
> temporary life (Quoted in Jeune, *De Graindorge à Barnabooth*,
> p. 215).

The admiration—or at any rate esteem—felt for American universities was not always quite so enthusiastic. It did nevertheless result in a new phenomenon: the practice of inviting French academics to the United States. Ferdinand Brunetière was invited over in 1897 by Johns Hopkins University and gave twenty-five lectures in six weeks. The philosopher Emile Boutroux was invited in 1909 and Gustave Lanson, the literary historian, in 1911, by Columbia. He drew on the experience to write a remarkable book, *Trois mois d'enseignement aux Etats-Unis* (1913), in which his innumerable French successors as teachers in the United States were to recognize their own essential impressions. I should also add that the Alliance Française was introduced to the United States in 1895, and that the Comité France-Amérique was founded in Paris in 1909, with Gabriel Hanotaux, the historian and former foreign minister, as its first president. At about this time a number of famous journalists began adding to the list of works left by previous visitors. André Tardieu, for example, who wrote for *Le Figaro* and *Le Temps*, published his *Notes sur les Etats-Unis* in 1908. Tardieu, incidentally, was later to become French high commissioner in the United States during 1917–18. There were also a number of other famous journalistic "investigators": Urbain Gohier, Jules Huret, Paul Adam, and the novelists Paul Bourget and René Bazin.

But it has to be admitted that if French travelers in America were touched at any time by genius, it was between 1830 and 1840, with Tocqueville and Michel Chevalier. The others were only carriers of their flame.

3. The reciprocal "images" of the two peoples

Travelers, however crammed with prejudices they often are, do, in theory at least, describe what they have seen. The remaining population of any country—in other words, the vast majority—tends to construct simplistic "images" of other peoples for itself. Admittedly, that majority will draw some of its raw material from travel books; but lacking any large immigrant group in the other country, as in the present case, they have very little to go on apart from contacts with tourists, certain literary works in translation, and whatever materials happen to catch the eye most, which means works of the imagination, plays, novels—particularly those that achieve great success.

We have a great deal of information about the images the French built up of the United States in these years thanks to two excellent books already mentioned: *Les Etats-Unis devant l'opinion française*, by René Rémond, and *De Graindorge à Barnabooth*, by Simon Jeune. We know a great deal less about the average American's image of the Frenchman, however, for reasons that we shall come to later.

The methods employed by Rémond and Jeune are different. The first examines all the possible kinds of contact between the two peoples; the second concentrates on the influence wielded by works of the imagination. Graindorge—a character invented by the historian and philosopher Hippolyte Taine, turned novelist and portraitist on this occasion (*Notes sur Paris: Vie et opinions de M. Frédéric Graindorge*, 1867)—was the Paris-based partner of a salt-pork business in Cincinnati. A. O. Barnabooth is another fictitious character, created in 1908 by Valéry Larbaud. He was an American millionaire perpetually and vainly striving to get Europeans to accept him.

There were fewer works of imagination relating to America during the previous period, that studied by Rémond. Of course there were vast numbers of translations of the works of James Fenimore Cooper and Edgar Allan Poe, as well as that of Mrs. Stowe's *Uncle Tom's Cabin*, but the great French novelists, even those specializing in the swashbuckling genre, sadly neglected America. There is nothing that stands out after Chateaubriand's *Atala* of 1801.

Simon Jeune's harvest, on the other hand, was bountiful. I will mention only a few isolated examples here. There was Jules Verne, for a start, who created quite a number of American characters. For Verne (as we see in the most remarkable of his American protagonists, the engineer Cyrus Smith, a Northerner who discovers the Mysterious Island by balloon) the American is above all a man of action, resourceful, wildly energetic, to whom no obstacle is insurmountable, thanks to his scientific knowledge. Similarly, it is Americans who build the vast gun that is to shoot a shell up to the moon. And when a brave but physically lightweight Frenchman, Michel Ardant, announces his intention to travel inside the shell, it is a pair of American scientists who go with him. This American "energy," already described by Tocqueville and Michel Chevalier, became one of the key

elements in the image. We have only to remember the fascination
exerted over the French by the almost symbolic figure of Theodore
Roosevelt, leader of the Rough Riders in Cuba, a president of great
prestige, and a big-game hunter. In 1904, the Abbé Klein, whom we
have already mentioned in connection with Roman Catholic "Americanism," produced a volume of American impressions with the
significant title *Au pays de la vie intense*. It includes a fervent eulogy
of Theodore Roosevelt. The latter, when he made a visit to Paris in
1910, after his term as president, was given official receptions not only
at the Elysée Palace by President Fallières but also at the Institut de
France, of which he was an associate, and at the Sorbonne.

The great playwright and writer Eugène Labiche, whose stature our
own age is now at last beginning to appreciate, also provided a
number of American types. His William Track in *Deux merles blancs*
(1858), a plantation and slaveowner, is "a madman perpetually
yelling oaths and leaping about with a whip or a pistol in his hand,
brutish and contemptuous of other people, while at the same time
being simple-minded and easily duped" (Jeune, *De Graindorge à
Barnabooth*, p. 24). In *Les 30 Millions de Gladiator* (1875), we find
another somewhat similar character. Gladiator is also a Southerner,
and he involves himself in the most extravagant expense simply in
order to win the favors of a tart and cut out his rival, the pharmacist's
assistant Eusèbe Potasse.

Thus, the figures of the serious-minded and intrepid American, and
that of the millionaire slaveowner, came to be accepted by millions of
French people as American stereotypes.

Two oddly similar conclusions emerge from Rémond's and Jeune's
analyses. The Great American Boor (as presented by Labiche), the
generous and philanthropic American businessman, and the loathsome and ruthless American capitalist are all in their own ways
"athletic males" who are "clumsy in the presence of women." The
American being described is usually a man of middle age visiting
Europe with his daughter. In business, he is more efficient than the
French. He is sometimes a high liver taking a no-expense-spared
vacation, floating in whisky and surrounded by chorus girls, sometimes buying up shiploads of antiques, sometimes in search of more
animal pleasures.

His daughter, on the other hand, is the heroine of heroines. She is virtuous, emancipated, practical, and ignorant of love. She goes out walking alone—thus arousing furious envy in the nice young ladies of the French *bourgeoisie*. And in an incredible number of plays or novels, true love, which carries everything before it, is revealed to her by a young Frenchman.

What we never find, on the other hand, is either the old American female or the young American male. This alone indicates how strong and at the same time false the stereotypes were and how very badly prepared the French were for the sudden appearance on French soil of two million such young males in the flesh. Just as indubitable, however, is the profound influence the image of the American girl had on the French life-style, even though it is true that, without the war, without voluntary nursing service, without the shortage of domestic staff, the young unmarried Frenchwoman would never have won the liberties enjoyed by her contemporary in the United States. Toward the end of this period, however, Jeune tells us, there was a "fragmentation of the original type": the "flirtatious ingenue" spawned a whole variety of secondary types: the "outdoor girl," the "feminist," the "straight talker," the "dumbbell," the "fast woman." Generally speaking, however, the American girl was always seen as too "masculine," at least until she had finally discovered love.

DID THE AMERICANS have a similar "image" of the Frenchman? In this case, the area of total indifference is much vaster. What possible interest could such a small and far-off country inspire in the midwestern farmer, often an immigrant from Germany or Scandinavia, at a time when political relations with France were so tenuous and trade with her was running at such a low level? Millions of American teetotalers were either wholly ignorant or else disapproving of those staple French exports, brandy and wine, both sources of sin. (It is worth noting that Americans have often tended to skate over the wedding in Cana, an episode viewed by some French people as the most telling in the entire New Testament!) What could distant France possibly mean to rugged frontiersmen, their minds wholly preoccupied with the struggle against the Indians or even, more concretely still, with the struggle for life itself?

To this indifference we have to add another and specifically American characteristic. The best works written on our subject by

Americans—*American and French Culture, 1750-1948*, by Howard
Mumford Jones (1927), and *American Opinion of France* by Elizabeth
Brett White (1922)—are wholly in agreement with the researches of
the social psychologists and cultural anthropologists on this point:
there existed among the American immigrant population a very real
"rejection" of Europe. France, being a European nation, shared in the
consequences of this rejection, despite the limited number of French
immigrants. The American immigrant was arriving in America, the
potential paradise, precisely because he or she was fleeing from
Europe, either for political reasons or in order to escape a life of
poverty. These people formed the "first generation." They adapted
themselves as best they could to their new environment, learning to
speak halting English, but feeling uncomfortable, deprived of the way
of life they had left behind. The second generation, born in the
United States, reacted violently against the first. Educated in American schools, they spoke English without an accent and made fun of
their older relatives' appalling pronunciation. The second generation
was so anxious to adapt, to be totally American, that it tended to be
chauvinistic and intolerant. It is only the members of the third
generation who are able to rid themselves of both their grandfathers'
yearning for Europe and their fathers' prickly Americanism. The result
is what Max Lerner termed "the slaying of the European father":

> In America the vigorous European elements were brought into play
> against the exhausted ones. It was free enterprise arrayed against
> mercantilism, *laissez faire* against cameralism, individualism against
> hierarchy, natural rights against monarchy, popular nationalism
> against the dynastic regimes, social mobility against caste, the
> pioneering spirit against the status quo (Lerner, *America as a
> Civilization*, p. 25).

> This psychic necessity for rejecting Europe has affected the whole
> spectrum of American social thinking. It is true that there is an
> underlying self-confidence in American thought. . . . In his
> spiritual isolation the middle-class American seems to suffer from a
> sense of encirclement and to identify with a "European" or
> "foreign" source whatever ills he feels he is subject to (*ibid.*,
> p. 27).

Indifference to Europe and rejection of it are thus widespread
attitudes that affect France just as they do other countries. Are there

nevertheless any American images specific to France? Yes, but they tend to fall into two opposing categories. The first, the unfavorable one, is that of the frivolous Frenchman, lacking in seriousness (unlike the German), even corrupt. "It is impossible to conceal from the world that a large portion of French society ... has for years been wallowing in a cesspool of corruption," the *Review of Reviews* informed its readers toward the end of the nineteenth century, thus echoing the words of Jefferson a century before (quoted by McKay in *The United States and France*, p. 93).

There are those who have found a certain charm in that frivolity: "The French," wrote James Russell Lowell in 1873, "are the most wonderful creatures for talking wisely and acting foolishly that I ever saw. . . . *Esprit* is their ruin, and an epigram has twice the force of an argument. However, I have learned to like them ... and to see that they have some qualities we might borrow to advantage" (quoted by McKay, *United States and France*, p. 92).

These qualities are ones that a minority of Americans have loved with passion (we will ignore the snobbery of certain social elites in this respect). The Daughters of the American Revolution, the Ivy League, the Colonial Dames of America (an association that was founded in 1890 and established a Parisian branch in 1901), the American Club of Paris (founded in 1900), and other such high-toned associations all professed pro-French sentiments. But that was simply the attitude of East Coast society in general at this period. After Washington had been destroyed by the British during the War of 1812, the plans for the new capital were drawn up by a Frenchman, Major Pierre L'Enfant, and although his intentions took several decades to realize, his tenacity was such that the physical appearance of the federal capital today bears concrete witness to the attraction then exercised by France. In 1881, at the celebrations marking the anniversary of the capitulation of Yorktown, a sizable French delegation took part. The then secretary of state, William Evarts, went so far as to declare that his country's friendship with France was closer than that with England: "Nothing can limit it, nothing can disturb it; nothing shall disparage it."

It was decided that a common monument should be raised by both countries to celebrate the War of Independence. The Americans were to provide the site and base, the French the statue. Such was the origin

of the famous Statue of Liberty, unveiled in October 1886 by
President Grover Cleveland. The French delegation was led by
Ferdinand de Lesseps, chief architect of the Suez Canal, later compromised and ruined by his difficulties in Panama; but there was no
French minister in attendance. In 1889, the American colony in Paris
gave France a bronze replica of the giant statue. In 1900 the Americans
sent over a statue of Lafayette. In 1902 the French riposted with a
statue of the comte de Rochambeau. In 1912 the Comité France-
Amérique presented the United States with Auguste Rodin's famous
statue *La France*.

Less superficial than these exchanges of sculpture however, more
genuine than this "fashion" and this "snobbery," was the remarkable
attachment felt by many people in intellectual circles of the eastern
United States to French culture and the French way of life. It was not
only painters who felt this way—though hundreds of painters did
spend long periods in Paris during the early part of the century—but
also teachers, writers, philosophers, and historians.

A great many such figures were already visiting France during the
early years of the nineteenth century. It is true that students from
Harvard tended to prefer the German universities, especially Göt-
tingen (as in Longfellow's case), to the French; but they traveled
through France to get to them.

> The salons were opened to them, they were treated as friends,
> almost as regular members of the circle, and these young students
> fresh from their little New England universities enjoyed the
> privilege that many a French student would have envied of
> spending a whole evening, of meeting in their homes, of conversing
> with Mme de Duras or the duchesse de Broglie, Benjamin
> Constant, Talleyrand, Lafayette, and a score of other equally
> celebrated people. And when they returned home they were to keep
> up numerous correspondences (Rémond, *Les Etats-Unis devant
> l'opinion française*, pp. 218–19).

Some of them even spent long periods in France, Washington Irving
from 1815 to 1823, James Fenimore Cooper from 1826 to 1833, Ralph
Waldo Emerson in 1833 and again in 1848. There were even some
American salons in Paris, such as that of Mrs. Childe, where Tocqueville was a regular visitor.

This trend was continued by the next generation. There were

numerous marriages between French aristocrats and wealthy American heiresses. The families of Choiseul-Praslin, Pourtalès, Rohan-Chabot, Polignac, Decazes, and Castellane all contrived to restore their fortunes by transforming American heiresses into duchesses. American wealth also flowed into France in the form of gifts from extremely wealthy francophiles: the restoration of Malmaison by Edward Tuck, the art collections presented to museums by J. Pierpont Morgan, the gift of Louis Pasteur's house to Dôle by John D. Rockefeller, the works financed by Cornelius Vanderbilt, the "Wallace fountains" in Paris, and the study grants endowed by Andrew Carnegie. Artists and intellectuals were arriving in greater numbers than ever. The emphasis shifted from society salons to more modest but also more genuinely cultured centers. Gertrude Stein, for instance, was beginning to gather around her in Paris the group of artists and writers that later, between the wars, was to provide the most prodigious explosion of talent American literature has ever known. Emerging as they did from her circle, John Steinbeck, William Faulkner, Taylor Caldwell, and Ernest Hemingway were to succeed Edgar Allan Poe and Mark Twain as favorites of the French reading public.

It goes without saying that this group of francophile Americans, restricted though it may have been to writers, thinkers, intellectuals, and members of "high society," did not fail to influence the image that Americans have of the French. That image can take an infinite variety of forms: the haughty aristocrat, the amoral young artist or student derived from Henry Miller, the paunchy, mustachioed chauvinist, or the arbiter of fashion exemplified by Boni de Castellane. The 1914–18 war was to add two further and contrasting figures: the heroic *poilu* or infantry private in the trenches, and the profiteer making his pile in safety behind the lines. On the whole, the result is that any Frenchman visiting the United States is sure of receiving a friendly welcome almost everywhere and, in certain more limited circles, a truly unforgettable one. Such is the meaning of the "image." It is more than an insubstantial shadow. To the visiting Frenchman, faced with America's immensity, it guarantees that somewhere a corner of warm friendship awaits him.

3

IN 1914, FRANCE ENTERED THE WAR with total good conscience. Once again, in the eyes of her citizens, the arrogant Prussian was attacking her. The national spirit was at first one of elated and almost universal enthusiasm; the army consisted wholly of eager young heroes. Then, as people became numbed by the shock of finding that the war was cruel and bloody, that it was going to be long and pitiless, the national spirit hardened into a sort of cold resolve that reached its culmination on the Marne (September 1914), then at Verdun (February–July 1916), but brought in its wake a mounting tide of lassitude and despair. The cause was a good one—that of justice, of right. What were the Americans going to do?

1. The frictions over neutrality

Woodrow Wilson, the professor of jurisprudence and political science who had been governing the United States since March 1913, was little known in France. Until 1917 the only available information about him lay fairly well concealed in one or two scant biographies published in very small editions, a few hard-to-find translations of his books, and a few articles of varying accuracy. The French image of Wilson varied according to people's own bizarre and contradictory prejudices. Sometimes he was seen as a woolly-minded visionary, a figure contemptuously referred to by the royalist Léon Daudet as "the Kantian," with reference to Immanuel Kant's *Perpetual Peace*; sometimes as the dispenser of justice, the supreme arbiter; sometimes as a timid mediocrity, too susceptible to German influence. No one knew the "stubborn fighter," the man of action; no one had realized that in a way he was a man of genius.

At first, the Western wind seemed favorable. To Anglo-Saxon solidarity, being fostered for all it was worth by the British Liberals then in power, and to the indignation aroused in the United States by the violation of Belgian neutrality, there was added, more powerful than ever, the "myth of Lafayette."

> Forget us, God
> If we forget
> The sacred sword
> Of La Fayette,

wrote the poet Robert Underwood Johnson.

However, having appointed as his secretary of state a rabid pacifist, William Jennings Bryan, the "Great Commoner," Wilson started off by proclaiming American neutrality. This neutrality, he added, was to apply not only to actions but to thought as well. Indeed, it is worth noting that a later president, an admirer of Wilson, Franklin Delano Roosevelt, was careful to say in September 1939: "This nation will remain a neutral nation, but I cannot ask that every American remain neutral in thought as well." The fact was that Wilson, in 1914, was only too well aware of three major factors that had naturally escaped attention in France. The first was that no American interests were engaged in the war that had broken out. In fact, if it was to be a short war, as was then supposed, American interests would be badly damaged by it, for there would be a sudden decline in exports to Europe and a corresponding fall of the dollar in the world money markets. The second factor was that Wilson was by no means convinced of the justice of the Allied cause. True, Britain and France were good democracies; but they were also in alliance with the worst of all regimes, that of the czar. Third, and most important, Wilson was afraid of seeing the United States ripped apart should it enter the war. Of the American population of 95 million at that time, 13.3 million had been born abroad and 12.9 million were the offspring of foreign-born parents. Of those 26 million forming America's "foreign white stock," 6.4 million were German in origin and 3.4 million were anti-British Irish. What would happen if all those people remained more attached to their countries of origin than to their land of adoption?

However, Wilson also believed that the land they had adopted was

superior to all others. Precisely because it was made up of white
immigrants from many different origins (Wilson, a Southerner by
birth, even went so far as to speak of the Aryan nature of the
Americans, thereby dismissing the country's blacks, Orientals, and
even Jews), it had a unique mission. The mission of the American
people was above all to reestablish peace and to act in such a way that
the peace would prove lasting. The president, who as an academic had
specialized mainly in domestic politics, was later to be "sucked in," as
it were, by his great ambition to reform international relations, to
create a "new diplomacy." As a start, since there had to be someone
in the world to defend the sanctity of international law, Wilson, as
leader of the largest of the neutral countries, was going to make
himself responsible for defending the rights of neutrals.

All this resulted, during the next three years, in a series of
complications that the French found deeply disconcerting. How much
they would have preferred Theodore Roosevelt, the earlier president,
the lion-hunter, who was shouting from the rooftops that the United
States ought to be joining the war on the Allied side, in which cause
he was proposing to raise his own regiment, successors to the Cuban
Rough Riders of 1898! Wilson frowned on this attitude, even though
it gave him a definite tactical advantage: it compromised his Republican opponents, so that his struggle for reelection in November 1916
could be based on the campaign slogan: "If you want Peace with
Honor, Vote for Wilson."

As champion of the neutral nations, Wilson proposed in August
1914 that in the matter of international trade the 1909 Declaration of
London should be applied. This document divided all exportable
goods into three categories: those that constituted "absolute contraband" (arms and munitions only), which were the only kind that the
belligerents had the right to seize unconditionally; those that were
termed "conditional contraband," which could be confiscated only if
found on their way to enemy ports and intended for use by an enemy
government; and, third, an extremely lengthy list of goods, including
food, that could not be seized under any circumstances. Since such
legislation favored the Central, "besieged," Powers, neither Britain
nor France would accept it unless permitted to make unending
additions to the list of "absolute contraband" goods. The result, right
up to 1917, was a series of almost daily minor disputes.

Oddly, the American historians who have made studies of this "quasi-blockade"—even the best of them, including Ernest May and Marion Siney—have omitted any mention of France's role in it. Because Britain was far and away the Entente's largest naval power, they seem to have viewed the blockade as a purely American-British affair. However, a young American historian named Marjorie Farrar has now begun to correct this emphasis, and Yves Henri Nouailhat, a young French historian, has been delving even deeper into Franco-American relations between 1914 and 1917.

If we look below the surface, we find an odd contradiction between the French and British blockade policies with regard to the United States. Whereas in London—at least until David Lloyd George's rise to the premiership in December 1916—the main concern was always to humor Washington and to defend the pound (while at the same time permitting the export of goods to Holland with a very dubious final destination), the French attitude was one of absolute intransigence. The French law forbidding trade with the enemy was much more severe than the corresponding British law. After all, since there was no chance of the Americans entering the war on the German side, why allow them to trade with Germany? Moreover, as a result of the submarine warfare initiated in February 1915 and the subsequent torpedoing of passenger liners, particularly the *Lusitania* in May 1915, and because of the creation of spy rings and sabotage networks in the United States (exposed in late 1915), the Germans had by now drawn on themselves a fair proportion of the American fury earlier reserved for the Allies as a result of the "blockade."

Meanwhile, despite the hard line being taken in Paris, the "myth of Lafayette" was still alive. Even the share of American anger directed at the Allies—in the form of daily indignant protests—fell far more on Britain than on France. In 1916, a very bad year for relations with the Entente as a whole, the Americans were breathless with excitement over the heroic changes of fortune in the Battle of Verdun, and the result, for France, was a wealth of indulgence that their ambassador in Washington, Jusserand, fostered with skill and stressed in his dispatches. Meanwhile, the British ambassador was being forced to admit that "the United States is pro-Ally but anti-British," and Wilson, inaugurating the illumination of the Statue of Liberty, proposed a

toast to the French president Raymond Poincaré and had the band
play the "Marseillaise."

The "mission" that Wilson had set himself—the restoration of
peace—took diverse forms. Colonel House, a friend of Wilson as well
as a champion of his mission, was increasingly favorable to the Allies,
as was Robert Lansing, who succeeded Bryan in June 1915 as secretary
of state. Naturally, given the sheer dimensions of the struggle,
everything went wrong: offers of "good offices" and even of "forced
mediation" were politely refused by both the Allied and German
sides. In 1916, on the advice of House, Wilson proposed a system by
which the Entente was to abandon the seizure of neutral shipping and
Germany was to end its submarine warfare. If the Germans refused,
then "the United States would enter the war against Germany."
Wilson had the word "probably" inserted into this sentence, wisely,
as it turned out, since the Germans declared themselves ready to
accept the offer, whereas the Entente ultimately rejected the plan in
August 1916.

Preoccupied as he was until early November of that year with his
electoral campaign, Wilson waited until he had been reelected before
putting forward a peace proposal of a quite different nature. For a
long time House had been pondering the problem of the belligerents'
"war aims." This was a subject on which the belligerents themselves
were reticent in the extreme, and mention of it was forbidden in both
France and Germany by the official censorship. In a famous book
published in 1961, *Griff nach der Weltmacht*, the German historian
Fritz Fischer has made it quite clear to what extent, in September 1914
at least, the aims of the German Chancellor Theobald von Bethmann-
Hollweg—supported by big business, the army, and most intellectuals—were both imperialist and hegemonic. In France, until 1916
at least, the government had never gone further than vague declarations in favor of the liberation of French and Belgian occupied
territories and the reannexation of Alsace-Lorraine, lost in 1871. But
apart from this—and Wilson shrewdly suspected as much—France had
also signed secret treaties promising control of the Bosporus and
Dardanelles to Russia, the Trentino, Trieste, and part of Dalmatia to
Italy, and so on.

It was Colonel House, at a meeting with the French premier Aristide

Briand, in February 1916, who put in the latter's mind the idea of probing more deeply into the subject. Briand, who had charmed House as only he knew how, set up an investigation among the military, the Comité des Forges (the leaders of the steel industry), and a number of intellectuals, all of whom were officially convened in early 1917 to form a study committee presided over by the historian Ernest Lavisse. The outcome was an excessively ambitious plan, the later avatars of which I shall be returning to later on.

The soldiers, for their part, were fighting not in order to achieve any particular ambitions, or for any consciously planned motives, but simply in order to defend their country. House and Wilson had not been mistaken when they thought that, by maneuvering the various governments into a *public* statement of their war aims, they would automatically force those governments to reduce them. Hence Wilson's note of 18 December 1916, requesting both sides to make clear declarations of their ambitions.

Where the American leaders did make a mistake, however, was in believing that such declarations could be made to lead to some kind of compromise. We now know that the Germans were absolutely determined never to give up Alsace-Lorraine and that for the French— including even some of the pacifist minority—the return of Alsace-Lorraine constituted a *sine qua non*. But the failure of this last bid for peace on Wilson's part did not stem from that misperception. Unfortunately, its date had been extremely ill-chosen. The Central Powers had just taken Bucharest and issued a haughtily worded peace offer to their opponents. The result was that in the eyes of the French people Wilson was an accomplice of the enemy. In France itself, Briand was then in the process of ousting Marshal Joseph Joffre and replacing him with the likable and charming Henri Nivelle, who was promising victory by the next spring. The Germans, by no means anxious to have Wilson taking part in any eventual peace conference, and already preparing for a new submarine offensive, rejected the American offer. The Allies took advantage of this refusal to expound their own aims in terms so vague that Wilson was bitterly disappointed and even offended.

He then decided to take up a new position, one calculated to stir up a veritable storm of imprecations, particularly in France. In his message to Congress of 22 January 1917, using somewhat abstract language, Wilson proposed a peace between equals, "peace without victory"!

2. France and the American entry into the war

Wilson's message to Congress was delivered on 22 January. Seven days later, to his profound amazement, he received a visit from the German ambassador Count von Bernstorff and was told that on 1 February Germany intended to launch a campaign of unrestricted submarine warfare. Until then, German submarines had attacked only *enemy* cargo vessels; moreover, Bernstorff had given Wilson an official pledge after the *Lusitania* affair that they would not in future sink liners carrying civilian passengers. This meant that before any torpedo attack the German U-boat commanders were obliged to make certain that the ship in their sights was an enemy vessel and not a neutral one, thereby enormously increasing the risks to themselves. Since all German cargo vessels were by now blockaded in port, so that the only vessels left on the high seas were all either Allied or neutral, and since the cargoes of neutral shipping were increasingly intended for the Entente, this new unrestricted submarine warfare was to consist quite simply in attacking *any vessel on sight*. It was a terrible blow to the rights of neutral nations, including, of course, those of the Americans. The calculation of the German High Command was that this new campaign would enable its navy to sink 600,000 tons of enemy shipping a month—an estimate that proved accurate—and that in six months, its lifeline cut, Britain would capitulate—which proved the weak point in their plans.

Let us turn to Georges Clemenceau, then only a senator and a journalist, to find out how the situation developed between 22 and 29 January. His reactions to Wilson's proposal are probably very revealing of what his compatriots were thinking: "Never before has any political assembly heard so fine a sermon on what human beings might be capable of accomplishing if only they were not human.... His eyes riveted on the abyss of the ages, gathering himself for a supreme bound, he leaps forward far beyond the limitations of time and space and soars high in the void, way above mere things, whose inferiority resides in the sheer fact of their existence." But as Clemenceau saw it, this idealism of Wilson's was not to be a substitute for national egoism: "We see him . . . sitting down at the future conference table in typical American fashion—before he has been invited" (*Homme enchainé*, 2, 3, and 25 January 1917).

Wilson's reaction to the German decision, which came on 1 February, was to break off diplomatic relations with Germany. He still hoped against hope that the German submarines would not actually dare to attack American shipping. He was determined not to enter the war except in the event of an "open act" of hostility on the part of the Germans, meaning the actual torpedoing of a United States cargo vessel. Since American shipowners kept all their vessels safely in port during the next few weeks, this "open act" did not occur until 12 March with the torpedoing of the *Algonquin*, followed by that of several other American vessels. Meanwhile the American public had learned to its fury that Germany was proposing an alliance with Mexico (through the "Zimmermann telegram"), while the Entente cause had suddenly been miraculously "purified" by the fall of the czarist regime and its replacement with a republic. In short, on 6 April 1917 the United States declared war on Germany, without any great enthusiasm, it is true, but with its usual good conscience and the widespread feeling that it had a vast and vague mission to accomplish—nothing less than the regeneration of Europe.

What was the reaction of the French to this happy event? On the part of the government—led since 14 March by Alexandre Ribot—there was overwhelming relief at the solution of a problem that the general public hadn't even been aware of. The Entente was on the verge of bankruptcy. It was true that Wilson had, after some hesitation, authorized American banks (Morgan's in particular) to make loans to the Allies. But in the spring of 1917 the Entente's credit had reached its lowest ebb. Now the Treasury of the United States, a country riding high on a wave of prosperity, was about to open its coffers. Instead of bank loans there would be state loans. Even so, after at first considering making France an enormous interest-free loan in memory of Benjamin Franklin, the Americans eventually proved more prudent, even mistrustful. Every month saw the necessity for yet another round of bitter and seemingly endless negotiations. But in the end the Treasury always gave way. The foundation for the future war-debt problem was being solidly laid—but while one's house is on fire one's first concern is always just to put out the blaze.

Largely unaware of these harsh realities, the French public was much
more occupied with the imminent arrival of American troops, with
thoughts of the Americans' enormous industrial capacity, and with
the boost to morale produced by "the arrival on the scene of the just
arbiter" (*Le Figaro*). The French government, on the other hand, was
only too well aware of the price to be paid for all this help. Its
ambassador in Washington, Jules Jusserand, was unfortunately a
friend of Theodore Roosevelt. Wilson was consequently wary of him,
and a number of French intellectuals were attempting to have him
replaced. As a result, in February 1917 the great philosopher Henri
Bergson was sent to the United States with official instructions to
improve relations with Wilson and government circles generally. In
fact, Jusserand, who had been in the United States since 1904, had acquired a very good knowledge of the American mentality. He knew the
repugnance it felt for overt propaganda, and it had been his intention
to play his cards discreetly, to urge the United States toward direct
action, but gently, without ever forcing its hand.

Was this enough? In Paris the answer was thought to be no, and
after the United States' entry into the war the French government
decided on two dramatic moves. The first was to send over a
delegation of high-ranking representatives headed by Marshal Joffre
and René Viviani, who had been premier in 1914 and became deputy
premier in 1917. Viviani was renowned as an orator, and Joffre
enjoyed enormous popularity. The aim of the visit was "to determine
without delay, and in their broad outline, directives for the cooperation of the American forces with the Allied armies. . . . Let the victor
of the Marne bring to the new soldiers of Liberty the fruit of his
glorious experience, since this will be an inestimable mark of
friendship and esteem for the Great American Nation" (André Kaspi,
Le Temps des Américains, p. 32). The idea proved a happy one.
Having dropped anchor on 24 April at Hampton Roads, the delegation proceeded to Washington aboard the presidential yacht. Joffre's
personal success was enormous. He produced the most amazing effect
on Wilson, House, Lansing, and the other American leaders. According to Lansing, he had the mind of a sage and the nature of a
child, possessing at once a will of iron and a tender heart. House
compared him to General Grant. When presented to the Senate,
Joffre replied to its enthusiastic acclamation with the simple words: "I

do not speak English. *Vivent les Etats-Unis!''* A long tour through the
country, during which he was constantly surrounded by crowds waving
the French flag, increased this success still further. In New York more
than a million people turned out to see him. The *New York Times* of
10 May, which devoted its first three pages to the event, claimed that
the welcome exceeded that ever given by the city to any man or group
of men. It then went on to greet these "representatives of the Nation
that after almost a hundred and fifty years is once again our ally."
There was also a famous photograph of Joffre saluting the statue of
Lafayette. "The Americans," writes André Kaspi, the author of a key
thesis on American aid, *La France et le concours américain*, "were
bowled over by this simplicity. Here was a professional military man
who really had all the facts at his fingertips" (Kaspi, *Le Temps des
Américains*, p. 37). Joffre also enchanted them on another score.
Unlike the other French military leaders, whom we shall come to later,
all he asked for was purely and simply the creation and dispatch to
France of "a great American army," with an advance guard of 50,000
to arrive as soon as possible.

The second major French initiative was the decision to create a
"High Commission of the French Republic" in the United States and
to appoint as its head the brilliant journalist and deputy André
Tardieu, who knew America well and in 1908 had published a book on
the subject, *Notes sur les Etats-Unis*. This high commission was set up
principally to deal with economic relations between the two countries.
In the end it had a staff of twelve thousand, including a propaganda
section headed by the teacher Louis Aubert and the journalist
Stéphane Lauzanne, whose efforts we shall hear of later.

Opinion in France, however delighted it may have been with its new
ally—or rather "associate," since Wilson did not wish to enter into
the commitments entailed by a formal alliance—was for some time
curiously reticent about saying so. This may partly have been because
the illusion of a swift victory that had gripped the French nation in the
spring of 1917 suddenly vanished with the failure of Nivelle's
offensive at Chemin des Dames on 16 April. The result was a period of
despair marked by a number of military mutinies (all minor in
themselves but nevertheless affecting two-thirds of all French divisions), by a wave of pacifism and defeatism on the home front, and by
strikes linked with rising prices.

The quotations in the following pages have been borrowed from André Kaspi's book, most of them deriving originally from the records of the postal censorship. The Americans had fewer than 20,000 soldiers, including their National Guard. An army isn't something one can improvise overnight. "The war is far from being over in my opinion," one French soldier wrote on 6 May. "On the contrary, the entry of the United States just means that it can be continued." In other minds, the discouragement implicit in such a prolongation was replaced by an illusion: that the Americans were going to take the place of French troops in the trenches and fight on their behalf. France was exhausted. "Quickly, let the Americans come over and replace us so that we can work behind the lines. I'm sure the French race will have shrunk a great deal" (letter of 29 June). Another source of uneasiness was the suspicion that, when peace came, Wilson was going to prevent France from attaining its legitimate aims. Hadn't he proclaimed that only the "military clique" in Germany was bad and that the German people were good? In France at that time, battered and bleeding as she was, it was an article of faith that all Germans were belligerent, arrogant, coarse, and barbarous.

It was not until June, with the arrival of General John J. Pershing, the American commander-in-chief, in Paris, and that of the United States First Division at Saint-Nazaire, that optimism was reborn and French enthusiasm reawakened. The welcome Pershing received was very moving. He was acclaimed by the people of Paris and went to the Picpus Cemetery to lay a huge wreath on the grave of Lafayette. Once again, Lafayette. "Lafayette, we are here!" was the symbolic phrase put in the general's mouth. On the Fourth of July an American battalion paraded through Paris on its way—naturally—to the Picpus Cemetery. The Stars and Stripes, displayed everywhere, was greeted with cheers. The American soldiers were "splendid fellows," "strong as oxes," "terrific and so athletic," fantastically well equipped, and with a great gift for organization. The very pessimistic found them a little lazy and, above all, ill-informed about the war—"as ignorant as schoolboys," in fact. "The Americans, although they're brave, do still have a lot to learn." Also, they had too much money and were sending prices up, to the great delight of profiteers of all sorts. The French soldier was "looking with all his soul toward the West, where paradoxically he can see a new sun dawning."

The Americans on their side were, in Kaspi's words, "discovering the country of Joffre." They arrived in France bursting with fellow feeling. The *poilus*, one American woman wrote home, "are heroes who have saved the world from the powers of darkness." The Americans also saw France's state of exhaustion. "The French are tired out," one airman wrote. "The Americans will have to take France's place or Germany will win" (letter of 1 June 1917). "Poor France" had to be saved. France "is depending on us, we mustn't let her down." The French propaganda department in the United States eventually began to be worried about such attitudes and to play down this potentially harmful picture of an enfeebled, already annihilated France. On 27 July, Tardieu wrote that sob stories were bound to have a disastrous effect "on a public opinion much more impressionable than is supposed in France, much more like that of the French than that of the English, and dominated above all by a passionate love of success."

Let us conclude with a quotation from Felix Frankfurter, sent over in July on an information-gathering mission to France: "The arrival of the American troops, and the idea that the United States is going to relieve France of a large part of its burden, have given France a great boost and checked the pacifist tendencies apparent in the spring" (from Newton D. Baker's papers, quoted by Kaspi, *Le Temps des Américains*, p. 137).

3. American assistance 1917–18

Once financial aid had been guaranteed, once the first American contingents had arrived (despite their purely symbolic function in a war involving millions of fighting men), the real problems emerged. It was on the solutions found to these problems that the final verdict on American assistance was to depend. Chauvinists on both sides of the Atlantic were later to pronounce contradictory judgments on this point. In America it was claimed that the Americans had not only saved the exhausted Allies but actually taken over from them completely. They had won the war. Not at all, came the retort from Europe. The Americans came too late, and they played no appreciable part in the war at all until September 1918. The war was finally won before any massive intervention on their part. It was won by the British and, above all, by the French, who lost 1,394,000 men as opposed to the Americans' mere 50,000.

It need hardly be said that these judgments, both equally categorical and dogmatic, are also both equally false, and that the question is really a very complex one.

The Entente was facing two tragic problems in 1917. The first was that of *shipping space*. In April 1917 the Germans set a record—one never surpassed in the Second World War—by sinking 850,000 tons of shipping. The Allies' recently adopted convoy system had lessened the losses, but it had also slowed down the turnaround of the ships involved. The American merchant fleet, largely concentrated in the Great Lakes, could not compensate for these losses until American shipyards were able to build up to full production. Civilian consumption in the Entente countries had to be cut back—hence the rising prices. It was as much as any of the Allies could do to keep their armies and their war factories supplied. Only through the Allied Maritime Transport Council—in practice a shipping pool—with its executive headed by the Englishman Arthur Salter and the Frenchman Jean Monnet, did it eventually prove possible to maintain a more equitable distribution of the ships available. But the Council was not created until March 1918, and even then the Americans did not actually become party to it until October, only a very short while before the armistice on 11 November.

The other problem was that of *manpower*. As it was, there was absolutely no possibility of the new Russian Republic's being able to persuade its troops to continue the fight; but then there came the October (Bolshevik) Revolution, and in November 1917 Russia withdrew from the war. The Germans began bringing back their best divisions from the eastern front and putting them into action in France. By late 1917, Philippe Pétain, the French commander-in-chief, was predicting that the Germans would have a superiority of twenty divisions by the end of March 1918 and of thirty divisions by the following May. Only the Americans, in theory, could possibly close this tragic gap, of which the German general Erich Ludendorff would undoubtedly take full advantage. But this problem itself resulted in a series of further difficulties, which became the subject of passionate argument during 1917 and 1918.

1. Could the Americans actually succeed in raising and training a

vast army? That was their business, and the Selective Service Act did resolve the problem to a great extent. The French, wishing to bring their influence to bear on this inexperienced army, sent instructors over to America and set up training camps in France. Were they too arrogant? At all events they met with polite but firm resistance. You are teaching us trench warfare, they were told, but the American army intends to reintroduce open warfare into the campaign. They were of course laboring under an illusion. In September 1918 the American headquarters at Montfaucon found itself quite unable to cope with the troop bottlenecks that occurred. But the fact remains that even though the Americans preferred French influence to British influence, a perfectly legitimate national pride still confined that influence to strictly technical areas.

2. Could an American army actually be transported with the inadequate shipping space available? By March 1918 the need for troops had acquired such urgency that absolute priority was given to troop transport, above all that of infantry. It is a fact that 1,000 men take up the same amount of shipping space as 5,000 tons of cargo. Almost the entire American merchant fleet was carrying soldiers. The British fleet also put sufficient vessels at the disposal of the United States to double the volume of troop transport. But was it *also* possible to ship heavy equipment, thereby making the fullest use of American industrial potential? As we shall see, another solution was found: *the equipment of the Americans by French industry*.

3. Where were the troops to be shipped? Ferdinand Foch, who had become commander-in-chief of the Allied armies in March–April 1918, wanted to reestablish the second front in Russia, which would have meant a massive American landing at Vladivostok in Siberia. Wilson disliked this idea, because he foresaw hostile reactions from the Russian people. Above all, the president, the American generals, and the War Department were "Napoleonic" in their attitude. The whole American military tradition was weighted in favor of a strategy of *concentration*: one should defeat the strong enemy where he is strongest—in other words, send everything to the French front through Brest, Saint-Nazaire, Nantes, Rochefort, Royan, and the Graves peninsula. Wilson did eventually resign himself to landing a small contingent of 7,000 men at Vladivostok, in August 1918; but on

the other hand he persisted in his adamant refusal to send anything
more than a few token detachments to the Italian front.

4. How were the American troops to be used? This was the main
subject of dispute. At a time when both the French and the British
divisions had been reduced to exhaustion by successive German
offensives, the Entente's political leaders, particularly Clemenceau
(who on 16 November 1917 had become French premier), as well as its
generals, especially Foch and Pétain, wanted *amalgamation*, in other
words, reinforcement of depleted French or British divisions with
American regiments. Fighting side by side with the Entente's veterans,
their argument went, the fresh troops from across the Atlantic, whose
courage was of course beyond question, would rapidly acquire the
necessary experience. Moreover, no Allied divisions would need to be
dissolved. Unfortunately, however, this solution once again clashed
with the legitimate pride, not only of Wilson, Secretary of War
Newton Baker, General Pershing, and General Tasker Bliss (the
American representative on the Interallied Council), but also with that
of American opinion in general. What was wanted, and as quickly as
possible, was an autonomous American army that would deal the
enemy blows of its very own. The advantage of this from the
Washington viewpoint would be not only psychological but also
political. Wilson saw the Europeans as dangerous imperialists, and he
wanted to impose on them a "new diplomacy" founded on morality.
But how was he to impose any such thing if he wasn't in control of his
own forces, if they were dispersed among Allied divisions with their
own chains of command? Joffre's popularity in the United States
stemmed in part from the fact that he alone of the top-ranking French
generals argued in favor of an independent American army.

How were these problems eventually resolved? André Kaspi, already
quoted, has made an extremely detailed study of this question, using
both French and American source material. I shall give not more than
a résumé of his findings here.

On 2 November 1917, the American Expeditionary Force in France
comprised 77,600 men, of whom 53,800 were actually combatants,
while the remainder provided the necessary back-up services. By 5
January 1918 the number had risen to 161,000 men, of whom 113,000
were combatants. The arrival rate during 1917 was thus quite low:

from April onward an average of 18,000 men per month. In the first three months of 1918 the figure rose to 40,000 a month. By 30 March, 284,000 in all had arrived, 173,000 of them combatants. On 21 March Ludendorff had launched the first of his big offensives, one that brought him within a hair's-breadth of victory and was to be followed by three more between then and 15 July. It was not until 18 July that the French generals Charles Mangin and Jean Degoutte launched the first successful counteroffensive. Meanwhile, on 29 July there were 1,102,000 Americans in France, 796,000 of them combatants. This means that in the preceding four months the arrival rate had been stepped up enormously: an average of 204,000 men had crossed the Atlantic every month. In the last three months of the war this figure was to rise to more than 250,000, enabling the Americans to reach the impressive total of 2,013,000 men in Europe by 11 November.

But this extraordinary success—not a ship was sunk—is partly to be explained by the French industrial effort. Since they were unable to bring over all their heavy equipment, the American troops were supplied with what they needed by France. This operation was in no way comparable to the "Arsenal of the Democracies" in World War Two. This point is so often misunderstood that I shall give a few figures. From 6 November 1917 to 11 November 1918 the French delivered to the American Expeditionary Force:

> 1,871 75mm guns ⎱   equal to three months' total French
>   762 howitzers ⎰   production in 1917
>   224 long-range field guns
>   10 million shells
> 57,000 machine guns and Lewis guns
>   206 million rounds of ammunition

Of the expeditionary force's 6,287 airplanes, 4,791 were of French manufacture. The 227 light tanks and 44 heavy tanks used from September to October 1918 were all French too. Thus France supplied the Americans with 100 percent of their field guns and howitzers, 100 percent of their tanks, almost 100 percent of their ammunition, 81 percent of their aircraft, and 57 percent of their long-range guns.

Once shipped over to France, equipped, then trained, the "Sammies," as they were called in France to distinguish them from the

British "Tommies," played a belated but rapidly increasing part in active operations.

The first battles in which they took part occurred in the spring of 1918. On 20 April, having been attached to the French Eighth Army, the U.S. Twenty-Sixth Division was positioned in what should have been a quiet sector of the front at Seicheprey, to the west of Pont à Mousson in the Meuse. Perhaps in order to test its fighting ability, the Germans attacked it. Lacking experience, despite putting up a brave fight, the Americans were forced to fall back, an outcome that General Gérard, the Eighth Army commander, attributed not to any defect on the part of the troops but to the American command, which according to him "was lacking in decision."

A month later, in a much more lively sector, the U.S. First Division was assigned to an operation at Cantigny, in the Somme. The plan of attack was drawn up by Lieutenant Colonel George Marshall, then at the outset of his great career and thought by the French officers to be excessively arrogant and "determined not to listen to us." The village of Cantigny was attacked and taken on 28 May, with the help of a hundred or so French guns. The French artillery officers in command of the guns had great praise for the American infantry, which suffered heavy losses. The attack was given very little coverage in France because on 27 May, the day before, Ludendorff had launched his third offensive and broken the French lines at Chemin des Dames.

While the Germans were advancing in the Marne sector, the U.S. Second Division was transferred to the neighborhood of Château-Thierry. There, at Belleau Wood, they fought a magnificent battle that was instrumental in preventing the Germans from advancing on Paris (June 1918). This time the French people did hear about it. The newspapers were full of nothing else. The Americans had saved the French capital. At last, after almost a year, American help was beginning to have some effect. Poincaré, the French president, as well as Clemenceau, Foch, and Pétain, all congratulated General Pershing, who had by then been in France a whole year. The bravery displayed by the Americans outside Château-Thierry played an important part in raising the morale of the Entente. "I am waiting for the Americans and the tanks," Pétain was supposed to have said in 1917. Now the Americans had arrived in earnest.

And the tanks too, as a matter of fact. Hundreds of them had secretly been massed on the western flank of the German salient in the forest of Villers-Cotterêts. To the north, along with a large number of French divisions and under the orders of the French general Mangin, were the First and Second U.S. divisions; to the south, under the command of General Hunter Liggett, was the U.S. First Army Corps, made up at that time of the Twenty-Sixth U.S. Division and one French division. At dawn on 18 July, emerging from the woods and advancing eastward through the misty wheatfields, the French and Americans broke through the German lines and gained several kilometers in one day. The First U.S. Division had lost 7,000 men, the second 4,000. It was the turning point of the war at last. At that time, in various sectors along the front, there were sixteen American divisions in the front line, five of them on the British front. "Your men have been, quite simply, splendid," a French general told his American colleagues.

From then on, the days of "amalgamation" were over. The American First Army was constituted on 22 July and given full responsibility for a sector of the front, a short sector, it is true, but an important one. Pershing's dream had been made a reality. Foch, too, came around to the same idea: "The cause of the Entente will be much better served by an American army than by a scattering of American units." Even Ludendorff was beginning to take the Americans seriously.

Finally the new First Army was entrusted with a major operation, that of eliminating the Saint-Mihiel salient. The Germans had held unbroken possession of this small town ever since 1914, and, facing south as it did, perched on a spur of the Meuse hills, it had enabled them to block the important Paris-Nancy rail route. Elimination of this salient would be clear proof of the Americans' skill in "open warfare." General Pershing, in his Chaumont headquarters, laid the most meticulous plans for the operation, not without a few clashes with Foch, whose directives as inter-Allied commander-in-chief he always accepted, but only, as it were, within the very strictest letter of the law. Ten American divisions, plus four French divisions under American command and four more American divisions held in reserve, were to take part in the battle. All the troops were transported to their positions by French trucks. The French provided the artillery, the tanks, and some of the aircraft (one air division, or 600 planes).

The U.S. First Army had 3,010 pieces of artillery at its disposal, 1,681 manned by American crews, 1,329 by French crews. All these guns, without exception, had been manufactured in France. The French army also lent 300 tanks. In other words, this battle under American command was to be one in which soldiers from both countries would be truly fighting side by side.

The offensive was launched on 12 September and proved successful. The Germans fell back and evacuated the salient. Fifteen thousand prisoners and 466 field guns were captured with relatively light Allied losses. "For the United States Army," Kaspi writes, "Saint-Mihiel was a milestone: its existence could no longer be questioned. Pershing had definitively won his battle against the partisans of amalgamation" (*Le Temps des Américains*, p. 289).

From the battle of Saint-Mihiel onward a remarkable change began to take place. Week by week the American sector of the front grew steadily wider, expanding westward from the Meuse toward the Argonne and Champagne, eastward into the plain of the Woëvre, between the Meuse and the Moselle. In other words, the Americans were now occupying the famous Verdun sector. They played their part in the triple offensive ordered by Foch on 25 and 26 September—the British in Flanders, the French south of the Somme, the Americans in the Argonne and the area around Montfaucon. The Germans were taken by surprise. But the results achieved by the U.S. First Army were less brilliant than Foch had anticipated. The Germans put up a savage resistance, and, due to the American staff officers' inexperience, a number of "indescribable" bottlenecks occurred. The roads became so blocked by troop trucks that the artillery couldn't be brought up. Rain, mud, fatigue, and the inadequate numbers of military police were the root causes of these difficulties. The French expressed concern, but American optimism remained unshaken. If the war had gone on until the summer of 1919 their ever-increasing divisions—large divisions of 25,000 men each—would by then have been holding a third, if not half, of the western front. Their role in the war would have become a leading one.

This explains why Pershing, backed by a large section of American public opinion, considered the armistice concluded in November 1918 to be premature.

1. The Armistice of 11 November

On 6 October 1918, the Swiss legation in Washington handed the State Department a German note asking for the opening of armistice negotiations on the basis of the American president's Fourteen Points peace program of 8 January 1918. This was the start of a period of intense diplomatic activity that was to result in the Rethondes armistice on the following 11 November. Those negotiations are now well known to historians, and we shall not follow all their intricacies here. On the other hand, it does seem essential to clarify the French and American positions.

President Wilson had taken his country into the war not in order to satisfy any territorial ambitions or even with the intention of acquiring new markets. It had been his wish to defend the "rights of neutrals" violated by the Germans' "unrestricted submarine warfare." But over and above that slightly abstruse reason, he had also entered the war in order to pursue the mission of the American people: to find the way back to peace and to act in such a way that the peace became definitive. Little by little the key elements of the "new diplomacy" had marshaled themselves in his mind. Under the protection of a League of Nations, states would be spurred on to practice a diplomacy based on morality. This latter quality, in Wilson's eyes, could flourish only within the framework of liberal democracy. What he desired, therefore, was a "world safe for democracy." He also wished to see acceptance of the equality of rights among nations, however large or small, with the consequent elimination of such time-honored practices of European diplomacy as the balance of power, the concert of Europe, secret military alliances, violations of international law, arms races, "strategic" frontiers, domination of one people by another (at least in the case of white peoples), and, at the same time, the implementation—including any economic adjustments that proved necessary—of the principle of self-determination. Having once expressed a desire for "peace without victory," he had now come to advocate "peace through victory," but in his eyes the peace was the same in both cases. Perpetually concerned over the seductive proclamations of the Bolsheviks, who had taken over the "peace without victory" idea for their own ends, he was now convinced that the war aims of the United States must be proclaimed publicly and that this statement of principles should be seasoned with a certain number of territorial considerations. Such were the intentions behind the Fourteen Points.

It was just before the promulgation of Wilson's Fourteen Points that the aging Clemenceau, the "Tiger," had been appointed prime minister of France by his old enemy Raymond Poincaré, the president of the French Republic. Poincaré was able to summon the necessary spirit of self-abnegation to appoint Clemenceau because, as a result of the pacifist troubles of 1917, the Tiger was one of only two possible options. Either a compromise peace was going to have to be patched together—in which case Poincaré would have had to turn to the pacifist leader Joseph Caillaux—or else, as was the president's own wish, the war was going to be fought to the bitter end, in which case it was Clemenceau—literally being clamored for by public opinion, socialists excepted—who was the only choice. "The country will know that it is being defended," Clemenceau said in his ministerial statement of 16 November. And once that iron hand had taken control, civil servants and administrators immediately began to toe the line, France's soldiers tensed themselves for one last effort, and morale soared, despite all the grave menaces lowering over the country.

Clemenceau had never taken a position on the Fourteen Points. One of them at least could have given him nothing but total satisfaction, and that was number eight, which stated: "The wrong done to France by Prussia in 1871 in the matter of Alsace-Lorraine, which has unsettled the peace of the world for nearly fifty years, should be righted." As for the other thirteen, all in good time. Moreover, Clemenceau had consistently refused to make any public statement of his war aims. "I am fighting the war," was all he would say. First prevent defeat. Then secure victory. It ought also not to be

forgotten that Clemenceau, an old radical-socialist, was in no way
hostile to Wilson's "new diplomacy." At most, his realism tended to
make him mistrustful of the abstract form in which Wilson's thought
was sometimes clothed. In any case, Clemenceau had always openly
stated that he was in favor of a "just peace based on international
law."

When Germany addressed its request for an armistice to the United
States alone and accepted the Fourteen Points—which included the
cession of Alsace-Lorraine to France—as a basis for discussion, the
French reaction was one of deep uneasiness. It was expected that
Wilson would immediately consult his associates. But he did nothing
of the sort. For three weeks he simply continued to exchange notes
with Germany and to make them public. Reassurance came quickly,
however. Wilson was not, as the Germans had hoped, going to play
the role of arbitrator between the two sides. His tone was that of a
victor: he demanded an immediate cessation of submarine warfare and
tried to take advantage of the circumstances to force Germany into
creating a democratic regime. In the event, the kaiser, William II,
abandoned by his supporters, did in fact abdicate on 9 November, and
a defeated Germany was soon ablaze with revolution.

In addition, the request immediately put forward by the Allies,
on 9 October, that military clauses should be inserted into the
armistice, preventing Germany from resuming the struggle, was
accepted by the American president without demur. Lastly, in the
middle of October Wilson decided to send Colonel House over to
Paris, where discussions with the Entente leaders took place from 26
October to 4 November.

For France there were two main problems. First, should the
armistice be signed before the military defeat of Germany had been
completed, especially since Pétain had persuaded Foch to agree to the
launching of a vast Franco-American offensive in Lorraine, set pro-
visionally for 15 November? Second, was it possible to accept the
Fourteen Points as a basis for the subsequent peace treaty?

As for the timeliness of the armistice, Poincaré and the ultranationalists feared that if it came too soon it might "break the spirit of
the French army." He wrote as much to Clemenceau, who retorted
very sharply. Clemenceau himself inclined more to the arguments of
Foch and Pétain. On 25 October Foch called a meeting at Senlis of the

commanders-in-chief of the three armies, Pershing representing the
Americans, Douglas Haig the British, and Pétain the French. Pershing
was hostile to the idea of an armistice. Aware of the growing role his
army was playing and avid for a greater share of glory, he was also
deeply imbued with the American tradition of unconditional surrender, as demanded of General Robert E. Lee at Appomattox Court
House in April 1865. Pershing wanted total victory. Haig, the British
commander, was the most pessimistic. In his judgment the main
burden of the war had been falling since March on his army. The
Germans were slowly falling back, but they were still resisting. Their
strength had not been broken. He thought that the most that could be
asked was an armistice stipulating the evacuation of occupied territories and Alsace-Lorraine. Pétain, echoing a note written by Foch
himself on 16 October, took up an intermediate position. An
armistice, yes! And as soon as possible in order to avoid further
bloodshed! But its absolute condition must be evacuation by the
Germans not only of the occupied territories but also, and within a
period of thirty days, of *the entire left bank of the Rhine.* Then
Germany would be truly defeated. But the Germans will never accept
that, countered Haig, who was in any case suspicious of French aims in
the Rhineland. Yes, they will, Pétain insisted. Furthermore, acceptance of the British plan would permit the Germans to shorten their
lines, thereby increasing their defensive capability.

In the end, Lloyd George gave his support to the French view, as did
House in Wilson's name. The first problem had therefore been
resolved.

There remained the second: the Fourteen Points. Wilson's position
on this matter admitted of no argument. The Germans had accepted
the Fourteen Points, therefore the Allies must too. If they didn't, then
the Americans had ways of bringing immense pressure to bear:
decreasing their financial aid, even concluding a separate peace. The
Entente had no choice.

Moreover, the main dispute was not between the Americans and the
French but between the Americans and the British. The latter, since
they were the possessors of the world's largest war fleet, were extremely
loathe to accept Wilson's point two, concerning freedom of the seas,
since it would deprive them of the power of blockade, a weapon that
had certainly proved its efficacy in the present war, having already

reduced Germany to misery and starvation. Even House's skill and obstinacy could not prevent the British from expressing a reservation with regard to point two. The main French request was much more acceptable, and House had no difficulty in obtaining Wilson's agreement on the subject. The French "comments" on the Fourteen Points program pointed out that it implied the payment by Germany of "reparations" for the damage suffered by the Entente's civilian populations. It should be noted that Wilson rejected the traditional notion of war indemnities, extracted from the defeated because they have proved the less strong: *Vae victis!* On the other hand, since he was as convinced as Clemenceau himself of the German government's "guilt" in starting the war, the idea of reparations seemed to him a just one.

On 5 November, therefore, Secretary of State Lansing informed the Germans, in the name of the Allied and Associated Powers, that their plenipotentiaries were invited to conclude an armistice. On 11 November, at eleven in the morning, the cease-fire was sounded along the entire front. And on 18 November everyone was staggered to learn that President Wilson would be coming to Europe in person to head the American delegation at the peace conference.

The conference was to be held in Paris. France, after all, was the country that had shed the most blood in the struggle. The American diplomats were apprehensive about the feverish anti-German atmosphere then reigning in the French capital, while the French were uneasy about having Wilson, a head of state, present at all. Since he outranked Clemenceau, might he not snatch the presidency of this conference of revenge from under the Tiger's nose? No. Wilson was to attend simply as head of his government. Everything was working out admirably, or so it seemed.

2. Psychological deterioration

It would be impossible to imagine a more widespread and more intense popularity than that enjoyed by Wilson when he arrived in France. From both extreme left and extreme right, for the moment reconciled, there came the same paeans of praise. Even *L'Action française*—the royalist paper run by Léon Daudet and Charles

Maurras—printed a "tribute to President Wilson," the age's outstanding man of action. The majority of newspapers, those supporting
Clemenceau, praised the American president above all as *the victor*.
The socialists, the only political group hostile to Clemenceau (at that
time making up about 20 percent of the electorate), saw Wilson
principally as the champion of the "new diplomacy"—the diplomacy
of peoples that was to eliminate war forever. The fact was that at that
time the French socialists had no great heroes of their own to inspire
the masses. Their own leader, Jean Jaurès, had been assassinated in
1914, and Lenin was still seen as no more than the leader of a minority
group. Who was there to set up in opposition to Clemenceau, the
"strike-breaker," other than Wilson? On 11 November, when the
Chamber of Deputies passed a motion declaring that Georges Clemenceau and Ferdinand Foch "had earned the gratitude of their
country," the socialists tried to add a further motion—not in fact put
to the chamber until several days later— declaring that President
Woodrow Wilson "had earned the gratitude of mankind." At all
events, the special number of the socialist newspaper *L'Humanité* put
out on 14 December was a ringing tribute to Wilson "the citizen of
the world." All the great left-wing intellectuals—except Romain
Rolland—added their own contributions, with Anatole France at their
head. "If Jaurès were alive," wrote the sociologist Lucien Lévy-Bruhl,
"he would be the foremost and the most enthusiastic of Wilson's
supporters."

As we shall see, however, from these peaks the American president's
popularity in France soon began a relentless decline, until by the end
of the next spring he was regarded with almost universal hostility and,
during the summer, with an indifference even worse than hate.

Considerably more serious was the disaffection produced between
the two nations by "mass" contacts. According to Kaspi, "a graph of
the Americans' popularity in France . . . would display two peaks. The
first occurred in the summer of 1917. The slope up to the second
began six or seven months later and by September of 1918 had reached
what one might term a record level. The troughs on either side of these
peaks vary somewhat in depth" (*Le Temps des Américains*, pp.
322-23). In the words of Yves-Henri Nouailhat, who has made a
detailed study of this problem with particular reference to the large

American bases at Nantes and Saint-Nazaire, this was "the period of disenchantment" following the "period of wild enthusiasm" (*Les Américains à Nantes et à Saint-Nazaire*, pp. 177, 201).

Everything the Americans did was now becoming a cause for criticism and complaint. Their wealth, which had contributed to a vast and useful public works program, thus providing a great deal of employment, now became a subject for bitterness. Prices were skyrocketing, and this too was laid at the door of the American troops. People claimed they were too well paid, ignoring the role played by French profiteers. The presence in France of hundreds of thousands of young men naturally gave rise, on the part of many French women, to a sometimes genuine but more often mercenary infatuation. And of course there were war marriages. In 1919, 22 percent of the marriages celebrated in Saint-Nazaire and Montoir were Franco-American. Many of those marriages were happy ones. The proportion of failures, those ending in divorce, was no greater than that for marriages between French partners. But there were all the other kinds of relationships as well. The French soldiers, away at the front, seethed with jealousy. As a result of their contacts with professional and semi-professional ladies, the American troops developed not only distressing diseases but also an extremely unjust image of the French female. In short, the American in France, with some exceptions of course, tended to meet two particular types of French people: rapacious tradesmen and women who were in varying degrees whores. He returned home disgusted. Jusserand, the French ambassador, expressed active concern in a number of telegrams dispatched during 1919 and 1920 over an absurd but typical myth that had grown up: that the French were so stingy they even *rented their trenches* to the poor boys who had come over to get themselves killed on their account!

The earlier image of the American as a good-hearted fellow, brave, athletic, elegant, and friendly, was replaced in French minds by that of the American as a tough guy, drawing his revolver at the slightest pretext, a brawler, drunk whenever he got the chance, and in general a source of alarm; the foundations were already laid for the Prohibition era, when America tended to be viewed by the French as a country entirely peopled by gangsters. The French expressed virtuous indignation at the moral depravity apparent in the vicinity of the American camps, as if such goings-on were a peculiarly American phenomenon,

not something caused simply by the presence of vast numbers of
healthy young males who unfortunately, despite all Pershing's directives, had made few vows of chastity.

Needless to say, it would be wrong to insist overmuch on the dark
side of the picture. It is more reasonable to assume—for the same
phenomenon was to be repeated in 1944-45—that any contact
between a civilian population and a large army, even a friendly,
liberating army, is always on the whole disastrous, since there is
inevitably a tendency to attribute the failings of an unpleasant
minority to every member of it. How can there fail to be some black
sheep among two million soldiers? Happily, however, among the
troops at the front, among the men who shared the same wretched
conditions and were directing all their energies toward the same goal,
relations were always good, and fair-mindedness prevailed, even to the
extent of overcoming the language problem. For thousands of training
and liaison officers it was a time that saw the beginning of lasting
friendships. On both sides of the Atlantic one can still meet elderly
men who remember with deep feeling the common struggle and
comradeship of their youth. In sum, the two elements to be found
throughout the history of Franco-American relations remained: friendship and incomprehension.

At the governmental level the misunderstandings were more serious.
All the more reason, therefore, to begin by exploding certain myths
that seem to die hard.

3. The Wilson-Clemenceau debate

We know little of Wilson's opinions with regard to Clemenceau.
Pershing, Lansing, and, above all, Colonel House were certainly
among the Tiger's great admirers. House even became a personal
friend of his, and there were very few years between 1920 and 1929
when he did not go to visit Clemenceau, sometimes staying with him
at his house in the Vendée, at Saint-Vincent du Jard. But, on the other
hand, Clemenceau was very free with his comments on Wilson. His
trenchant wit led him to express somewhat variable judgments on the
subject. On 29 December 1918, during a famous session of the
Chamber of Deputies, he referred, somewhat slyly, to the American
president's "noble candor." Since he knew English extremely well,

the phrase must certainly have been chosen with some malice aforethought. For though "candor" in English signifies honesty, *candeur* suggests simple-minded guilelessness to the French.

That Clemenceau was always mistrustful of Wilson's idealism, that he was constantly apprehensive of a certain ignorance of the European situation on the American president's part, as well as of a lack of realism, is incontestable. In his last book, *Grandeurs et misères d'une victoire*, we find a typical judgment along those lines: "President Wilson, the inspired prophet of a noble and idealistic undertaking of which he was most unfortunately to become the prisoner, possessed an insufficient knowledge of this Europe that lay in fragments before him. . . . He acted to the best of his ability in circumstances whose origins lay outside his field of vision" (p. 140).

Given such a statement, it is only a step to concluding—as the great economist John Maynard Keynes did in chapter 3 of his famous book *The Economic Consequences of the Peace*—that the two men were total opposites, Wilson a "blind and deaf Don Quixote," Clemenceau, much more intelligent but also cynical, "the French Bismarck." It is a step that has also been taken by innumerable French and even more American historians. But in taking it they seem to have been ignoring two very crucial facts. The first is that Clemenceau too was an idealist, in the sense that he was in love with justice. During the whole of his long life he constantly sacrificed both career and wealth to his insistence on justice and republican order. Even though his opponents are sometimes justified in saying that he went too far in the direction of order, it is worth remembering that he did not achieve ministerial rank until the age of sixty-five, despite the fact that he could have done so twenty times over at the cost of a few compromises, and also that he died, if not poor, then at least not at all well off. His means were such that he was unable to buy even his modest house in the Vendée.

The second fact is the real friendship that existed between Clemenceau and Wilson. On 29 June, the day after the signing of the Treaty of Versailles, when Clemenceau accompanied Wilson to the station where the president was to take train for Brest, the Tiger was deeply moved and said: "I feel that I am losing a true friend." In 1922, when Clemenceau undertook a final and triumphal visit to America, he paid the ailing and discouraged Wilson a long visit and expressed great affection for him. One could go on indefinitely noting the differences between the two men, the Presbyterian pastor's son, deeply religious and in love with idealistic abstractions, versus the atheist republican, born into a tough fighting tradition in the Vendée; the optimist brimming over with faith in humanity versus the cynical pessimist. But both shared a total faith in democracy, the same desire for justice, even though their conceptions of it differed, and the same taste for the universal. To treat Clemenceau as a "Bismarck" is to believe that he put nation above justice, a notion given the lie by his entire career. To treat Wilson as a "Don Quixote" is to ignore the energy, the realism, and even the tactical ingenuity he displayed on many occasions.

All this adds even further to the fascination of following their debate in retrospect, one of those debates that have weighed heavily in the scales of history. It ended in compromises, and that perhaps is where the misfortune lay. But was it possible, given the forces involved, to avoid imperfect solutions? Moreover, they were not alone. There was also Lloyd George, the subtle mouthpiece of British opinion.

The first observation that ought to be made is that there was one essential historical dimension that largely escaped the attention of both leaders: the problem of postwar economic organization. From what had been a purely liberal economy in 1914, particularly as regards international trade—the state could act only by means of tariffs, quotas, trade treaties, and taxation of private importers and exporters who enjoyed a total autonomy—the world had progressed to what we today term "planned economy." As the result of a slow but steady process, reaching its culmination in mid-1918, the various states involved in the war, and the interstate organizations they had created, were now directly controlling the problems of cargo space, supplies, raw materials, and armaments. In October 1918 the Americans had finally accepted membership in all the inter-Allied committees, which had their headquarters for the most part in London. When the war ended, two courses were possible. The first was to continue, for a time at least, to make use of those committees, that is, to treat economic recovery and reconstruction as an inter-Allied undertaking, one in which governments would play a large role. This was the course favored by France and vigorously advocated by a remarkable trade minister, Etienne Clémentel, himself inspired by his young representative in London, Jean Monnet. The other possible course was an abrupt return to free enterprise and the dissolution of all the inter-Allied organizations. This was the course favored by the whole of American "big business," which had found a perfect advocate for its cause in a member of Wilson's own circle, the director of the Food Administration, who had been given responsibility for aid to Europe— Herbert Hoover, the "great engineer" and future president of the United States.

What may with certainty be said is that neither Wilson nor Clemenceau felt any passionate interest in this problem. Neither was an economist. The British were divided in their opinion but had decided to go along with the decisions of the world's largest economic power, the United States. In January 1919, Wilson settled for the course advocated by Hoover. It was probably inevitable. But it seems likely that this return to a savage economic nationalism had a profound effect on subsequent world history.

For Wilson, as for Clemenceau, the essential lay elsewhere, in the realm of pure politics. Both clearly shared the same aim: to guarantee peace for a long time to come—for what, on our human scale, we term "forever." But the methods they envisaged to achieve that aim were not the same; they not only reflected two dissimilar temperaments, they also expressed convictions rooted in two essentially different geographical situations and political viewpoints.

Wilson, leader of the world's largest economic power, secure from any possibility of direct attack—given the weakness of its Latin American neighbors and the tradition of good relations with Britain and the Dominion of Canada—put his entire trust in the League of Nations, proposed in his fourteenth and most solemnly formulated point. He was so deeply convinced of its rightness that he demanded: (1) that the League's Covenant should be included as an integral part of the treaties and constitute their first articles; and (2) that all other business, including all the territorial questions so essential in the eyes of the European delegates, should be suspended in order to discuss it. The result was that the first four weeks of the conference, from 19 January to 14 February, were spent producing a draft of the Covenant that was thereafter modified only very slightly. Wilson was so confident of his plan that he rejected the French proposal, put forward by the radical-socialist Léon Bourgeois, that an international army should be created directly answerable to the League. It would be wrong, Wilson said, to replace national militarism with an international militarism. It should also be added that the American president, like Lloyd George, felt a certain mistrust of the man who would have been appointed to command such a force, that is, Foch, the generalissimo of the Allied armies, who was in Wilson's eyes far too independent.

Clemenceau was certainly not hostile to the League. He spoke of it to House with great warmth and declared himself convinced of its value. But for him, before the League could be in a position to start guaranteeing a future peace there were concrete measures that had to be taken. He intended to guarantee the security of France, a depleted nation of forty million inhabitants, against any possible aggression from a Germany with a population of sixty-five million whose nationalists still refused to accept their defeat. In their eyes, only a "stab in the back," from the socialists, or the Jews, or the democrats, could possibly explain the signing of the armistice.

There was nothing of the imperialist in Clemenceau. Whereas certain right-wing ultranationalists, such as Maurice Barrès, were demanding annexation of the west bank of the Rhine, thus reverting to the old tradition of the nineteenth-century French republicans, Clemenceau had never even dreamed of such a step. Alsace and Lorraine, yes, because their inhabitants wanted to be French. The Rhineland absolutely not. "Is it my fault," he was to say during the debate on the ratification of the Versailles Treaty, "is it my fault if, when I go to the Rhine, I find the people there are Germans?" But Clemenceau, who before 1914 used to go every year to take the waters at Carlsbad, had formed his own very personal image of the Germans. "I know the Germans better than anyone," he was given to saying. He saw them in fact as a nation apart, easily dominated by evil forces, and with a respect for power and power alone. How could their submission be ensured? The best expert in the field, as Clemenceau saw it, was Foch, and Foch was an energetic champion—as we know from his notes of 27 November 1918 and 10 January 1919—of the following thesis: the Rhineland (that is, the west bank of the Rhine) should be militarily occupied by the victors; it should be detached politically from Germany and reconstituted as one or several independent states. "The Rhine must henceforward be the military frontier of the German peoples."

In December 1918, Clemenceau adopted this thesis as his basis for bargaining. Unlike Foch, who believed it to be absolutely essential, it is likely that Clemenceau viewed it with some skepticism. He did his utmost to keep his maneuvers secret and refused to reveal his aims to the French parliament. The result was a paradoxical situation in which, for six months, from November 1918 to May 1919, the French remained in almost total ignorance (apart from one indiscretion by Foch in March) of what their government was demanding. The Tiger would have preferred personally to move straight into the attack, get the negotiations off to a brisk start, and follow the traditional course of signing a set of simplified "preliminaries to the peace" that would have resolved the problem. But how was he to inject any urgency into things with Wilson unable to arrive in Paris before mid-December, then spending a month visiting all the Allied capitals, a second month on the negotiations over the League (which, he insisted, must have priority), and a third month (14 February to 14 March) on a trip back to the United States?

Thus, real negotiations began only after 15 March, with the daily meetings of the Council of Four: Wilson, Lloyd George, Orlando, and Clemenceau. We have a record of their deliberations, thanks to the historian-interpreter Paul Mantoux (*Les délibérations du Conseil des Quatre*). Few documents are of equal importance to a knowledge of Franco-American relations. It must be said at once that the French proposals were severely undermined at the very first meeting. House, it appeared, had already given them his "provisional" approval. This made Wilson furious, and his fine friendship with House never recovered from this blow. The furthest he would go was to support a proposal put forward by Lloyd George: in exchange for the abandonment of the French plan for the Rhineland, the United Kingdom and the United States offered France two treaties guaranteeing solidarity in the event of any German aggression.

The really hard bargaining continued on this basis from 24 March until 17 April. Clemenceau relinquished the idea of the *political detachment* of the Rhineland from Germany in exchange for the two "guarantee treaties"—ratification of which by the American Senate seemed from the outset extremely doubtful. But he stuck tenaciously to the notion of a *permanent military occupation* of those territories. Ultimately he settled for a *temporary* occupation (of fifteen, ten, or five years, according to the particular area), but accompanied by an article on which he was pinning all his hopes, article 429 of the future treaty, which stipulated that, in the event of Germany's failing to observe any of the treaty provisions, not only could the occupation be continued beyond the periods laid down but evacuated territories could even be reoccupied. Convinced that Germany would eventually act in bad faith, Clemenceau believed that article 429 would in practice produce a permanent occupation. Foch, on the other hand, was furious and from then on allowed himself to become a figurehead for France's most nationalistic forces, who always accused Clemenceau of having sabotaged the peace, to which Clemenceau had only one reply: We did not win the war alone. We cannot impose our own viewpoint in its totality on our allies and associates.

Oddly enough, however, it was not over this fundamental problem that the Wilson-Clemenceau debate took its bitterest form, but over a tiny stretch of territory on the left bank of the Saar river, including the towns of Saarlouis (founded by Louis XIV) and Saarbrücken. Under the first Treaty of Paris of 1814 France had been permitted to keep this area; then, under the second treaty, signed in 1815, she had been forced to relinquish it. Urged on by the military, who wanted a strategic frontier, and by big business interests, with their eyes on the Saar's steelworks and coal (even though the most productive mines were on the right bank of the river), Clemenceau demanded that there should be reparation of "the wrong done to France" not only in 1871—meaning the restoration of Alsace-Lorraine—but also in 1815. A number of extracts from the dialogue with Wilson merit quotation. According to Mantoux, the date was 28 March 1919.

> WILSON: The annexation of these regions to France has no sufficient historical basis.... The map of Europe is covered, I know, with old injustices that cannot all be made good....
> CLEMENCEAU: I take note of President Wilson's words and excellent intentions. He is eliminating feeling and memory....
> You are seeking to do justice to the Germans. Do not believe that they will ever forgive us ... nothing can assuage the fury of those who have attempted to bring the world under their domination and who thought they were so close to succeeding.

I shall never forget that our American friends, like our English friends, came over here to aid us in a moment of supreme danger....

I am old. In a few months I shall have left political life forever. My disinterest is absolute.... I shall go before Parlement and support the conclusions we have reached together. But here, between ourselves, permit me to tell you that you will lose one more link in the chain of affection that binds France and America together....

You are prepared to do us justice from the economic point of view, and I thank you for it. But economic necessities are not everything. The history of the United States is a glorious one, but it is also short. A hundred years for you is a very long time; for us, it counts very little.... We have our own conception of History that cannot be quite the same as yours....

WILSON: I thank you for the very fine words you have just uttered; I appreciate all their gravity.... I believe as you do that feeling is the most powerful force there is in the world.... The feeling that united peoples from all corners of the earth in combat was the feeling that they were fighting together for justice. That is why I have on occasion felt able to say here that we are representing not so much states as world opinion. This passionate aspiration toward a just solution will be replaced by a cynical skepticism if there is any feeling that we are not observing the rules of justice we have laid down.

It was in vain that André Tardieu, Clemenceau's principal collaborator, put forward argument after argument, even going so far as to say—without the slightest justification—that there were "150,000 French people" living in the region. Wilson's argument—the principle of nationality—carried the day. We cannot, Lloyd George added, create an Alsace-Lorraine in reverse. Tension was running very high, and it was at this point, on 7 April, that the rumor began of Wilson's imminent departure on the *George Washington*. Clemenceau was forced to accept a compromise. The territory of the Saar, including the coal mines on the right bank, was to be separated from Germany and placed for fifteen years under the administration of the League of Nations, after which time—that is, in 1935—a plebiscite was to be taken. France was to be ceded absolute ownership of the mine as compensation for the wanton destruction of its own northern coalfields by the retreating German army.

These, then, were the points that produced the greatest tension. The French press, on the whole, took the side of Clemenceau and adopted an offensive tone in its treatment of Wilson that both wounded him and infuriated the hundreds of American journalists in Paris at the time. These clashes unfortunately distracted attention from the many other issues over which Wilson and Clemenceau were in almost total agreement: the restitution of Alsace and Lorraine to France; the payment by Germany of heavy reparations, the amount of which was not to be fixed until 1 May 1921 (Wilson would have preferred an immediate lump-sum payment but came around in the end to this idea); demilitarization by Germany of the Rhineland and also of a thirty-mile strip along the east bank of the Rhine; reduction of the German army to 100,000 men; the trial (not possible, as it turned out) of the Kaiser and war criminals, and so on.

The extent to which France and America were in agreement was revealed in all its fullness in June 1919. The Germans received the text of the treaty on 7 May. Taken completely aback, they announced indignantly that they would never sign it. Meanwhile, opinion in Britain, with Lloyd George as its mouthpiece, had moved away from the idea that the Germans must be thoroughly punished toward the notion that it was more important to resume profitable trade with them, and therefore they must not be treated too harshly. In the face of the German indignation Lloyd George therefore made a statement advocating considerable modification of the treaty's terms. Clemenceau, only too well aware that French public opinion considered the treaty far too lenient as it was, refused to make any concessions. It was up to Wilson to arbitrate. Since Wilson was convinced that the compromises reached in April were fully consonant with his own principles, he was hostile to any relaxation in the terms: "The question is whether our previous decisions were just or not.... But I am not swayed by the argument that Germany will not sign, unless it can be shown that in making our stipulations we have infringed our principles.... It is not up to us to make concessions to the Germans simply because they do not wish to sign some given stipulation" (3 June; Mantoux, *Les délibérations*, p. 191).

Thus in the dispute between Lloyd George and Clemenceau Wilson wholly endorsed Clemenceau's viewpoint, and the treaty was modified hardly at all. Foch announced that he was quite certain, in the event of a German refusal, that he could be in Berlin within a week. After a change of government, Germany resigned itself to an acceptance of the Entente's ultimatum, and its plenipotentiaries duly arrived to sign the treaty, an event that took place on 28 June 1919 in the Hall of Mirrors in the Palace of Versailles, the very same spot where, on 18 January 1871, the German Empire had been proclaimed. At that moment the Franco-American *entente* was total. There was no doubt that it was Wilson who had forced Lloyd George to accept the French point of view.

4. Defeat

In the months that followed, however, the situation deteriorated. The reason for this was not any divergence of opinion between Clemenceau and Wilson but an exclusively American development: the Senate's refusal to approve, by a two-thirds majority, the Versailles treaty, including the League of Nations and the military guarantee to France. This "nationalist" position, as opposed to Wilson's "international-ism," was established by two separate votes on 19 November 1919 and 19 March 1920. And that was not all. In the November 1920 election it was the Republican candidate, Warren G. Harding, who was elected president (his slogans were "Back to Normalcy" and "America First"), not the Wilsonian Democrat, James M. Cox (whose choice to run with him for the vice-presidency was the young Franklin Delano Roosevelt, Wilson's assistant secretary of the navy).

During the entire period in which this tragedy took place, marked as it was by Wilson's own illness, there can be no question of claiming that Clemenceau and Wilson were ever at variance on the essential points. Wilson, for instance, was convinced, and remained convinced, just like Clemenceau, that Germany was *guilty* of having deliberately started the war. Their positions with regard to the Bolsheviks were also similar. After a very brief attempt at conciliation in January 1919, which earned him a great deal of criticism from the French right-wing press, Wilson never ceased to express his profound hostility to what he saw as a minority government put in power by a violent revolution. Clemenceau, it is true, would have liked to go as far as armed intervention, which Wilson would not agree to; but Clemenceau was not, as Winston Churchill was, committed to the idea of a new war.

The intervention he envisaged was one without massive French participation. He came around without difficulty to Wilson's notion of a *cordon sanitaire*, of leaving Bolshevism, as Wilson put it, "to stew in its own juice." Like Wilson, Clemenceau deluded himself that the Bolsheviks would be unable to maintain their position of power for very long. And even though he was rather less anxious than Wilson to raise the blockade of Germany, he concurred with the American's belief that an excess of privation in that country could well provoke a Bolshevik revolution. Like Wilson, Clemenceau became annoyed by Marshal Foch's political interference. Like Wilson, he was hostile to General Mangin's policy of fostering the spurious separatist movement in the Rhineland, and he let him know as much in no uncertain terms. The Italian claims were likewise viewed by both men in the same light. Naturally France was obliged to support those incorporated into the London treaty of April 1915—not, of course, signed by the United States—but Clemenceau made no secret of the fact that he himself would never have agreed to such a treaty. Finally, during the whole of the period in 1919, from August to October, when the French Parlement was debating the ratification of the Versailles treaty, Clemenceau believed—or affected in public to believe—that the treaty would ultimately be approved by the American Senate.

It is true that Wilson's supporters in France were becoming scarcer. The socialists, who had been using Wilson as a political stick with which to beat their internal enemy Clemenceau, announced on 15 February 1919 that they were deeply disappointed by the Covenant of the League. As Marcel Cachin wrote in that day's issue of *L'Humanité*: "We cannot conceal the feeling of disillusionment that our first perusal of this long agreement causes us. . . . In its present form this pact could never, by any means, win the support of the democracies and the people's parties. Instead of the great, new, bold organization that our ravaged people had been led to expect, they are being given a revised edition of the Hague Conference." On 8 May, when the treaty terms were made known, the socialists rejected this "peace by force" and from then on spoke of "Wilson's defeat." "His defeat is the defeat of bourgeois idealism, which may occasionally be sincere, but is always weak; it proves to all mankind that through socialism alone can order and fraternity be achieved" (*L'Humanité*, 9 May 1919). Later the socialists were even to talk, like Lenin, of "the hypocrisy of

Wilsonism." At the opposite extreme, the nationalist press was vigorously attacking Wilson's lack of realism. As for the other newspapers, the majority, which supported Clemenceau, remained for the most part courteous in their treatment of Wilson—contrary to what has been said by many American historians—but they did express reservations as to the merits of the compromises.

Most serious of all, however, was the fact that, as the months went by, people in France were believing less and less in the possibility of a just peace with the United States as its guarantor. More and more, Wilson and America were being literally *forgotten*. Out of fifty-eight speeches made in the Chamber of Deputies between 25 August and 25 September, during the ratification debate, Wilson's name was mentioned only a hundred and eight times. Nineteen of the fifty-eight speakers did not even allude to him at all. Of the others, very few indeed were fair in their judgment of him. I shall quote here only that made by Henry Franklin-Bouillon, a radical with nationalist leanings: "There is little doubt that after having been continuously applauded, President Wilson is now being severely criticized. Let us be fair: President Wilson came here armed with the best intentions toward France. Like all our American friends, he was somewhat ignorant— naturally so—of the details of the European situation." Clemenceau for his part declared: "I would personally consider it a crime to identify myself with the slightest bit of the criticism that is being directed at him."

Two coincidences, compounded with this growing indifference, are sufficient to explain why the two votes in the United States Senate passed almost unnoticed in France: that of 19 November 1919 because there was a newspaper strike on; that of 19 March 1920 because the Senate's decision coincided with Wolfgang Kapp's ultranationalist *coup d'état* in Berlin, an event infinitely more disturbing to a French public still deeply uneasy over the moves being made by the "revenge party" across the Rhine.

IT IS ALWAYS FUTILE to try rewriting history. Asking ourselves what the fate of the world might have been if the three great Western democracies—the United States, France, and the United Kingdom—had succeeded in achieving perfect agreement, if the United States had become a member of the League of Nations, if Wilson's dream of a "world safe for democracy" had been realized, would be the merest academic and superficial exercise. Could those powers have prevented the rise of a new type of political regime, fascism? Would they have won over a Soviet Russia whose very essence—whatever tactical tergiversations she may have indulged in—was struggle against the capitalist system? Would they have managed to avoid the great economic crisis that began in 1929? Would Hitler and national socialism have remained a merely secondary phenomenon as far as Germany was concerned, too weak to seize power and destroy the Weimar Republic? All are questions to which there can be no clear reply. This historian's role is rather that of understanding why it was that dissension, fear, cowardice, and irresolution came as they did to dominate a postwar world in which nothing any longer conformed to the traditions of the past.

In the history of Franco-American relations, what must be analyzed first and foremost is the great dispute that dominated the 1920s, that of France's war debts, which was scarcely stilled even by the illusion of the 1928 Kellogg-Briand Pact. It was from this dispute, and from the unprecedented economic crisis following it, that the central fact of the 1930s stemmed: isolationism, a domestic American phenomenon over which France had no control.

1. The war-debts dispute

When today's economists, wise from the experience of others and armed with the theories of John Maynard Keynes and his disciples, discuss the problem of the war debts owed by the Entente countries to the United States, they are unanimous in denouncing the long list of "errors" committed at that time by the governments concerned and their experts—the economists of the generation before.

As I have already mentioned, before the United States entered the war, both France and Britain secured private loans from American banks, in particular that of J. P. Morgan and Company. These loans were quickly repaid and posed no problem. However, from April 1917 onward the foreign payments of France and the other Allies were to a large extent met by the United States Treasury, in other words, out of public funds, and this aid was continued through part of 1919. The Americans had lent the Entente about \$10 billion in this way, or 50 billion gold francs. Of this total, France owed about \$4.2 billion (21 billion francs), including \$400 million representing the sale of American army surplus in France (a most distasteful operation for the French, who were in any case to recoup only about half that figure in the process). Moreover France also owed about 15 billion francs to Britain, which brought her total foreign war debt up to about 36 billion gold francs. To appreciate this figure, it might be well to set it beside France's annual budget expenditure figure for 1913: a mere 5 billion gold francs. The debt was, in short, enormous, and its repayment posed unprecedented problems.

There was another side to the coin, however. The Treaty of Versailles had stipulated that Germany should pay reparations, the total of which was not fixed until 1 May 1921, when it was decided that it was to be about 150 billion gold francs, of which France's share was to be 52 percent, or about 80 billion.

Let us suppose that Germany could have paid such a sum, that the annual payments eventually fixed were adhered to, until the last scheduled disbursement was finally made in 1988. Let us suppose, in other words, that three successive generations of Germans would have gone on calmly paying off these reparations imposed as the result of a defeat suffered by their fathers and grandfathers. In that case, France would of course have had the ultimate gain. But could such an

outcome be counted on? At all events, the French were very anxious to
obtain from their American creditors what was termed a "guarantee
clause," which meant that a direct link would be established between
payment of the reparations by Germany and repayment of France's
own debts, in particular those to the United States. If for any reason
Germany ceased to pay up, then France would be entitled to do
likewise.

The Americans, however, had never ratified the Versailles treaty.
Moreover, since they wanted to increase their trade with Germany,
they were not particularly concerned that the reparations should be
paid. Indeed, their only policy in that respect consisted in acting so as
to encourage the European nations to reduce, or even to cancel, the
German debt. They were totally opposed to the guarantee clause.

Toward the end of 1918, according to Mlle Denise Artaud, who has
written an important thesis on this problem, both the British and the
French made discreet approaches to the United States Treasury to see if
the latter would agree to cancel, or at least reduce, their debts. Neither
Wilson, nor his son-in-law at the Treasury, William G. McAdoo, nor
the Treasury's experts, nor Congress, nor public opinion generally—
despite a few discordant voices—would hear of any such thing.
Whereas the German reparations were "political debts" as far as the
Americans were concerned, that is, debts created by a treaty and
therefore susceptible of cancellation by a further treaty, the war debts
were "commercial debts." In a free-enterprise system—the ideal of
the vast majority of the American people—nothing was more sacred
than a commercial debt, since it was the very symbol of the law of
property. Moreover, the European loans had been financed by huge
domestic borrowings, to which American citizens generally had made
massive contributions. The federal budget, like any national budget
anywhere in the world, was obliged to include on its list of expendi-
tures the interest charges on its debt. It was therefore only reasonable,
the Americans felt, to expect that the European nations too, even if
they could not immediately repay the principal they had borrowed,
should at least pay interest on the sum in the interim, at a rate initially
set at about 5 percent.

According to the pre-Keynesian economic doctrines of the day, the
finances of states had to be managed no differently from the finances
of private individuals. Any sum due had to be paid, otherwise the

creditor would suffer a loss. The idea that a state has the ability to manipulate its money supply, and is in a fundamentally different situation from its individual members, was one that had not occurred to the experts of classical economics. The dollar was stable because it was linked to gold. The European currencies, on the other hand, were now unstable, because early in the war it had become necessary to abandon the convertibility of paper money into gold and impose compulsory currency of notes. The British returned to the gold standard in 1923, at the 1914 parity, a disastrous measure that was to wreck their balance of trade for a long while to come. The Germans saw their currency, the mark, collapse completely in 1923, and they were finally forced to create a new one, known first as the rentenmark and later as the reichsmark. The French, whose considerable prewar investments abroad had been mostly swept away in the whirlwind of the war (Russian loans, Austro-Hungarian loans, Turkish loans, and so on), also experienced a serious monetary crisis up to 1926, and the franc was not returned to the gold standard until 1928, at about a fifth of its 1914 parity (the "Poincaré franc").

Another idea, that it may be better to cancel a debt in order to reestablish the economic health of a trading partner—a notion familiar to the British, who were for that reason favorable to a reduction in the German reparations—seems to have eluded both the American experts (in relation to the war debt) and the French experts (in relation to the reparations). It must be admitted, however, that political preoccupations were not absent from these simplistic reasonings. With a debtor, one can always exert political pressure, in this case pressure in the sphere of international relations; the American authorities were only too well aware of this fact.

Since the French—or at all events Poincaré, who played the principal role in the France of the 1920s—were insisting that the Germans should pay their reparations, what arguments could they possibly use in the attempt to repudiate their own debts? There were two principal ones.

The first was of a moral nature: You, the Americans, did not enter this war we have won together until two years and eight months after it had started. During that period of neutrality you acquired enormous wealth, whereas we were pouring out not only our economic substance but also our blood. The French casualties were 1,394,000, those of the

United States 49,000. We have already paid dearly for our participation in the common struggle. Do not now play Shylock and seek to cut off yet another pound of flesh. Moreover, your loans were made only on condition that they be used exclusively for the purchase of your own goods. We paid the highest prices for those goods, and now you want us, by repaying you, to finance the vast war profits of your businessmen.

When tension between the two countries was at its highest, the aging Clemenceau emerged from the silence of his retirement to write an open letter, dated 9 August 1926, to President Calvin Coolidge:

> Yes, we threw everything into the abyss, blood and money, as did England and the United States also. But it was France's own soil that was scientifically ravaged. Three mortal years we waited for those words from America: "France is the frontier of liberty." Three years with our blood and our wealth streaming from every pore. Come and read in our villages the endless lists of our dead, and make comparison, if you wish. Was that not "money in the bank" to us, the living energy of those young men lost? (*Grandeurs et misères d'une victoire*, pp. 369-72).

Coolidge, unmoved by this argument, merely remarked that he was negotiating with the French government, not with private individuals, and declined to answer Clemenceau.

The second argument the French used was that they quite simply hadn't the money to pay, especially as long as Germany continued to avoid making its reparations payments. The return to power of the Republicans, in March 1921, merely hardened the demand for reimbursement. Successive presidents—Harding, Coolidge, Hoover—all refused to budge an inch from the position laid down by Wilson: France must pay everything, principal and interest as well. But how was France to pay? The only possible way would have been by increasing French exports to the United States, which would earn the necessary dollars. But this was precisely what the "nationalism" of the Republicans made impossible by its restrictive policies: prohibition of alcohol (entailing a ban on a number of traditional French exports), immigration laws, and, above all, sky-high tariff barriers: the Fordney-McCumber Act of 1922 set up an average tariff of 38 percent, as against 21 percent under the Underwood Act previously in force. In 1930, at the beginning of the slump, the Smoot-Hawley tariff raised the figure to 59 percent. Moreover, the American Tariff League, a zealous protector of American goods, enjoyed the good will of Hoover, who before becoming president had been secretary of commerce. Meanwhile, because of the war, France had been experiencing a considerable deterioration in its balance of trade—traditionally adverse even before the war—as well as a great reduction in the invisible income that had once compensated for its trade deficits (tourism and, above all, income from foreign investments). It was only the crisis of the franc that, by improving the export situation, enabled the country to maintain a favorable over-all balance of trade for three successive years (albeit not with the United States). The problem, quite simply that of obtaining dollars, thus seemed insoluble.

There did exist one possible way out, and that was to borrow dollars—from the United States! But alas, as the result of an official agreement drawn up between Secretary of State Charles Evans Hughes, Secretary of the Treasury Andrew Mellon, and Secretary of Commerce Hoover, on the one hand, and J. P. Morgan in the name of the principal American banks on the other, no further money could be loaned to foreign countries not yet in repayment of their state debts to the United States.

Thus, while in France the Americans were seen as vampires sucking the blood of their exhausted associates, in America the French were seen as a dishonest lot who "paid no taxes," were brutally harrying the Germans to make sure they kept up their reparations payments, and were maintaining an army that made France the number one military power in the world at a time when the United States—whose security was, to be honest, total—was dreaming only of disarmament. In short, as the result of a problem to which economic realities alone had any relevance, the massive involvement of both press and public opinion, on both sides of the Atlantic, was literally poisoning relations between two peoples who a few years before had been fighting side by side for the same cause.

Needless to say, neither of the governments involved was inactive. That of the United States was attempting to persuade France to present a plan for repayment by annual installments, to include both principal and interest. That of France was attempting to obtain a reduction in the principal, the fixing of a favorable interest rate, and, if possible, the notorious "guarantee clause," linking its debt with the reparations.

By an act of 9 February 1922, Congress created the World War Foreign Debts Committee, and on 24 April the American ambassador, Myron T. Herrick, notified France of the committee's readiness to hear the French proposals. That date marked the start of long, hard, complex negotiations that were not finally concluded until 29 April 1926, with the signing of the Mellon-Berenger Agreement (whereas Britain had signed an agreement with the United States in 1923, Italy in 1925). This agreement established the amount of the debt at about $4 billion. France was to repay this in sixty-two yearly installments—in other words, the final payment would not be made until 1988!— with the exception of the $400 million representing the French purchase of surplus American goods, which was to be repaid in a single installment on 1 August 1929, *if the agreement was not ratified*.

In fact, the matter was far from closed. For one thing, it was still necessary for the French Parlement to ratify the agreement. And the French Parlement did not happen to share the opinion of Senator William Borah, chairman of the Senate Committee on Foreign Affairs, who was on record as saying that "the generosity of the United States was without parallel in the history of the world." The majority of French deputies and senators thought the agreement a loathsome document. This opinion was shared by Raymond Poincaré, who returned to power in July 1926 at the head of a government of national unity that finally managed to save the franc. Poincaré accordingly informed the government in Washington that in his opinion there would be no ratification from his Parlement. The result was an even worse storm of recriminations. Subsequently, as the result of a series of provisional annual agreements, France did actually pay the sums fixed by the unratified Mellon-Berenger agreement; but even this did nothing to lessen the tension.

In reality, these annual payments by France were made possible by an absurd arrangement. As a result of the 1924 Dawes Plan, Germany did in fact make the reparations payments due from 1925 to 1930, the transfer in foreign-exchange stock being effected by a "general reparations agent" working from Berlin, who happened to be a brilliant young American named Parker Gilbert. France then used the exchange stock received from Germany to make the annual repayments on the French war debt. But, in order for the Germans to pay in the first place it had been necessary for the Americans, who had reserves of excess capital in hand, to pour loans, credit, and investments into Germany (since, in accordance with the internal American agreement mentioned earlier, they were refusing to lend money to France). The result, therefore, was a financial merry-go-round that produced no profit whatever for the main parties concerned: American loans to Germany, reparations payments by Germany to France, annual repayments by France to the United States.

As the fateful date of 1 August 1929 loomed nearer, with France clearly in no position to pay a lump sum of $400 million, Poincaré finally persuaded the French Parlement, in late July, to ratify the Mellon-Berenger agreement. It was his last political act. After three years of government, illness forced him to hand in his resignation, thereby ushering in a period marked by extreme instability of the executive power in France.

Moreover, at the very moment when everything at last seemed settled, just when the 1929 Young Plan had fixed the amounts of Germany's annual payments so as to achieve final amortization in 1988 (the same terminal date as for French repayments to the United States, the aim being to establish a kind of parallelism to replace the notorious "guarantee clause" still rejected by Washington), the entire structure collapsed.

The reason for this was the world-wide economic crisis thought of symbolically as striking on "Black Thursday," 24 October 1929, on Wall Street. This crisis was closely linked to the unbridled capitalism exemplified for the rest of the world by the United States of the Hoover era. Confidence vanished overnight. The value of stocks and shares collapsed, resulting in the closure of a great many banks. Industry, starved of credit, responded by cutting back production, thus producing widespread unemployment. Willy-nilly, the population at large responded in its turn by decreasing consumption, so that, as the result of an excess of goods, prices shot down, thus producing further bankruptcies, ruining farmers operating on credit, and setting the whole vicious circle spinning even faster. It is enough here to record that America's national income fell from $87 billion in 1929 to less than $42 billion in 1932.

The year 1930 was the last in which any of the international payments
were made as agreed. The Americans were already calling home with
all possible speed whatever they could salvage of their German
investments. As a consequence, the crisis spread to that country in the
spring of 1931. Paul von Hindenburg, the German president, begged
Hoover to propose a general suspension of international debts,
reparations and war debts alike. Hoover agreed, and proposed a
year's moratorium, from 1 July 1931 to 30 June 1932, on all such
debts. The French, in the summer of 1931 still not affected by the
crisis, accepted with some reluctance. But by the autumn of that year
they themselves were pulled into the decline as well.

Was this not a good moment for all parties to rid themselves of the
intolerable millstone that these reparations and debts had now
become? The sums involved, when measured against the magnitude
of the crisis, were so minimal that common sense demanded such a
course. That at any rate was the opinion of the American secretary of
state, Henry Stimson, who put forward to Hoover a simple but
effective method of achieving it: prolonging the moratorium for
another year, then another, and so on until such time as world
prosperity had been reestablished. But in the United States 1932 was
an election year. Bowing to public opinion—which naturally didn't
understand the technicalities involved—Hoover refused. In the summer of 1932, at a meeting in Lausanne, the European nations decided
to put an end to the German reparations. However, they also came to
a "gentleman's agreement" that this decision was to be applied only
in exchange for cancellation of their own war debts. Hoover, Congress,
most of the American press, and finally the new president-elect, the
Democrat Franklin Delano Roosevelt, protested indignantly.

There ensued a development that was at once totally illegal from the
standpoint of international law yet literally unavoidable: America's
European debtors refused to pay. The French premier, Edouard
Herriot, did in fact suggest making the payment due on 15 December
1932, but the Chamber of Deputies rejected the proposal, thereby
bringing down his government and enabling France to suspend
payments. The British took what they believed to be a more subtle line
by offering to make a "token" payment. The United States rejected
the suggestion. The result was a definitive rift between America and
Europe at the very moment when, on 31 July 1932, 230 Nazis were

being elected to the German Reichstag, and when, on 30 January 1933, President von Hindenburg appointed Adolf Hitler as chancellor of the German Reich.

2. The pacifist illusion

Between 1928 and 1931, despite the thorny war-debt problem and the acrimony it stirred up, the French and the Americans had nevertheless moved slightly closer together on the political level. However, as we shall see, this *rapprochement* was founded on an illusion.

Between April 1925 and January 1932, France's foreign policy was in the hands of an extemely subtle man with great powers of conciliation and eloquence—one of history's greatest orators, in fact—Aristide Briand. Along with Poincaré, he was France's best-known statesman, had already headed governments many times, and enjoyed world-wide recognition. Briand, who later came to be known somewhat grandiloquently as "the apostle of peace," was much less set than Poincaré on exacting a remorseless "execution" of the Treaty of Versailles and payment of the reparations from Germany. Indeed, he sincerely wanted a *rapprochement* with the Germans and was even prepared to make major concessions to that end. He was a supporter of the League of Nations and still hoped that the United States would one day become a member of its Council.

Briand was very concerned over the tension between France and the United States produced by the war-debt problem. Knowing a good deal about how people's minds work, he had established good relations with a number of American pacifists, despite the slight difficulty presented by the fact that there were two categories of pacifists in the United States. One group, consisting mainly of Democrats and disciples of Wilson, was campaigning for United States membership in the League. Their main organizations were the Carnegie Endowment for International Peace (which had a European branch in Paris, at 175 Boulevard Saint-Germain) and the World Peace Foundation in Boston. Its leaders were the president of Columbia University, Nicholas Murray Butler, and Professor James Shotwell. But apart from this group the country was also swarming with a variety of more radical pacifists who were hostile to the League because its Covenant endorsed the use of military sanctions—in other words, war.

These radical pacifists were grouped into innumerable and very active
small associations, and their great leader was the journalist Salmon O.
Levinson, chairman of the American Committee for the Outlawry of
War. Levinson's reasoning was at once simple and exactly what one
might expect from the citizen of a country enjoying almost total
security. War, like slavery, is an institution. Just as national laws had
put an end to slavery, so they could also declare war illegal. All nations
should enact such laws, and a kind of international tribunal should
then deal with any infringements. Unlike the League, however, this
tribunal would punish such infringements solely by means of individual sanctions against the statesmen who had violated the law.

It is beyond doubt that Aristide Briand harbored few illusions as to
the possible efficacy of such a scheme. But he was more interested in
psychology than in law, and what he was after was some kind of shock
treatment he could administer to American public opinion in the
hope of mitigating its present bitterness toward France. Taking
advantage of the tenth anniversary of America's entry into the war
(6 April 1927) to make a resounding proclamation in favor of peace
seemed to him a good method of inspiring a vast outpouring of
sympathy on the other side of the Atlantic. He talked the notion over
with Shotwell, whom he met on 22 March and who helped him with
the actual wording of the proclamation. With great astuteness, Briand
introduced the phrase "outlawry of war, to borrow an American
expression." On 6 April he publicly addressed a message to the
American people—the government in Washington was not officially
sent the text until later—proposing that France and the United States
should enter into a solemn pledge never to make war on one another.
Levinson, who learned of the message while crossing the Atlantic with
his family to take a European vacation, greeted it with enthusiasm,
and as soon as he had landed rushed to see Briand and congratulate
him.

At first, Briand's maneuver proved successful. The American press,
on the whole, reacted favorably. The French, always more given to
skepticism in any case, happened to have a quite different event to
enthuse over just then, since it was on 21 May 1927 that Charles A.
Lindbergh landed outside Paris in the *Spirit of St. Louis*, after the first
successful Atlantic air crossing. He had in fact succeeded in the very
exploit, though in the opposite direction, that the French aviators

Charles Nungesser and François Coli had recently attempted at the cost of their lives. He was given a hero's welcome, and it was on the occasion of a reception given in the great aviator's honor that Briand asked Myron Herrick, the American ambassador, to pass on his peace message to the American government officially. Ever a man of intuitions and spur-of-the-moment decisions, he was hoping in this way to kill two birds with one very inexpensive stone: two birds, because he was expecting not only to rally support among one section of American opinion in the name of pacifism, but also to nudge the French, with their passion for alliances, into believing he had achieved some kind of pact with the United States; and a very inexpensive stone, because the likelihood of France and America ever making war against each other was more or less nil.

The American secretary of state, Frank Kellogg, however, was extremely embarrassed by Briand's move. Kellogg, who was later to be awarded the Nobel Peace Prize, had nothing of the pacifist about him. He had no faith in the League of Nations, or in collective security, or in the "outlawry of war." He loathed the kind of "alternative" diplomacy that men without political responsibility like Shotwell and Levinson were carrying on with Briand. In consequence, despite having received Briand's memorandum, he remained obdurately silent on the matter until December.

It was Senator Borah who got him off the hook. Borah, the "lion of Idaho," though in fact a Republican, was totally independent in his behavior and something of a bugbear to the State Department because of the vast influence he wielded as chairman of the Senate Foreign Relations Committee. Borah, who was violently opposed to the League, happened to be a friend and disciple of Levinson. The latter persuaded him that the Briand proposal could be used as a means of outlawing war once and for all. As a result, Borah suggested to Kellogg that he answer Briand with a counterproposal: instead of a bilateral renunciation of war by the United States and France, *let the declaration be extended to all the countries of the world*. On 28 December, Kellogg—who would personally have preferred a series of bilateral arbitration treaties, like the one actually signed with France on 6 February 1928—handed an American reply to the French ambassador (the great writer Paul Claudel) proposing the outlawing of war by all nations of the world.

It was Briand's turn to be embarrassed. On the one hand, the illusion of a bilateral agreement with the United States, replacing the notorious and stillborn "guarantee treaty" of 1919, had evaporated. On the other, ceaselessly accused as he was by the nationalist right of making too many concessions to the Germans, of putting too much faith in the efficacy of collective security, of being a dangerous utopian, Briand was well aware that such a project would be greeted with the biggest barrage of sarcasm his "realist" opponents could muster—which is precisely what happened.

Nevertheless, it was essential to put a good face on things. Members of the League of Nations couldn't outlaw war totally, since the Covenant specifically referred to the possibility of military sanctions ordered by the League's Council; but after negotiation an acceptable formula was finally agreed upon: the signatories of the new pact were to pledge themselves to renounce war "as an instrument of national policy in their mutual relations." In addition, war was condemned as a means of resolving international conflicts. Thus the only form of war authorized in future would be collective war ordered by the League against an aggressor. Contrary to the ideas of Levinson, no international tribunal was envisaged for the punishment of politicians adjudged responsible for starting a military conflict.

The response of the American pacifists was on the whole enthusiastic. While Frank Kellogg was crossing the Atlantic on the French liner *Ile de France*, on his way to the signing of the pact in Paris (an event that took place on 27 August 1928), the American Senate was so inundated by delegations, pamphlets, articles, and signed declarations, which arrived in their millions, that it was eventually forced to give its approval to the "renunciation of war" pact by a vote of 85 to 1 (15 January 1929). The fifteen signatories of the Paris Pact were later joined by the majority of the world's remaining countries, including the Soviet Union, which had at first viewed the whole thing, not untypically, as a "maneuver of encirclement" directed against itself. Only Arabia, Yemen, Brazil, Argentina, and Bolivia refused to sign. Nineteen twenty-eight of course marked the very peak of the years of prosperity, and prosperity makes people optimistic. There were many who sincerely believed that war and all its attendant sufferings were done with forever. Many others, knowing nothing of Briand's and Kellogg's real intentions, saw this curious Franco-American initiative as proof that the two countries were once again bringing the message of true progress to the world, exactly as they had in the late eighteenth century. But many more denounced the dangerous illusion inherent in condemning war without providing for sanctions against future violators of the pact. Although Briand's initiative, as transmuted by Borah and Kellogg, achieved enormous success in the United States, the same was not true in France, where the "nationalist" offensive against Briand redoubled in vigor.

It was not long before the economic crisis, with its terrible political consequences, proved the cynics and ironists right, on the surface at least. In September 1931, when Japan—a signatory of the Kellogg-Briand Pact—launched a war of conquest in Chinese Manchuria, the members of the League of Nations, in particular France and Britain, and the nonmember United States had every reason to trust in their own solidarity. Henry Stimson, the American secretary of state, did in fact send a representative to Geneva with an offer of "independent aid" to the League. But neither the League nor the United States had any real intention of taking vigorous action. President Hoover, of Quaker stock and therefore a pacifist, worked out the most restricted interpretation possible of the "Stimson Doctrine" of 7 January 1932, which went no further than moral condemnation of conquests made by force and of violations of the Kellogg-Briand Pact. In that same month of January 1932, Briand, the "apostle of peace," sick, disappointed in all his hopes, ceaselessly accused by an ever more powerful opposition of betraying France's true interests, left the Ministry of Foreign Affairs. He was to die two months later.

Taking a longer view of things, it is permissible to see the Kellogg-Briand Pact as possessing a very real historical significance. Until that time, international law had authorized war, on condition that it observed certain rules specifically laid down over the course of the centuries. After the pact, war itself stood condemned, at least in certain cases. Later, at the trials of the major German and Japanese war criminals in Nuremberg and Tokyo in 1946, apart from the charges relating to specific war crimes, the Kellogg-Briand Pact made it possible to add the supreme accusation: that of having provoked a war of aggression and conquest. It is true that the circumstances in 1946 were exceptional. Too many people, too many statesmen, even today, still look on war as a normal method of attaining their aims, or, in

Clausewitz's words, as "the continuation of politics by other means."

As far as our present subject of Franco-American relations is concerned, let us remember that this notorious pact, the result as we have seen of half-hidden diplomatic confusions, had the advantage of demonstrating yet again that the two countries, despite their use of profoundly differing methods, were still at one in their ideals of democracy and peace.

3. American isolationism and a humbled France

The year 1932, marked by the death of Briand, the peak of the economic crisis, the cancellation of both war reparations and war debts, and the election in the United States of an exceptional president, Franklin Delano Roosevelt, also saw the opening of a dark era in the history of the world. Within five years in the Far East, and within seven years in Europe, the world would be irrevocably on the brink of war, a second war even more terrible than the first.

It was as though the great nations of the world had no other choice but insane aggression or cowardice. The German Nazis, the Italian Fascists, and the Japanese warlords all opted for aggression and madness. The French, the British, and the Americans chose cowardice and selfishness. The British believed they could appease Hitler by giving way to his superficially arguable demands: the annexation of those territories where German was spoken. It was necessary for the *Führer* to seize a non-German-speaking territory, Czechoslovakian Bohemia (on 15 March 1939) before the British prime minister, Neville Chamberlain, finally discovered that Hitler was "not a gentleman." The French, after a war that had decimated them, did not dare practice any foreign policy that would isolate them from the British. For them, it was less "appeasement" that carried the day than "self-effacement." As for the Americans, shattered by the worst crisis in their history, angry with these immoral Europeans who would not pay their debts, they simply withdrew into themselves. What in the 1920s had been termed "nationalism," in opposition to Wilsonian internationalism, now took a systematic form and was transmuted into "isolationism." And if our picture is to be complete, we must not forget the Soviet Union. In those years Russia was by no means a peaceful haven from the tempests raging elsewhere. It was the era of

Stalin's appalling purges, which today the Russians themselves admit cost millions of human lives.

To return to our own subject, Franco-American relations, the first observation that needs to be made is their very nullity on the political level right up to 1939. A perusal of the *Documents diplomatiques français* and the corresponding documents in the United States, *Foreign Relations of the United States*, makes it clear that diplomatic relations between the countries had been reduced to their lowest common denominator: the presence of ambassadors, who limited their role to that of observers and suppliers of information and who had almost nothing to do in the way of negotiation, or at any rate nothing of the slightest importance. There is really not enough material to make an "account" of these dealings possible. It would be more useful to look into the essential facts underlying this diplomatic void.

The first of these is the disparity between the two countries' situations. For France, the period between 1932 and 1939 was totally dominated by the growing threat from Hitler. For the United States, security, at least for the near future, seemed just as total in 1939 as it had in 1932. Let us for the moment leave aside the Far East, where France, despite its colony of Indochina and its islands in the Pacific, could never have played more than a secondary role. As far as Europe was concerned, the Americans knew that before they could even be attacked by Hitler—whom they loathed totally, for his anti-Semitism, for his will to conquest and aggression, for his insane antidemocratic fury—the *Führer* would first have to smash two lines of defense both external to the United States but nevertheless viewed as bulwarks by it: the French army and the British navy. To make American impregnability complete, all that was needed was the creation of "Fortress America." Charles Lindbergh, the wealthy aviator who had been the first to fly the Atlantic and who was now one of the leading proponents of isolationism, was of the opinion that all the United States needed was a powerful air force. In fact, all the efforts previously made to achieve world disarmament were soon to prove vain. As far as land forces were concerned, the disarmament conference in Geneva finally faded from the scene in 1934, and in 1935, in London, the Japanese refused to adhere to the policy of naval disarmament.

But while the Americans were feeling themselves secure, despite the weakness of their land forces, the French were watching their situation with regard to Germany deteriorate year by year. With Hitler's accession to power on 30 January 1933, his country was taken over by an extreme nationalism dedicated to revenge. In *Mein Kampf*, Hitler made no secret of the fact that before conquering a vast *Lebensraum*, or "living space," to the east, it was necessary to smash France. But was not the French army the largest in the world? And the German army had been reduced to a mere 100,000 men by the Treaty of Versailles. Moreover the Rhineland, plus a thirty-mile strip along the Rhine's eastern bank, had been completely demilitarized, thus making any attack on France impossible. Within three years Hitler had swept away all these advantages. In October 1933 he left the League of Nations and the disarmament conference and began openly to rearm. On 16 March 1935, he repudiated the relevant clauses of the Versailles treaty and resumed a two-year period of compulsory military service in Germany. On 7 March 1936 he invaded the demilitarized Rhineland, and the French, even though they still possessed military superiority, did not dare to react. Having got that far, Hitler was then able to begin constructing his "western wall," a fortified line sufficiently formidable to deter France from going to the aid of her Central European allies, Poland and Czechoslovakia. By 1937, thanks to an all-out rearmament campaign, the *Wehrmacht* had become more powerful than even the French army. It was also more effective, because it had adopted modern theories on the use of tanks and air cover then being advocated in Germany so successfully by General Heinz Guderian—and so unavailingly in France by Commandant Charles de Gaulle.

But, surely, was not Germany completely isolated? France had alliances with Poland, with Czechoslovakia, and secondarily with Yugoslavia and Romania. In 1920 she had concluded a secret military alliance with Belgium. In 1934, one of her great foreign ministers, Louis Barthou, the only one during this period who dared to practice a policy independent of that followed by Britain, laid the foundations of a "realistic" alliance with the only great nation capable of aiding France: the Soviet Union. Barthou was assassinated in October 1934. But his successor, Pierre Laval (who in October 1931, as prime minister, had made a much-publicized visit to the United States) nevertheless signed the Franco-Soviet pact of mutual assistance in May 1935. Finally, the Italians, disturbed at seeing Hitler threatening Austrian independence, seemed to be ranging themselves on the side of the French and British.

Alas! Within three years this splendid diplomatic structure lay in ruins. In January 1934, their heads full of illusions, the Poles had effected a *rapprochement* with Germany. In 1935, the Italian attack on Abyssinia estranged Italy from the Western democracies. The reoccupation of the Rhineland, as we noted earlier, made France's alliances to the east valueless. At the same time, Belgium repudiated her military agreement with the French. General Francisco Franco's rebellion in Spain, supported by the Nazis and the Fascists, was the first step toward the establishment of a hostile regime on France's southern frontier. It also led Italy to come to an arrangement with Germany, the Rome-Berlin Axis of October 1936, to be followed by outright alliance and the "Pact of Steel" in May 1939. The Soviet Union, disgruntled by France's waverings—Pierre Laval refused to accompany the alliance with a military agreement—moved gradually away from her, until it finally reversed its alliances, on 23 August 1939, by signing the German-Soviet pact. The sum total of all this was that France, until 1935 the world's foremost military power, surrounded by allies, now found herself not only facing a rising Germany, more powerful and dynamic than herself, but also losing all her allies, one after the other, with the exceptions of a Britain busily practicing appeasement and a Czechoslovakia under threat of extinction.

Moreover, the French knew that there was absolutely no question of their counting on support from the Americans. Not only was the vast majority of the country isolationist, committed to the time-honored tradition of nonentanglement advocated by Jefferson, as well as by Washington in his Farewell Address of 1796, but also, between 1935 and 1937, Congress was passing a series of "neutrality acts." The essence of these acts was to tie the hands of the executive by blocking the mechanism that it was thought had dragged the country into war in 1917. It was essential, the argument went, to avoid aiding any belligerent nation whatever, since the financial interests involved in such aid, naturally hoping for an eventual return on their investment, would be anxious to ensure victory for the side they had assisted and would therefore work to ensure American intervention. In consequence, as soon as the president was apprised of a state of war between two or more countries, he was to place an immediate embargo on all exports of arms and munitions to those countries, victim as well as aggressor. As for goods other than arms and munitions, in their case the "cash and carry" clause would be applied, meaning that the belligerents would be obliged to pay cash for all goods, thereby avoiding the building up of war debts, and also to transport them on non-American vessels, thereby avoiding the torpedoing of United States shipping. Moreover, it was only by a very narrow margin that its opponents defeated a constitutional amendment, proposed by Congressman Louis Ludlow of Indiana, making any declaration of war dependent, not on a simple vote in Congress, as before, but on a referendum! In short, the United States had made any active foreign policy on its part an infringement of its own laws.

Faced with this strange situation, what was the reaction of the remarkable man governing the country at that time? First, we must remember that Franklin D. Roosevelt was elected because he provided a hope of resolving the economic crisis. During the first three years of his presidency his entire energies were devoted to the New Deal. He left the conduct of foreign policy to his secretary of state, Cordell Hull, whom he had chosen for that office much more on account of the influence he had with Congress than because of any particular competence in international affairs. The proof of this is that as soon as Roosevelt decided to concentrate on foreign policy himself, in 1937, he appointed as undersecretary of state Sumner Welles, and thereafter consulted him much more frequently than he did Cordell Hull, who felt somewhat bitter in consequence.

The New Deal, a series of empirical measures tending to replace unrestricted economic liberalism with what was in fact a federally controlled "planned economy," was a conception that fitted in very nicely with the "nationalist" line taken in the 1920s. Whereas Cordell Hull dreamed of returning to a higher level of international trade, which he was hoping to foster by lowering America's tariff barriers and signing multilateral agreements, Roosevelt, who in his electoral campaign had rejected the idea of United States membership of the League of Nations, kept firmly to the old path and thereby guaranteed the failure of the World Economic Conference held in London in the spring of 1933. In April he had devalued the dollar, and he refused to enter into any agreement on the international stabilization of currencies. "With his characteristic optimism," the French ambassador, André Lefebvre de Laboulaye, wrote after a private dinner at the White House, "he is already anticipating the success of his experiment and counting on the dollar once more becoming one of the world's healthiest currencies. Once that has been achieved, it will be possible for the United States to carry out effectively the policy of international cooperation that he assures me he still holds to" (*Documents diplomatiques français*, first series, vol. 3, no. 460, 6 July 1933).

While waiting for that day, however, the United States continued to remain silent and actively uninvolved. At the most decisive moment of all for France's future—the reoccupation of the demilitarized Rhineland in March 1936—its reaction was nonexistent.

> Replying to questions put to him by press correspondents, the Secretary of State confined himself to the comment that Germany's action did not concern the United States, since it did not violate the peace treaty his country had signed with Germany. Senator Borah, for his part, expressed delight at the abolition of the Versailles treaty, which he had never considered viable, and added that the position taken by Germany was "not of a nature to lead to war." (*DDF*, 2d series, vol. 1, no. 347, 9 March 1936, telegram from Ambassador Laboulaye)

It was in 1937, far in advance of American opinion as a whole, that Roosevelt began to foresee the extent of the danger. Possibly the unleashing of a ruthless war of conquest in China by Japan, in July 1937, had played at least as great a role in his thinking as Mussolini's and Hitler's first displays of strong-arm tactics or as the Spanish Civil War. At all events, in his "quarantine" speech, made in Chicago on 5 October 1937, he took up a firmer position for the first time:

> The peace, the freedom, and the security of 90 percent of the world are being jeopardized by the remaining 10 percent who are threatening a breakdown of all international order and law. Surely the 90 percent can and must find some way to make their will prevail. . . . When an epidemic of physical disease starts to spread, the community approves and joins in a quarantine of the patients in order to protect the health of the community against the spread of the disease.

Needless to say, the mere idea of establishing a distinction between aggressors and victims was sufficient to inflame isolationist opinion. To the isolationists, the suggestion that a move of any kind might be made against the aggressors seemed fraught with dangers. As they saw it, the American government was free to decide between United States entry into war and the maintenance of peace. Roosevelt, much more of a realist, understood that war is a ruthless mechanism capable of dragging nations into itself against their wills. He had no great faith in the first line of defense—the French army—and he was critical of the British—whose navy was America's second line of defense—for their excessively conciliatory policy. He was therefore conscious of a mounting danger. But faced with an isolationist majority, he knew that he could not act in the immediate future. The "quarantine" speech was the first step in his extraordinary attempt at the "education" of American opinion, which was to continue until 1941 and succeed in making his fellow citizens increasingly aware that they were facing a mortal peril.

The French were quick to grasp the purport of his Chicago speech: "No president since Mr. Wilson has made statements of such high moral import," wrote the French chargé d'affaires Jules Henry. "It would be illusory to draw the conclusion from Mr. Roosevelt's speech that the United States is now departing abruptly and definitively from the line of conduct it has followed in recent years in matters of foreign policy," but this statement does constitute "a warning and an appeal to American public opinion" (*DDF*, 2d series, vol. 7. no. 33, 7 October 1937).

On the surface, it was true that little seemed to have changed. The year 1938, marked on 11 March by the *Anschluss* (Germany's annexation of Austria) and on 30 September by the Munich accords (German annexation of the Sudetenland from Czechoslovakia) brought no large-scale American initiative. In September, when the American ambassador to France, William Bullitt, in the course of unveiling a monument outside Bordeaux commemorating the arrival of the "Sammies" in 1917, remarked that perhaps the United States would not remain forever aloof from the conflict, his words were promptly qualified by Roosevelt as being the ambassador's own opinion. Just before Munich, Roosevelt did in fact suggest that an international conference should be held at The Hague, including delegates from

Czechoslovakia; but he made it plain at the same time that the United States would be unable to attend. At Munich, Czechoslovakia was stripped of the Sudetenland without even being consulted. France had literally betrayed her ally. To Chamberlain, enchanted by the "success" of his appeasement, Roosevelt dispatched an enigmatic telegram: "Good man."

In April 1939, after the total dismemberment of Czechoslovakia, Roosevelt made an even more dramatic gesture. He sent Hitler and Mussolini a list of thirty nations and requested a pledge from the two dictators that they would not attack them. In exchange, he offered a plan affording them unrestricted access to raw materials. Such an offer of course minimized the *territorial* aspect of Nazi ambitions. Influenced, as he was by his geopoliticians, Hitler was much more concerned with the actual "room" implied in his *Lebensraum* than with any economic considerations. Thus Roosevelt's initiative would have to be interpreted as extremely naïve if he was really expecting by such means to halt Hitler and Mussolini in their hungry pursuit of conquests. In fact, it should be interpreted above all as a skillful psychological maneuver made for the benefit of the American public. Since he was certain that the two dictators would arrogantly refuse to make the peace pledge demanded, what Roosevelt was actually angling for was proof from their own lips, as it were, that their policies had been and still were aggressive in intent, so that the American people would be forced to draw the only possible conclusions.

In reality, behind this diplomatic façade Roosevelt had already entered upon a much more important course of action. As a result of secret negotiations carried out on behalf of the French government by Jean Monnet (whose role in 1918 we have already mentioned, and whose name will recur a great deal later on), contracts had been signed between France and various American aircraft manufacturers to reequip the French air force. France was even prepared to make capital investments in the United States in order to hasten this process. At the time of Munich the French were making thirty to fifty planes a month, and the Germans at least two hundred fifty. Roosevelt, aware that aid to the democracies was essential, took action on at least two levels in this operation. In December 1938 he instructed Henry Morgenthau, secretary of the treasury, to facilitate financial arrangements with Britain and France. He also recommended that the American air force should pass on information about its most advanced aircraft. He was even considering a revision of the neutrality laws.

An incident connected with these moves rendered such a revision impossible, however, at least for the moment. On 23 January 1939, an ultramodern military aircraft, equipped with secret new devices, crashed in California. There was general consternation—and indignation in the case of the isolationists—when it was learned that one of the victims was a French air force officer. The rumor spread that the government was negotiating an alliance with France. Roosevelt was forced into vigorous repudiation of a remark being attributed to him to the effect that the frontier of the United States lay on the Rhine. In fact there did exist a very small minority of Americans who were openly advocating such an alliance, among them a former secretary of state, the Republican Henry Stimson, who in July 1940 was to be appointed by Roosevelt as his secretary of war. In addition, a Gallup Poll revealed that 65 percent of Americans approved the sale of military aircraft to France and Britain. In other words, an erosion of absolute isolationism had begun. But Congress was still disinclined to revise the neutrality laws, and on 3 September 1939, when the United Kingdom and France declared war on Germany as a result of the invasion of Poland, President Roosevelt's first act ought to have been the proclamation of an immediate embargo on the arms and munitions that American factories were beginning to manufacture on behalf of both European democracies.

THUS MUTUAL INCOMPREHENSION, exacerbated during the 1920s by the war-debt question and divergent attitudes with regard to Germany, had simply increased further during the 1930s. The harm done by the economic crisis was not confined to the material sphere. It plunged tens of millions of people into anxiety; and from anxiety one can slide only too easily into mistrust, then hate. The most extreme example was that of Germany, where a regime founded on hate and violence succeeded in seizing power—by legal means.

When they looked across at the Americans during the period of world prosperity that lasted from 1925 to 1929, the French—themselves experiencing a great economic expansion—perceived with some misgivings an America now very sure of itself, a proud symbol of the triumphs attained by capitalism on the grandest scale, the foremost economic power in the world, and by then even challenging London's position as the principal center of world finance. They observed with stupefaction the progress of standardization, of "Taylorization," of advertising, of mass production, of "Fordism." Was that to be the future of the world? Georges Duhamel, in an unfair and prejudiced book that nevertheless became a best seller, his *Scènes de la vie future* (1928), claimed just that, and deplored it. A much more objective observer, André Siegfried, also published an important book on the same subject, his *Les Etats-Unis d'aujourd'hui* of 1927, in which he analyzed the system and demonstrated its limits.

Of course, these political and financial considerations held very little interest for that small but astonishingly vivid group of American writers, painters, and musicians who had migrated from Greenwich Village to Paris. Everything drew them there: America's Prohibition, the egoistic nationalism of the 1920s, and the cultural confusion left in the wake of a war in which, in the absence of any threat to their own country, two million Americans had been engaged. "You are the lost generation," wrote Gertrude Stein to Hemingway. This "lost generation" was not to conquer the French public until the end of the 1930s, and its great success, marked by translations and literary influence, was not realized until after the Second World War.

Our purpose in this book is not to study literature and art. The importance of these "Americans in Paris" for the general history of the relations between the two peoples in not, however, slight. Around Gertrude Stein, who lived in the rue de Fleurus, and especially around Sylvia Beach, who in the rue de l'Odéon established her famous bookstore, Shakespeare and Company, near to the Café Voltaire, there was a whole world of young writers—American, English, and French—who met, talked, influenced each other, produced, were creative. The American friends of Sylvia Beach numbered among them Hemingway, Scott Fitzgerald, and Gertrude Stein, William Faulkner, John Dos Passos, Sinclair Lewis, and T. S. Eliot. The American composer George Gershwin drew on this experience for a pleasant operetta, *An American in Paris* (1928), and from this, in turn, a film was produced in 1950. Henry Miller, for his part, chose as his base of operations the Café Sélect and the nearby Montparnasse quarter.

But if we are to avoid anachronism, we must take note that the American writers who enjoyed success in France in the 1930s were not the members of this burgeoning "lost generation." The best sellers were Sinclair Lewis (Nobel Prize for literature in 1930), Pearl Buck (who received the same prize in 1938), and, above all, Margaret Mitchell. Her novel, *Gone with the Wind*, published in 1937, was devoured in France during the war and the exodus from occupied France, because its situations seemed so relevant: Sherman's March through Georgia; Scarlett O'Hara's flight before the advancing Northern troops; famine; occupation. It was therefore after 1945 that Faulkner, Hemingway, and Steinbeck obtained the Nobel Prize (respectively in 1949, 1954, and 1962), as did the French: André Gide, François Mauriac, Albert Camus, and Saint-John Perse (1947, 1952, 1957, and 1960).

I would like to speak here of the increasing influence—finally gigantic—of American films, but this would require a book in itself. Obviously, they exerted their effects more on the imagination than in the political sphere, which is the center of our study. Moreover, it would require refined research to grasp the nuances between the influence of the silent films—which coincided with the prosperity of the 1920s—and that of the talking films, which made their appearance at almost the same time as the economic crisis.

With this, everything collapsed. Whereas France, with its family-based mixed farming, its tariff barriers, and a number of relatively unaffected archaic sectors in its industry, managed to scrape through the crisis with scarcely more than a million unemployed at any one time, the United States, with only four times the population, had more than fourteen million out of work. Between 1933 and 1939, neither France nor the United States succeeded in eliminating all the consequences of the crisis. Whereas by 1939 both the Germans and the British, by different methods, had raised production considerably above their 1929 levels, the United States had still only barely equaled theirs, and France was not to succeed in doing so except for a very short period, the first eight months of 1939.

However, the Americans were at least spared the incoherencies of France's successive economic policies, since they had the benefit of their New Deal. France, until the brief left-wing Popular Front government of 1936-37, continued to practice deflation and refused to devalue; espousing the old prescientific economic myths, she became the champion and leader of the "gold bloc." Then, with the advent of the Popular Front, she raised wages and devalued her currency several times, a policy that might have succeeded if she had not at the same time brought in a national forty-hour week. Was it reasonable to cut back the nation's labor rate so rigorously in a period of crisis, or the labor rate of one's war factories during a period of external threat? There are very few economists who still think so today.

As a consequence, the French followed the progress of Roosevelt's New Deal with passionate interest and mostly with incomprehension. Admittedly the communists, in whose eyes nothing good could ever emerge from a capitalist regime, condemned the New Deal out of hand and in their newspaper, *L'Humanité*, depicted America as a country whose strikes were the symptom of an inexorable class struggle. But superimposed on this doctrinaire and unrealistic reaction there was that of the socialists, avid to discern measures in the New Deal conforming with their own theories. In fact, with the exception of the Tennessee Valley Authority, which did have socialist aspects, the New Deal was largely a heterogeneous collection of ad hoc measures that certainly constituted state planning but were entirely without socialist inspiration. To the right and the moderates, these measures provided proof that capitalism was capable of overcoming a crisis by capitalist methods. Thus there was a great deal of mental confusion in France as to the real significance of the New Deal and the political reforms that accompanied it.

Finally, Roosevelt enjoyed an undoubted popularity in France, which continued to grow after his "quarantine" speech. The dominant impression in the country, as far as one can judge, was that Roosevelt did ultimately want to help the democracies and would one day come to the help of a threatened France. This vision of the future proved correct. What no one knew, unfortunately, was that he would arrive too late to spare the French one of the greatest disasters in their long history.

6

THE SECOND WORLD WAR very quickly brought a new dimension to Franco-American relations, and in that it differed profoundly from its predecessor. Superficially, the general scenarios of both wars were nevertheless the same: a war unleashed in Europe involving the two principal democracies there, the United Kingdom and France, led the Americans to proclaim their neutrality. They intervened only later in the war, when the Allied situation was inauspicious. Their efforts contributed to the final victory without their losses in terms of human life being comparable to those of the European nations. Their economy received a boost from the war, and their national product doubled in a few years.

What had changed totally were the proportions. First the early neutrality: it came to grief on a violent repugnance for Hitler and the Nazis. Second the inauspicious situation of the European democracies: this time it was catastrophic. France had been totally defeated, half her territory occupied in June 1940, the remainder in November 1942. Third, the American intervention: it was just as late coming in the European theater, but this time it was decisive and indispensable. Moreover, in contrast to the previous war, the Americans not only equipped a nine-million-man army of their own this time, they also lavished military aid on the Allies, including the tiny French forces that were either continuing the struggle or resumed it later. Another difference was the fact that the struggle on this occasion included other essential and largely independent theaters of war outside western Europe: the eastern front, where the Russians "broke the back" of the *Wehrmacht*, as Churchill put it, thus making the Normandy landings possible, and the battle for the Pacific, in which France was hardly involved at all (despite the "Pacific Battalion" recruited in the French Pacific islands). Lastly, as a result of mass bombing, the material destruction suffered was far greater, and of all the major nations involved in the war only one escaped physical damage: the United States. As a result, the American nation was to emerge from the conflict, militarily, politically, and economically, an overwhelming victor.

1. The fall of France

It was neither the Nazi aggression against Poland (1 September 1939) nor the British and French declarations of war against Germany (3 September) that breached American isolationism. The most those events achieved was to produce a reform of the United States neutrality laws in favor of the democracies with their control of the seas: on 4 November 1939 Congress raised the embargo on arms and munitions. The French, who had made extensive investments in America, particularly in the area of aviation, were greatly heartened by this move and began to have hopes of future dividends, in 1941–42.

The real catastrophe, the event that truly shook the Americans, was the fall of France. "Fortress America" had possessed two "bonus" advance defenses: the French army and the British navy. Now the first of these had been destroyed, annihilated in six dramatic and appalling weeks. The French premier, Paul Reynaud, sent Roosevelt a desperate telegram on 14 June asking for the immediate intervention of the United States: "I know that the declaration of war does not depend on you alone. I must tell you, however, in this critical hour for us and for you, that if you cannot, in the next few hours, give France that assurance that the United States will enter the war in the very near future, the fate of this world will be changed." Naturally, neither public opinion nor Congress was prepared for such a reversal of American policy. Roosevelt could do no more than promise arms and urge the French colonial empire and the French navy to continue the struggle. But he added: "I know that you will understand that these statements carry with them no implication of military commitments. Only the Congress can make such commitments."

The United States government, with which Churchill was in the process of establishing solid bonds, became extremely anxious when the French signed their armistice with Germany, particularly as regards the future use that might be made of the French fleet, and President Roosevelt gave his approval to the extreme action taken by the British at Mers-el-Kebir. But we must look at the effects of France's defeat from a more distant viewpoint. Three such effects stand out immediately.

1. American opinion, stunned by the event, suddenly realized that the United States itself was now under direct threat. Various opinion polls, by this time a widespread phenomenon (they had been invented by George Gallup in 1935), demonstrate this change very clearly. In November 1939, when asked what action America should take in the war, only 1.7 percent were in favor of an immediate entry into the war, with 10.1 percent in favor of entry into the war if the democracies were on the verge of defeat; 12.2 percent thought that the Americans ought to provide the democracies with the maximum possible quantities of arms and munitions, though without entering the war themselves; 36.9 percent were in favor of neutrality, accompanied by supplies of arms in accordance with the "cash and carry" clause; 6.4 percent were hostile to any sale of arms but accepted the sale of other products. On the other hand, 23.7 percent thought that the United States should refuse to trade in any way with the belligerents, and 0.1 percent were in favor of aid to Germany. In total, then, 24 percent were firmly pro-Allies, as against 0.1 percent pro-German. But 67 percent were still decidedly isolationist.

France's fall perceptibly increased the number of those in favor of an American entry into the war—from 14 percent on 25 June 1940 to 26 percent on 9 September 1941, extremely high figures if one takes into account the natural repugnance that all peoples feel for war. When questioned not about whether America *ought* to enter the war but about the *likelihood* of United States involvement, in August 1939 38 percent thought that the Americans would inevitably be drawn into it. This figure had shot up to 65 percent in June 1940. Lastly, to the question "What is our main duty, to keep out of the war or to aid England even if it involves serious risk of war?" the answers changed as follows:

	Stay out of war	Aid England	No opinion
23 May 1940	64%	36%	—
11 December 1940	37	60	3%

In other words, the shock administered by the fall of France did not succeed in making the Americans eager for war, but it did lead them to realize that war was now for them a possibility, even a probability, and that the cause of Britain, now standing alone, had to be defended, despite the clear risks involved.

2. The immense prestige enjoyed in the United States since 1918 by the France of the *poilus*, the France of Joffre, Foch, Clemenceau, the Marne, Verdun, and Villers-Cotterêts, suddenly collapsed. Affection for France persisted, it is true, but admiration was replaced by pity. Since the Americans are realists, this eclipse, which many saw as definitive, immediately became an item in their calculations. Pierre Laval's son-in-law, René de Chambrun, a descendant of Lafayette and therefore an American citizen, went over to Washington to offer Roosevelt his views (which he later expanded in a book) on the theme: "I saw France fall. Will she rise again?" To Roosevelt, whose attention was by then concentrated entirely on Britain, that resurrection seemed improbable. The American chargé d'affaires, Robert Murphy, writing in his book, *Diplomat among Warriors*, of a visit to Washington in the summer of 1940, remarks that he had great difficulty in arousing any sympathy for the French and that many Americans were very harsh in their judgments on France and her defeat. Roosevelt, long a convert to anticolonialism, was to speak on many occasions during the war of the necessity for ousting the French from Indochina. In January 1943, at Casablanca, he was to encourage the sultan of Morocco to seek independence. He often simply ignored France altogether. "Ultimately," General de Gaulle was to write, "the American leaders accepted France's permanent eclipse as a fact." Whereas, in de Gaulle's own view, "in the depths of American opinion General de Gaulle's undertaking aroused a deep emotional response." It was certainly a fact that all the private or public initiatives made by French refugees in the United States—in particular the creation of an Institut Français in New York with the great art historian Henri Focillon at its head—received more than warm support from the Americans.

3. The Americans were going to have to face a problem that had not existed during the First World War: Which was the legitimate government of France? As the result of an entirely legal process, Marshal Pétain had become prime minister on 16 June 1940, in Bordeaux. He promptly asked for an armistice. Without waiting for

that armistice to be signed, a brigadier general and expert in tank warfare who had recently been an undersecretary of state, Charles de Gaulle, was given permission by the British to use the facilities of the BBC for his famous appeal of 18 June. For him, the request for an armistice had in itself rendered Pétain's government illegitimate. La France had to continue the war. The small group he formed under his leadership, France libre, and later France Combattante (the Free French and the Fighting French), was therefore committed on the one hand to increasing its influence over the remnants of French power (the colonial empire, resistance groups in France, reformed fragments of the armed services outside the overrun metropolitan territory) and on the other to substituting itself gradually for the Pétain government in Vichy as the legitimate and recognized government of France. In the beginning, Washington did not even recognize that a problem existed. As we know from Murphy's book, no one even thought of questioning the legitimacy of the Pétain government. Not until 1943 was General de Gaulle seen as presenting a clear alternative to the Vichy government. What Murphy and many other highly placed Americans seemed to ignore, however, is that the reason for this delay lay largely in Roosevelt's own policy. The relations between Roosevelt and de Gaulle at this time had incalculable consequences for the future of Franco-American relations.

2. Roosevelt, Pétain, and de Gaulle

Hundreds of books, memoirs, articles, and compilations of documents have been published on this subject. I shall simply try, in a few pages, to sum up what is most important in them without distorting the reality by introducing value judgments conditioned by subsequent events. It is possible, in my view, to single out one central and decisive factor here: the total lack of understanding between FDR and de Gaulle, which poisoned their relations from start to finish.

In the early days, the Americans were still not at war, while de Gaulle was almost unknown and beset by a series of unfavorable circumstances. The British action at Mers-el-Kebir had deprived his movement of the many French soldiers and sailors then in England. In the colonies, he obtained support only from the poorest countries (French Equatorial Africa) or those furthest away (the Indian enclaves,

New Caledonia, the Pacific islands). Then the failure of the Anglo-Gaullist Dakar expedition, in September 1940, clearly demonstrated the limits of his powers of attraction. In the summer of 1940, the immense majority of the French themselves, stunned by their country's defeat, were in favor of Marshal Pétain, "the victor of Verdun," whom they were expecting to play some sort of wily double game with the Germans.

But the marshal was very old and very easily influenced. In 1940, Vichy turned into the "national revolution," a kind of paternalist, religious, and corporatist reaction on the part of the extreme right, a mishmash of ideas from Maurras, the Boy Scout code of honor, and appeals for moral order. Pétain saw nothing in the war but one more twist in the old rivalry between France and Germany. He lacked the vision of General de Gaulle, who grasped from the outset that the war was going to be global. On 13 December the leaders of the "national revolution" succeeded in getting rid of the politician Pierre Laval, the inspiration behind the "policy of collaboration," and the Americans were exultant. Their celebration was premature, however, since, for one thing, his successor was Admiral François Darlan, a great realist and a cynic, who in exchange for German permission to return the French fleet to service was prepared to hand over the French bases at Bizerte in Tunisia, at Dakar in Senegal, and also those in Syria. Moreover, the Germans, who had unlimited ways of bringing pressure to bear—they were occupying two-thirds of France, had taken a million French prisoners, and so on—eventually obtained the return of Laval in April 1942.

During this entire period, despite strong opposition from public opinion, the Americans had been assiduously carrying out a policy, originally adopted in summer 1940, of maintaining good relations with Vichy. The argument was as follows: since the rift between London and Vichy was total, ever since the armistice and Mers-el-Kebir, only the Americans could exert any influence on the marshal's government capable of counterbalancing that of the Germans. The American line was therefore largely to ignore the Free French, despite the obvious sympathy they were arousing in the United States, and maintain close diplomatic relations with Vichy. Since the American ambassador William Bullitt had returned to the United States, Robert Murphy had been left as chargé d'affaires. But it was felt necessary to appoint a new ambassador with some aura of prestige. Roosevelt thought at first of the aging General Pershing, Pétain's comrade-in-arms in 1918. But Pershing's health was failing. Finally it was a personal friend of the president's, Admiral William Leahy, who was appointed, while Murphy was sent as consul general to Algiers, with responsibility for the whole of French North Africa.

While Leahy was in Vichy, doing his best to restrain Pétain from making increasing concessions to Germany, Murphy had hopes of winning over the French commander-in-chief for North Africa, the brilliant General Maxime Weygand, a former colleague of Foch, to the idea of resuming the struggle against Germany. In vain. Weygand was determined to remain faithful to Pétain and in any case felt he was too old for such exploits. (He was to die in 1965 at the age of ninety-seven.) Moreover, in November 1941 the Germans managed to obtain his recall. In fact, while the Germans had the marshal's government so completely by the throat, what could the Americans really offer, apart from fine words? An agreement was reached guaranteeing the neutrality of the French Antilles—where all the gold from the Banque de France was stockpiled!—on the authority of the Vichyite governor there, Admiral Robert. There was also the Weygand-Murphy agreement of February 1941, which did produce a slight easing of the North African blockade in exchange for official inspection rights of American goods imported by the various vice-consuls in Tunisia, Algeria, and Morocco. But one seeks in vain for any dramatic diplomatic success. The great American historian William Langer has offered a skillful defense of this "Vichy policy" in a well-known book commissioned by Cordell Hull, *Our Vichy Gamble*, but it fails to carry total conviction. Laval's return to power in April 1942 brought this phase to an end, and the United States ambassador to Vichy was recalled.

Meanwhile, with rare pertinacity and limited means, General de Gaulle was carrying out a far-reaching program that he himself has defined as follows: "What was the point of simply providing auxiliary forces for another power? No! In order for the effort to be worth the trouble, it was essential to succeed in bringing back into the war, not just Frenchmen, but France." However, this presupposed "recognition by foreign powers of the fact that France, as such, had never stopped fighting." The general had "no illusions about the obstacles to be overcome." Not only the might of the enemy, skepticism, moral and material difficulties, rival undertakings, the divisions among the French people, but also "the tendency of the great nations to take advantage of our present weakness to urge their own interests to the detriment of France" (*Mémoires de guerre*, vol. 1, pp. 69–70).

In the event, of all those great nations it was America, or at least the American government, that put the greatest difficulties in the way of the Gaullist movement. It is difficult to imagine a more total incomprehension than that which existed between Roosevelt and de Gaulle.

The most surprising part of all is that it began long before they even knew each other, for their first actual meeting did not occur until 22 January 1943, at Anfa in Morocco. In Roosevelt's mind, de Gaulle was from the word go a man lacking in lucidity—was his failure at Dakar not sufficient proof of that? But it was Cordell Hull, the secretary of state, who carried this stereotype of the Free French leader to its extreme.

The tiny islands of Saint Pierre and Miquelon, south of Newfoundland, had remained French after the Treaty of Utrecht of 1713. With a population of only five thousand, their strategic importance was minimal. But since they were under the authority of the Vichyite governor of the Antilles, Admiral Robert, they could have been used as bases for the transmission of meteorological reports by radio to the German submarine fleet. De Gaulle, disturbed at the thought of a possible Canadian takeover, suggested that the islands should be occupied by Free French naval forces, only to be met with a polite refusal from the Americans, who had signed a pledge with Admiral Robert to maintain the status quo. De Gaulle decided to go ahead anyway, and several days after Pearl Harbor, on 24 December 1941, while the Japanese were daily conquering and occupying vast islands and whole archipelagoes, the Free French landed on Saint Pierre and Miquelon, and an immediate plebiscite expressed almost unanimous approval of their presence there. In such a period of defeats, American opinion was jubilant: there were two islands at least that had changed hands in the right direction. Minuscule islands, true, but they were a symbol.

Cordell Hull, on the other hand, was outraged and allowed his fury to lead him into an uncharacteristic blunder. "Our preliminary reports," he announced,

show that the action taken by the so-called Free French at Saint
Pierre–Miquelon was an arbitrary action contrary to the agreement
of all parties concerned and certainly without the prior knowledge
or consent in any sense of the United States Government. This
Government has inquired of the Canadian Government as to the
steps that Government is prepared to take to restore the *status quo*
of those Islands (Sherwood, *Roosevelt and Hopkins*, p. 482).

To restore liberated territories to a regime viewed as pro-German
was unthinkable to American opinion. And the use of the phrase
"*so-called* Free French," applied to men who had voluntarily chosen
to fight on against the Germans, was more than the Americans could
stomach. The State Department was inundated with telegrams addressed to the "So-Called Secretary of State," and many newspapers
began referring to the "So-Called Department of State." Hull, a very
worthy man, who thought of himself, so Sherwood tells us, as
sacrosanct, had no sense of humor. His wrath was terrible. The
conclusion he drew was that de Gaulle was some sort of dangerous
adventurer, a budding dictator, despite the fact that Roosevelt
affected not to take the matter at all seriously, partly perhaps because,
on 30 December, Churchill delivered an eloquent speech in praise of
the Free French. As time went by, however, Roosevelt allowed himself
to become increasingly influenced by Hull, and he continued to treat
de Gaulle in an offhand manner. The Comité National Français was
not invited to sign the United Nations Declaration of January 1942 as
a recognized government.

The most dramatic result of this affair was what might be termed
the search for the "third man." When the Americans had been
persuaded by the British, despite their own preference for a landing in
Europe, that it was essential to acquire control of North Africa first,
they decided that they needed to find another French leader, someone
between Pétain and de Gaulle who would be capable of bringing the
French colonial army back into the war. They hit upon General Henri
Giraud, who in April 1942 had escaped from the Koenigstein prison
in Germany. The choice was an excellent one from the American point
of view. A good general, Giraud knew nothing whatever about
politics, though he was instinctively right-wing in his views, hostile to
both communists and Jews. Totally lacking de Gaulle's visionary cast
of mind, he himself very succinctly summed up the essential nature of

his plans in the title of his memoirs: *Un seul but, la victoire.* De Gaulle stubbornly upheld the principle that France, despite her present misfortunes, had been a great power for fifteen hundred years and must still be treated as such by the Allies. Apart from his own natural pride he possessed an unshakable conviction that any compromise on this point must be rejected out of hand. Churchill, even though he did have violent differences with de Gaulle, nevertheless appreciated the nobility of this attitude. Roosevelt, too convinced of always being right, could not accept such opposition. With Giraud he had no worries on that score.

The result was that in November 1942, when the French in North Africa reentered the struggle after the American landing, it was Giraud (after a brief interregnum, during which the former Vichy leader Admiral Darlan took command) who was placed at the head of the bizarre regime there. The Americans even ended up supporting a French committee, the "Conseil impérial," which was maintaining concentration camps for Jews and communists in southern Algeria.

Speculation will continue for many years on the wisdom of the "third man" policy. It was certainly true that de Gaulle was very unpopular in certain North African military and civilian circles. But the French resistance at home, right-wingers and left-wingers alike, refused to tolerate the maintenance of the antidemocratic Vichy régime in the liberated empire. De Gaulle was seen as the leader of this silent army, a fact that Roosevelt failed to grasp.

He tried reconciling de Gaulle and Giraud by subordinating the former to the latter, the initial step in this attempt being the first de Gaulle–Roosevelt meeting, at Anfa near Casablanca, on 22 January 1943. It had taken what amounted to an ultimatum to get de Gaulle to Morocco at all. Roosevelt, who knew how to charm better than most men, failed totally with de Gaulle. There were armed police concealed behind the hangings in the presidential office. "As a result of these vague presences, the atmosphere in which Roosevelt and I conducted our first conversation was a strange one indeed. . . . He seemed very anxious to establish contact between us, employing charm rather than arguments in order to convince me" (de Gaulle, *Mémoires de guerre*, vol. 2, p. 79). Roosevelt's charm suffered a defeat that day comparable to the one it met later on with Stalin at Yalta. The distorted image of de Gaulle as dictator took firm shape in his mind.

But that meeting likewise succeeded in imprinting a false and ineradicable image of Roosevelt and the Americans in the general's mind. The following quotation from his war memoirs has an immense historical significance—a significance that did not fully emerge until long after Roosevelt's death, during those eleven years in the 1950s and 1960s when de Gaulle was to govern France. After a period of isolationism, de Gaulle suggests, the all-powerful United States, inspired by a kind of "messianic mission," had embarked upon "vast designs."

> The United States, amazed at the scale of its own resources, feeling that its dynamism no longer had sufficient scope for action within its own frontiers, wishing to aid all those in the world then living in poverty and subjection, yielded in its turn to the temptation of intervention, a cause in which the spirit of domination then became enlisted. . . . But as soon as America was at war, it became Roosevelt's intention that the ensuing peace should be an American Peace, that he himself should be in a position to dictate its organization, that those states crushed by the ordeal should be subjected to his judgment, that France in particular should accept him as its savior and its judge. In consequence, the fact that France had risen once more at the height of the battle, not in the form of mere fragmentary and therefore easily handled resistance groups, but as a sovereign and independent nation, ran counter to his intentions (*Mémoires de guerre*, vol. 2, pp. 79–80).

In short, just as Roosevelt saw de Gaulle as a man of overweening ambition burning to set himself up as a dictator—wrongly, as subsequent events showed—so de Gaulle believed Roosevelt to be engaged in nefarious maneuvers ultimately intended to lead to a Pax Americana, consisting of a world of docile nations, all looking up to the Americans because of their lofty ideals and all willing in consequence to accept American domination. In fact, he was just as mistaken as Roosevelt, in my view, for although Roosevelt did have every intention of purging the world of the Nazi and fascist virus, his plans for the peace to follow were deliberately vague in the extreme, and the idea of domination, even indirect domination, was certainly very far from both his mind and his heart.

The true picture, therefore, is that of a clash between two types of great men, both characteristic of the nations they represented.

Raymond Poli, in a paper written for the European Association for American Studies, has delineated very clearly the differences between the American "great man," typified by Roosevelt, and the French "great man" as exemplified by Napoleon, Clemenceau, and de Gaulle. The American great man must be a kind of sublimation of the average American. He stands out from the crowd of fellow citizens around him, not because of any differences from them but because of the high degree to which he possesses those characteristic qualities to be found scattered throughout tens of millions of families. He is therefore likable, smiling, easy to talk to, hospitable, modest, and kindly. He is the very essence and soul of the whole people. The French great man is in a way set apart from other men. His greatness is a solitude regarded with awe. The people, Victor Hugo wrote with reference to Napoleon,

> Gazed at the thunder-girdled Louvre
> As at another Mount Sinai.

Even though Clemenceau does somewhat belie this image, General de Gaulle certainly accepted it and cultivated it, as something forced on him by destiny. Moreover, his task was that of hauling France back up from the very depths of the abyss. "As for me, now about to dare the attempt of such a peak, I was nothing at the start. Limited and alone as I was, and precisely because I was so, I had to reach the heights and never again descend from them" (*Mémoires de guerre*, vol. 1, p. 70).

Roosevelt, as all his colleagues and all those close to him have testified, was an incredibly complex and ultimately mysterious man. Outwardly, however, he succeeded in clothing his immense ambition with an extremely natural and smiling affability. Leader of the world's most powerful nation, he always strove on the surface to bridge the gap between himself and the average man. De Gaulle, his very authority in question, building on the ruins of a country shattered by misfortune, always cultivated his natural tendency to solitude and intransigence, because, as he said, "the slightest weakening would have brought everything crashing down." De Gaulle did perceive Roosevelt's greatness, but he imputed to it an imperialist tinge that Roosevelt in fact strove to avoid. Roosevelt thought he was always

right, loathed opposition, viewed that of General de Gaulle with
vexation, and was never able to appreciate the Frenchman's greatness.

3. American delaying tactics

We now come to one of the least pleasant and least clear-sighted
aspects of the great American leader's policy. The fact that Roosevelt
enjoyed only moderate popularity in postwar France, a popularity
much inferior to that of Harry Truman or General Dwight Eisenhower,
was a direct result of his resolutely anti-Gaullist attitude in 1943 and
1944. After the meeting at Anfa in January 1943, Roosevelt remarked
that de Gaulle—whom he had already described as a prima donna—
seemed to think he was Joan of Arc or Clemenceau. Before long he was
saying that de Gaulle *had compared himself* to Joan of Arc and
Clemenceau. It is only too easy to recognize in that subtle shift a
process typical of prejudice at work. Actuated by this idea, more
emotional than rational in origin, Roosevelt did his utmost to prevent
de Gaulle from playing a decisive political role.

His first move was to send Jean Monnet over to Algeria. Monnet, an
eminent Frenchman who had chosen not to join the Gaullist movement in July 1940 but instead to play a part in the process of America's
economic mobilization, had in the course of his stay become friendly
both with Roosevelt and with the latter's close adviser, Harry Hopkins.
Disturbed by the continuing rift between the French in London and
the French in Algeria, despite the fact that both groups had now
rejoined the struggle against Germany, Jean Monnet was hoping to
achieve a reconciliation between de Gaulle and Giraud while at the
same time fostering the plans of the United States. Was it practical of
de Gaulle, with a maximum of 70,000 fighting men at his disposal, to
aspire to a status of equal importance with the full might of the
United States of America? Roosevelt believed that it might be possible
for Monnet (who arrived in North Africa on 27 February 1943) to
persuade de Gaulle into an outright acceptance of Giraud as "civil and
military commander-in-chief."

Jean Monnet realized immediately that Giraud had to be made to
adopt a more democratic stance. He persuaded him to make a speech,
on 14 March 1943, that Giraud himself was to describe naïvely in his

memoirs as "the first democratic speech of my life." In addition to
the liberation of the political internees and Jews, already under way,
Giraud promised a return to popular sovereignty after France had been
liberated: "The people of France will then become master of its own
destiny.... The people of France will then form its own government
in accordance with the laws of the Republic." Long negotiations
began between the Gaullists, represented in Algeria by General
Georges Catroux, and the Giraudists. I will not enter into the details
of them (they have been excellently covered by André Kaspi in his
book *La Mission de Jean Monnet à Alger*), since it is more relevant to
our theme to concentrate on the course taken by Roosevelt. In
practice, this consisted in delaying de Gaulle's arrival in Algeria until
the defeat of the Axis forces in Tunisia had been achieved. General
Eisenhower and Murphy, the American representative in Algiers, were
both apprehensive of possible Gaullist demonstrations that might sow
discord in the area, and even of some sort of Gaullist coup aimed at
the removal of Giraud. Moreover—as had become evident after the
triumphal reception in New York of the majestic *Richelieu*, the sole
battleship to survive the scuttling of the French fleet by its own crews
off Toulon in November 1942—the soldiers and sailors under Giraud's
command had been known to go so far as to "desert" in order to join
de Gaulle's forces, who were better paid, it is true, but also more
intransigent and trailing greater glory as a consequence of the heroic
battle of Bir Hacheim in the Libyan desert during June 1942. While all
these delaying tactics were in progress, de Gaulle sent Catroux a telex
both "imperative" and imperious: "I fail to understand Giraud's
delays in a matter already settled in the minds of the vast majority of
Frenchmen even in North Africa.... I intend to come to Algiers in
daylight and with dignity." From all sides, and particularly from
occupied France via the Underground, messages and telegrams were
arriving in Algeria from county and municipal councils, from unions
and trade associations, expressing support for de Gaulle. Monnet
himself was fully aware how far de Gaulle's political position was
superior to Giraud's. After a few months, as we know from Murphy, it
became apparent to the Americans in North Africa that Monnet's
conception of French unity was diametrically opposed to Roosevelt's.
Ultimately, all Giraud had in his favor was his age (he was eleven years
older than de Gaulle), his higher rank (five stars as opposed to two),

and, above all, the good will of the Americans, who were by then sending him large consignments of military equipment.

De Gaulle finally arrived in Algiers on 13 May 1943. On 1 June there followed the creation of the Comité Français de Libération Nationale (CFLN) under the alternating presidency of Giraud and de Gaulle, a body that one year later was to become the provisional government of the French Republic.

But then, having accepted de Gaulle's arrival, Roosevelt did everything he possibly could to limit the general's power. De Gaulle wanted to replace Pierre Boisson, the governor-general of French West Africa, who had remained a Vichy supporter up to November 1942. Roosevelt was of the opinion, as he wrote to Churchill, that all the talk about a Gaullist takeover in Dakar was too serious for him to remain passive. Neither he nor Churchill, he felt, really knew just how far de Gaulle might go. De Gaulle wanted the command of French troops to be answerable to the CFLN, in conformity with the democratic tradition of the superiority of the civil authority over the military. The Americans were insisting that Giraud, copresident of the CFLN, should remain as commander-in-chief *as well*. They would not continue with the rearmament of the French army unless it remained under the command of the only leader in whom they had confidence—Giraud. On 19 June, Eisenhower was instructed to pass this ultimatum on to de Gaulle. De Gaulle has left an account of this conversation, in which he replied with characteristic hauteur: "Are you aware that I, for my part, have duties toward France, and that in virtue of those duties I cannot accept the interference of any foreign power in the exercise of French powers?" Nor did he fail to remind Eisenhower that France, as we saw earlier, had equipped the American army of 1918 with French arms: "Yes, during the first world war you, the Americans, fired no guns that were not our guns, rode in no tanks but our tanks, flew no aircraft but our aircraft. Did we, in return, demand from the United States the appointment of such and such a leader, or the setting up of any predetermined political system?" (*Mémoires de guerre*, vol. 2, pp. 115–16).

In the event, de Gaulle won, for two reasons. The first was Giraud's political ineptitude. He allowed a Gaullist majority to develop in the CFLN, then left for the United States, in response to an invitation pointedly addressed to him alone, and failed to demand that he be treated as a head of state. On 6 November 1943, de Gaulle succeeded in removing Giraud from the CFLN, then the next April in depriving him of the military command. The Americans themselves had by then grown weary of supporting their "third man," and according to Murphy even Roosevelt was referring to him as a soldier with a rather limited mind. The other reason was the role played by Eisenhower. "It was a happy result of the alliance," de Gaulle wrote, "that Dwight Eisenhower discovered in himself, not only the prudence required to deal with these thorny problems, but also the attraction of those larger horizons that history was opening to his future career. He succeeded in being shrewd and flexible. . . . He was also capable of taking a risk." Although he did not allow the French army the role due to it, "that was because . . . the policy, originating in Washington, that dictated his conduct, imposed on him a degree of reserve. . . . Deep down, this great soldier felt in his turn the mysterious sympathy that for almost two centuries had brought his country and mine together in the great events of the world. It was not his fault if this time the United States gave less ear to our distress than to the call of domination" (*Mémoires de guerre*, vol. 2, p. 117).

These events explain, though they do not justify, Roosevelt's stubborn opposition to the great powers' recognizing the CFLN in Algiers as the provisional government of France. The Soviet Union was the first to declare its readiness to do so, on condition that its major allies were in agreement. The British position was more or less the same. Of the Americans in Algeria, Eisenhower and even Murphy were ready to agree. When Roosevelt was informed of this project, he cabled Eisenhower and in the most energetic terms forbade him to make any gesture that would imply, even tacitly, the slightest hint of recognition for this "government." Since the Lend-Lease Act of 11 March 1941, the United States had of course been providing the French with arms and aid. In the case of the Gaullists in London this aid was for a long time supplied through the intermediary of the British. In the case of the colonies in Gaullist hands (French Equatorial Africa, the Pacific Islands), the Americans made use of the system of "local authorities" already in existence. This practice was convenient in that it avoided taking up any position on the future status of France, even though Eisenhower and Murphy had promised that she would reestablish her authority over the whole of her colonial empire.

The result of Roosevelt's position was that the CFLN was not even recognized as a *de facto* government. Of the various forms of partial recognition adopted by the Russians, the British, and the Americans, that of the Soviet Union was the broadest and that of the United States the most narrow.

This attitude led to tragicomedy. Convinced that de Gaulle was merely the creation of his own propaganda, Roosevelt was accustomed to remark, as he did to Stimson, "that de Gaulle will crumple and that the British supporters of de Gaulle will be confounded by the course of events" (Henry Stimson and McGeorge Bundy, *On Active Service in Peace and War*, p. 551). In July 1944, Roosevelt was to go further and claim that de Gaulle was supported by less than 10 percent of the French people. One would be staggered at finding the most powerful of the coalition leaders so incredibly ill-informed unless one took into account the emotional nature of his statement. As a matter of fact, American military circles, beginning with Secretary of War Henry Stimson, a Republican, were perfectly well aware of the vast popular support de Gaulle enjoyed in France. In January 1944, when he was in the thick of preparations for D Day, Eisenhower tried to persuade Roosevelt that an agreement ought to be made with the CFLN entrusting the latter with the government of France after liberation. Roosevelt opposed the idea. He was all for simply creating an allied military government in France, exactly like the one set up in Italy after the defeat of its Axis rulers. The most that could be obtained was an agreement from Hull, made in March, that the allied military government would use the machinery being set up by the CFLN to facilitate the task of governing a liberated France.

The indignation of General de Gaulle when he learned of these plans may be imagined. "The refusal to recognize us as the national authority in France was in reality a cover for the American president's determination to make himself the arbiter in France. This belief in his power to trample upon our independence was something I felt myself in a position to render vain in the event" (*Mémoires de guerre*, vol. 2, p. 211). Eisenhower was very embarrassed by this turn of events. Invested by Roosevelt with the authority to govern France, it was he, finally, who was to take the responsibility of not setting up an allied military government. But before that happened, there was still to be one last screech of protest from the diplomatic machinery.

On 2 June 1944 de Gaulle was invited to London, where first
Churchill, then Eisenhower, told him of the imminence of the great
landing in Europe. But when de Gaulle was shown the proclamation
that Eisenhower was to make on 6 June to the nations being liberated,
he found it unacceptable. After having spoken to the Norwegians, the
Dutch, the Belgians, and the people of Luxembourg simply as a
soldier, Eisenhower then asked the French to

> carry out his orders. . . . In short, he was making it look as though
> he was going to assume full authority in our country, for which
> he was in fact no more than an allied general, skilled in the com-
> mand of troops but without the slightest right to intervene in its
> government, quite apart from the fact that he would be extremely
> embarrassed at having to do so. There was not a word in the state-
> ment about the French authority that had for years been en-
> couraging and directing France's war effort.

Since the text of the Eisenhower statement was too sacrosanct to be
altered, de Gaulle refused to make his expected broadcast to France on
the morning of 6 June. He did go on the air that evening, however,
when he made a completely separate statement (*Mémoires de guerre*,
vol. 2, p. 225).

In the event, everything was to be decided in the first small French
town actually liberated, Bayeux, famous for its Queen Mathilda's
Tapestry depicting the details of another celebrated landing: that of
William the Conqueror in 1066 on the shores of Britain! On 14 June,
with what emotion may be imagined, de Gaulle set foot on the coast
of France. He hastily sent on ahead Commissioner of the Republic
François Coulet (who had taken over the functions of the subprefect of
Vichy) in order to forestall the British and American "political"
officers. Then he made his entry into Bayeux, where the crowd formed
into a procession behind him "amid a display of extraordinary
emotion." The "plebiscite" of the French people in favor of General
de Gaulle, which was to culminate in the famous procession down the
Champs-Elysées in Paris on 25 August, was to make it clear to
everyone's eyes, even those of Roosevelt, that the man of 18 June had
become the embodiment of France.

Later there came the general's visit to Washington, where Roosevelt
welcomed him on 6 July "all smiles and cordiality." "I listened while

Roosevelt outlined his plans to me. How human it was, the way he cloaked his will to power in idealism.'' But although the mutual incomprehension persisted, at least the two men moved closer on a moral level. ''A great mind,'' de Gaulle added, ''the American president feels a real predilection for France. But it is precisely because of this feeling that he is, in his heart of hearts, disappointed and angered by our recent disaster and by the contemptible reactions it elicited in so many Frenchmen'' (*Mémoires de guerre*, vol. 2, p. 239).

At the very moment when liberation was within grasp, in August 1944, a last effort was made with the help of certain American secret agents (though probably without Roosevelt's knowledge) to hand over power to Edouard Herriot, one of the best-known politicians of the Third Republic. It was Pierre Laval, the Vichy prime minister, later sentenced to death and shot, who had Herriot released from the hospital where he was imprisoned and brought to Paris. But Herriot, an ardent patriot and an unswerving democrat, laid down conditions that were not accepted. In any case, the Gestapo, having been excluded from the plot, broke it up and removed Herriot to Germany, where he was to remain until the German capitulation.

4. Liberation and rejoicing

Nothing in this world is unalloyed, and the de Gaulle-Roosevelt conflict somewhat darkens the picture of delirious joy the French have of their liberation from four years of occupation and suffering. There were other shadows in the picture too, in particular a bloody and excessive zeal in some areas to ''purge'' the country of collaborators. Then there were the material problems—food supplies, wages, war damage, total hiatus in the national economy, hatreds among the French themselves, political rifts—all of which swiftly made themselves felt.

However, on the morning of 6 June, when the French learned that the Allies, accompanied by French contingents, had landed in Normandy, there was joy everywhere. It was to redouble at the news of the Avranches breakthrough in late July. As the Allies approached Paris, where the Resistance had organized an uprising, de Gaulle persuaded Eisenhower to change his plans slightly in order to forestall massacres and destruction in the city, and the American general had the tact to order that the entry of the Allied troops into Paris should be headed by the famous Second Armored Division of General Jean Leclerc. During those days the brotherhood-in-arms was total. Gratitude toward the liberators overcame all differences. Anyone who actually saw, all over northern France, the sight of the Germans hurriedly evacuating the towns and villages, using every imaginable form of transport, and the unending columns of tanks and trucks pouring in from the south, manned by innumerable khaki-clad soldiers, so stolid and relaxed, followed by that tremendous tide of supplies of all kinds, has it imprinted on his memory forever.

What part did the French play in all this? A limited one, as we know, especially in Normandy, despite the delaying action of the Resistance movement, which held up German reinforcements at the cost of appalling reprisals. It was much larger in Italy, however, where the French contingent was much more sizable and played a considerable role, especially west of Monte Cassino and during the taking of Rome. But the culmination of the French effort came on 15 August with the landing on the coast of Provence. Not only did the *maquis* in the southeast, helped by their knowledge of the terrain, achieve successes not expected by the Allied leaders, but the principal role in the campaign was played by the French First Army under General Jean de Lattre de Tassigny. With his tremendous dash—which earned him the same sort of popularity in America that General George Patton enjoyed in France—de Lattre managed to march into Marseilles twenty-six days ahead of the date set him and into Lyons seventy-two days ahead!

The joy of the liberation was tinged with sadness. Total American casualties in the Second World War were 225,000. Those of France, with only a quarter of the American population, reached 625,000. Of this number 70,000 were victims of Allied bombing, unavoidable bombing, no doubt, but involving a number of misjudgments—the pointless flattening of Royan by the United States Air Force due to erroneous intelligence, for example—which thereby provided fuel for Nazi propaganda. However, once the American breakthrough at Avranches had occurred, in July, the liberation of France took place without excessive losses, except in Normandy. In November and December, with the conquest of Alsace and Lorraine, almost the whole of metropolitan France had been liberated, the only exceptions being the Atlantic "pockets" contained by the French Forces of the Interior. Paris was saved. In the rectangle formed by the Loire, the Rhone, the Pyrenees, and the sea, there was little Allied penetration. It was the French Underground that liberated that area and harried the retreating Germans.

General de Gaulle's independence of spirit, and his concern for the interests of France, led to a serious incident involving Eisenhower. Strasbourg and part of Alsace had been liberated when the Germans launched a powerful counteroffensive in the Ardennes. Eisenhower decided that prudence required a withdrawal on his right wing, which happened to include the French First Army under de Lattre. De Gaulle, as president of the provisional government, ordered de Lattre not to retreat.

> The evacuation of Alsace, and in particular of its capital, might seem logical from the viewpoint of Allied strategy. But France as a nation cannot accept it. That the French army should abandon one of our provinces—and that province above all—without even having done battle to defend it; that German troops, followed by Himmler and his Gestapo, should be allowed to march back in triumph into Strasbourg, into Mulhouse, into Selestat, would be an appalling wound inflicted upon the honor of the nation and its fighting men, an appalling motive for despair hurled in the Alsatians' faces by their own country.... Clearly I cannot consent to it (*Mémoires de guerre*, vol. 3, p. 143).

The American order was issued on 28 December. De Gaulle reacted swiftly and informed Eisenhower "that France would defend Alsace on her own with the means at her command." The risk was enormous. But it would not be the first this amazing man had taken. With Churchill's support, he succeeded after a "heated argument" in persuading Eisenhower to cancel his instructions. It was a serious incident, there can be no doubt, but one that contributed ultimately to a strengthening of the mutual esteem between the American commander-in-chief and the French leader, as well as to Eisenhower's popularity in France.

Finally, on 9 May 1945, in Berlin, General de Lattre de Tassigny, who had led the final campaign in Bavaria, signed the German capitulation in the name of France. "What? The French too!" Fieldmarshal Wilhelm Keitel exclaimed.

France had contributed to the victory. Her role had been modest, it is true, simply because of her defeat in 1940. But the fact that she was able to play any role at all was thanks to de Gaulle. Thanks also to the British and the Americans. For although the main brunt in Europe was borne by the Red Army, the true liberators of France had in the main been the Americans—and that is something the French have not forgotten.

IN THE MAJESTIC, undoubtedly partial, but superb and penetrating account he gives of his relations with Roosevelt, de Gaulle is, to begin with, in the right. The American president, before the liberation of France, was grossly mistaken as to the real situation. However, the third volume of the *Mémoires de guerre* is less convincing. After the liberation of Paris, albeit without ever developing any great love for the incomprehensible Frenchman, Roosevelt did make numerous conciliatory gestures. Yet not only did de Gaulle consider these inadequate, in relation to France's "rank," but he continued to scent perfidious ambitions, which take on a posthumous character after FDR's sudden death on 12 April 1945.

In his both impressive and utopian desire to restore France to her place among the great powers, the general did achieve considerable success. He achieved this, thanks to British help, true, but also with American support. The provisional government, by then head-quartered in Paris, was finally recognized *de jure* by the three major Allies on 23 October 1944. On 11 November 1944, France was admitted to membership in the European Advisory Commission, formed to deal with the myriad questions relating to the fate of a defeated Germany. At Yalta (February 1945), Churchill and Roosevelt eventually persuaded Stalin to accept France on an equal footing as an occupying power in Germany, on condition that the French occupied zone be carved out of the British and American zones. Roosevelt, originally reluctant, had been persuaded to back this request during the preliminary meeting on Malta. The three great powers then asked France to take part with them in the San Francisco Conference (April to June 1945), which was to be the first step toward the creation of the

United Nations Organization. De Gaulle refused, on the grounds that he had not been party to the preliminaries. France nevertheless obtained a permanent seat on the Security Council, with a right of veto, along with the United States, the Soviet Union, the United Kingdom, and China. At the three-power Potsdam Conference, France was likewise invited to take part in the council of foreign ministers, composed of representatives from the same list of powers that was to draw up the peace treaties.

Yet the general was not at all satisfied. He still perceived the maleficent designs of the United States everywhere: in Indochina, where it is true that American secret service agents were encouraging the communist leader Ho Chi Minh to declare independence; in Syria and Lebanon, where the Americans, anticolonialist by temperament, by tradition, and out of genuine democratic concern, were in favor of total independence for France's former mandates; and in Europe, where the Americans refused to arm ten or twelve additional French divisions. But there was a shortage of shipping space, so wasn't it perfectly logical of the Americans, wishing as they did to carry the greatest weight in any future negotiations, to reserve any available arms for their own reinforcements? And when France was conceded an occupied zone in Germany, the general complained that it was too small.

One could go on citing such examples. The most important of all was the general's reaction to the Yalta Conference, to which I shall return. De Gaulle took the fact that he hadn't been invited as an insult, and he soon let the fact be known in dramatic fashion. Unlike Churchill, Roosevelt had not made an official visit to France, despite the general's invitation. His health was failing. On his way back from Yalta, he asked de Gaulle to come and meet him in Algiers, in order to spare his declining energies. On 13 February de Gaulle sent a refusal.

He was happy to learn that President Roosevelt was planning to visit a French port. [He] added that the invitation he had received to visit that port himself had caught him unprepared, at a time when a great many matters were requiring his presence in Paris, and on the heels of a conference between the three leaders of the Allied governments, their advisers, and their experts, a conference in which

France had not taken part and of whose many aims she had still not
been apprised (De Gaulle, *Mémoires de guerre*, vol. 3, p. 400).

1. The Yalta myth and the neutralist era

There was world-wide consternation when news got out of what
seemed to many just one more proof of de Gaulle's eccentricity.
American opinion took it as an insult, as was soon apparent from the
sharpness of American comments. In France there were some who
appreciated the loftiness of his reaction and saluted his inflexibility.
But France was in ruins, and her need for American help was so great
that public opinion was in general critical of what it saw as excessive
intransigence. In reality, the general had laid the foundation stone of
a theory that was to achieve lasting success, a theory that I shall call
"the Yalta myth."

There were a good many reasons why de Gaulle was not asked to
join the three great powers at Yalta or their previous meeting in
Tehran. Stalin thought exclusively in terms of armored divisions,
sneering at the pope for having none and at France for having so few.
As a result, he completely dismissed the alliance pact that de Gaulle
had signed in Moscow the previous December. Churchill was mistrustful of the influence wielded by the French communists and also
wished to preserve the British special relationship with the United
States. For Roosevelt, as we have seen, de Gaulle was the archetypal
gate-crasher.

De Gaulle on his side saw Yalta as something quite other than a
mere inter-Allied conference. In his view the Soviet Union and the
United States—escorted by its "brilliant second-in-command,"
Britain—were meeting in order to divide the world up into zones of
influence, taking care to exclude France. De Gaulle was to remain
convinced of the truth of this interpretation for the rest of his life, so
much so that others came to believe in it too. One of his supporters,
Arthur Conte, was even to publish a book in 1964 with the significant
title: *Yalta ou le partage du monde*. Yet anyone who reads carefully
through the relevant American records and the memoirs and remi-
niscences of those present is bound to admit that at no point during the
Yalta Conference was any mention made of zones of influence.
Moreover, Roosevelt struggled with all his might against the very

principle of zones of influence, eventually created, on the Soviet side, by the presence of the Red Army in eastern Europe and Stalin's desire to establish his domination there. Roosevelt had certainly been entertaining the idea that the great powers should maintain a world-wide preponderance of power for the purpose of preserving peace, but *in association*, without any partition and without geographical boundaries. He loathed the very notion of zones and had expressed unequivocal disapproval of the Churchill-Stalin conversations in Moscow during the previous October. At Yalta, by means of the Declaration on Liberated Europe, and his negotiations over Poland, he attempted to preserve a certain degree of American control in eastern Europe, in exchange for acceptance of similar Soviet control in western Europe. On 11 February 1945, at the end of the conference, he felt that he had to a large extent achieved what he wanted. It was not until *after* Yalta, and only as a result of Stalin's determination, that the Soviet zone came into existence and that certain Americans, such as George Kennan and Charles Bohlen, the State Department "Sovietologists," together with Dean Acheson, James Forrestal, and a few others, thought up the "containment" theory: preventing the Soviets from enlarging their zone since it was impossible to "liberate" it. I remain convinced, in other words, that *Yalta, far from being an occasion for world partition, marked the last attempt of the Western powers to prevent it.*

Nevertheless, following as it did the infuriating experience of the wartime negotiations, it was de Gaulle's view of the Yalta Conference that formed the basis upon which what one might term "Gaullist anti-Americanism" was firmly established. It was directed against what the general saw as the Americans' hidden resolve to impose their will inside "their zone of influence," in which they included France. But France wished to remain independent and had perforce to show the world that she was capable of that independence. Saying no to the Americans was one day to become the governing principle of Gaullist policy.

After organizing the referendum of October 1945, which resulted in the creation of a new Republic, the Fourth, and the election of a National Constituent Assembly, de Gaulle abruptly resigned on 19 January 1946. Believing as he did that he represented the very essence of France, he decided that it was futile to wear himself out fighting the excessive influence of the political parties. He proved at every turn, contrary to what Roosevelt had believed, that he was a genuine democrat, the very antithesis of a budding dictator.

It is a fact that the influence of the French Communist party was then reaching its apogee, and it would be true to say that during the next twelve years the whole of Franco-American relations was to be dominated by the problem of communism, both Soviet and French.

Having been badly weakened by the shock of the Hitler-Stalin pact signed on 23 August 1939, the Communist party in France began making headway again when it abandoned the amazing "war of imperialism" doctrine it upheld in the latter part of 1939, under Stalin's influence, and switched to its "patriotic war" line as a result of the German invasion of the Soviet Union. Moreover, the communist "base" in France had not waited until June 1941 to begin the anti-Nazi struggle, and it soon created, parallel with the noncommunist resistance, an almost autonomous resistance network of its own that supported de Gaulle only grudgingly but nevertheless fought the same fight with admirable courage. This acknowledged valor, plus the growing and immense prestige of the Red Army, explains the fact that in 1944 the Communist party occupied such an important position in the country. The Americans, despite their official attitude, which was to extol the alliance with Russia and Allied brotherhood-in-arms, certainly took some umbrage on this score, and everything seems to suggest that the relative parsimony of their arms drops to the *maquis* was not unconnected with a desire to keep the communists from being too well armed when the moment of liberation came.

General de Gaulle played absolutely fair, and although publicly excluding the communists from the ministries of war, home affairs, and foreign affairs, he agreed in November 1945 to the formation of a three-party government, a third of the cabinet being from the Communist party, a third Socialist, and a third Mouvement républicain populaire (Christian Democrats). In the various general elections of 1945 and 1946, the votes cast in favor of the Communist party varied between 26 and 28 percent (as against 21 percent in 1973). There were a number of attempts to seize power, though these in fact originated with a group of communist military leaders rather than the party itself, and in any case de Gaulle was able to nip them in the bud. The Communist party conducted an active campaign against him, but finally the essential fact became apparent that the majority of the French people were hostile to it, and that its participation in the government was only tolerated at the very most.

It was this very participation, however, continuing as it did until May 1947, that ensured France's noninvolvement in the dispute then developing with ever-increasing intensity between the Soviet Union and the United States. General de Gaulle had set an example by seeking to practice an even-handed policy, of which the December 1944 Franco-Soviet treaty was the principal manifestation. Georges Bidault, the Christian Democrat and former president of the underground National Resistance Council, who became foreign minister in September 1944, tried to remain faithful to this "neutralism" as long as he remained in office, which, apart from a break of one month, was until July 1948. Until 1947 he did in fact continue the general's policy.

This neutral stance implied a willingness to play the role of arbiter—but how is one to arbitrate if one is weak? It did, it is true, make possible a superficial diplomatic success in the conflict between Italy and Yugoslavia over Trieste. The "French line" was adopted in the delimitation of the two spheres of influence. But France had not brought pressure of any kind to bear. The only merit of the "French line" was that it lay midway between the "Soviet line," favoring the Yugoslavs, and the "American line," favoring the Italians. In addition, if this policy of neutrality was to be carried out successfully, a certain coherence was essential within the French government itself. And the fact was that, throughout the three-party period, each of the three parties was simply attempting to defend its own interests, and in the end both the Socialists and the Christian Democrats became profoundly mistrustful of the Communists. Yet the three parties continued governing together, even though they no longer had a man at their head capable of playing an independent role.

It was in these sorry conditions that France rejected a first constitution (May 1946), elected a second Constituent Assembly, which drew up an almost identical constitution, then adopted that constitution by a tiny majority, with almost a third of the electorate abstaining. On 1 January 1947 the Fourth Republic came into being, with the socialist Vincent Auriol as its president. For eleven and a half years France was to live in the strange situation of a country almost lacking any real

executive power. It was a most unpleasant situation, and one she had
already experienced under the Third Republic. Under the Fourth,
however, the difficulty became even more acute, because the pre-
posterous political machinery built into it made every crisis interminable. Under the Third Republic a crisis used to last three or four days.
Under the Fourth it would often go on for a month or more. For
eleven years France was simply not governed.

However, it was the weak governments of the Fourth Republic that
caused France to swing from her neutral position into the "American
camp."

2. France opts for America (1947–49)

The year 1947 was one of exceptional importance in the history of the
United States, as it was in that of France. It was the year of "the great
turning-point."

In the United States, President Harry Truman, the little man from
Missouri, soon to reveal his true mettle, had acceded to the White
House, unprepared for such a move. He had only one desire: to carry
on Roosevelt's policy. But FDR was so mysterious a man that no one in
the spring of 1945 knew exactly what his plans had been with regard to
the Russians, who had by now, in Churchill's words, lowered an "iron
curtain" across the center of Europe. Was the right course to continue
a policy of concessions until Stalin's trust was finally won? That was
the opinion of Secretary of Commerce Henry Wallace, who in
September 1946 even went so far as to advocate presenting the
Kremlin with all of America's atomic secrets. Or would it be wiser, as
was insisted by Secretary of the Navy James Forrestal, Undersecretary
of State Dean Acheson, and the State Department "Sovietologists,"
George Kennan and Charles Bohlen, to interpret the Marxist-Leninist-
Stalinist doctrine strictly according to its letter? In that case no trust
was even possible between capitalists (or partisans of a liberal
economy) and communists. Stalin was seeking to conquer the world
for communism by no matter what means. It was essential to prevent
the "free world" from "swinging over" into the other camp. Since
there was no possibility of winning back their "liberty" for the
peoples in eastern Europe already under the Soviet yoke, since no one
wanted or was in a position to unleash a third world war, the least that

must be done was to "contain" communism, to prevent any expansion of its sphere of action: "containment."

It was in January 1947 that Truman opted for containment. At that time he appointed as his secretary of state the principal American wartime military leader, General George Marshall. The latter had just returned from a mission in China, where he had become convinced that the whole of that vast country was about to be won over to the communist cause. Western and southern Europe at least must be prevented from doing the same. While interminable and futile negotiations were still continuing with the Russians, Truman switched in no uncertain manner to a new policy. On 12 March 1947 the Truman Doctrine announced the granting of economic and military aid to Greece (then in the throes of civil war) and also to Turkey (threatened by Russian territorial claims). On 5 June 1947, at Harvard, the Marshall Plan for economic aid to Europe was announced. The act creating the European Recovery Program was passed in April 1948, though, even before that, aid had already been granted to the two countries where communism was strongest, France and Italy.

At the same time as the Americans were putting this major policy change into effect—a change that put an end to the great alliance of the war period and ushered in the "cold war"—an analogous change was taking place in France. France had ceased to be a great power. But there were many French people, de Gaulle chief among them, who believed that she could recover that status thanks to her colonial empire. Hence the obstinacy with which the French were to resist the vast independence movement that was gathering strength through all the world empires. In December 1946 there came the outbreak of the war in Indochina, which was to last for seven and a half years. The position of the Communists in the French government became untenable, because they were in favor of Ho Chi Minh's communist regime and opposed to the French attempt at reconquest. This attitude, added to social difficulties at home, led in May 1947 to the removal of the Communist ministers from the cabinet. A series of terrible strikes, both social and political in origin, shook the country until the end of the year. But the Communists were forced to give way. Since that time they have never again participated in any French government.

During the three-party-government period it had been the Com-

munists alone who were pro-Russian and pro-Stalin without murmur
or hesitation, ready to approve of everything Stalin did, including the
concentration camps—of which they nevertheless denied the existence—the bloody purges, the takeovers in Hungary and Czechoslovakia, achieved by simply eliminating all opposition, and so on.
Despite the assurances of the Communist party, however, a vast
majority of French people (including many who voted Communist for
reasons to do with French domestic policies) believed in the reality of a
Soviet threat. We know now that Stalin did not in fact want war and
that he was waiting—vainly as it turned out—for the onset in the West
of another economic crisis that would weaken the capitalist camp as
the one in 1929 had done. In 1947–48, however, the Soviet leader's
desire for peace was considered very doubtful. The Americans even
believed on several occasions (in March 1948, at the time of the Berlin
blockade, and during the early days of the Korean War, in June 1950)
that the Russians might be going to start a third world war. For the
French in those days, that meant the Red Army in Brest within two
weeks.

The series of new and very precarious governments formed after May
1947 were groupings of what was termed the "third force," whose
task was to resist the country's two extreme groups, the communists on
the one hand, violently hostile to any *rapprochement* with the United
States, and the Gaullists on the other, outraged by this Fourth
Republic, which they saw as responsible for France's debility and
"satellization." This "third force" was therefore drawn from the
center of the political spectrum, extending from the Socialists on one
side to the non-Gaullists of the right on the other, and including the
Christian Democrats of the MRP and the Radicals in between. Since
there were so many points on which they disagreed, these groups could
only form unstable coalitions, which fell to pieces at the first bump in
the road.

It was in the sphere of foreign policy, however, that the "third
force" displayed the most unity and continuity. Its policy was one of
alliance with the United States of America. During 1947, Georges
Bidault, the foreign minister, increasingly abandoned the great
Gaullist tenets: autonomy of the Rhineland and the Ruhr and
fragmentation of Germany. Toward the very end of 1947, having
enjoyed British and American support during a clash with Russia over

the economic annexation of the German Saar region to France, Bidault agreed to the principle of West German unification. He even agreed to the French zone being incorporated into the Anglo-American economic "joint zone." Finally, he took part in negotiating, then signed, the London agreement of 1948 providing for the creation of a German Federal Republic, to become effective in September 1949. In short, he gave increasingly clear support to American ideas and plans.

But the Franco-American *rapproachement* was connected above all with the two great tragedies of the immediate postwar years: the dollar gap and the cold war.

3. France, the dollar gap, and the Marshall Plan

In 1945, not only was the United States the only industrial power that had suffered no material damage within its own frontiers, but its economy had received a tremendous boost from the war. From $101.4 billion in 1940 (a figure slightly lower than that of 1929), its gross national product had risen to $215.2 billion in 1945. As against this tremendous expansion, the rest of the world, and France in particular, was in a wretched economic state. No country could have undergone defeat, four years of occupation and pillage, the absence of two million of its work force (deported war prisoners, doing forced labor, and so on), and then the liberation campaign, without being economically drained. In 1944, production was less than a third of what it was in 1938, itself a very poor year. Nine hundred thousand dwellings, 3,125 bridges and works of art had been destroyed, as well as thousands of factories, two-thirds of the country's harbor installations, three-quarters of its locomotives, and nine-tenths of its road vehicles. In addition, the French were facing imminent famine.

In order to remedy these ills, thoughts might well have turned to German reparations, in particular the dismantling and confiscation of factories. But Germany was in an equal state of ruin, and the experience of the post-1918 era was in fact to lead to the abandonment of reparations as early as 1950. The only path open was to get down to organizing the return to work of a country whose industrial capacity was very large and whose economic mental habits were undergoing a radical transformation. According to the American economist Charles Kindleberger (*Economic Growth in France and Britain*, passim), the economic renaissance of France after the war was due to the reorganization of the economy by new men with new ideas. The difficulty, however, was "priming the pump." Either the food and machinery France lacked could be purchased from the United States—but how, since France had no dollars and was scarcely in a state to export anything whatever to so wealthy a country?—or else ruthless rationing would have to be maintained, together with the introduction of compulsory saving, thus sacrificing the population's standard of living in order to achieve a slow rebuilding from the ruins. The first alternative inevitably entailed American aid in order to bridge the dollar gap; the second presupposed a strong government capable of making the French accept long and heavy sacrifices. Historical circumstances were such that a communist regime alone could have succeeded in such a course.

In short, the dollar-gap problem resolved itself quite simply in France's case into a choice of regimes: either the preservation of a liberal Western type of democracy, with American aid, or the setting up of a "people's democracy," in other words, a party dictatorship. One may justifiably claim that up to the spring of 1948 the fate of France hung in the balance.

From the American point of view, aid to the countries ravaged by war was far more than a mere charitable undertaking. The purely "commercial" mentality displayed after 1919 in the war-debt imbroglio was a thing of the past. What had to be achieved before all else was full employment in the United States itself, since large-scale unemployment would have spelled disaster. But how was that to be achieved if the country's world trading partners, reduced to ruin by the war, were unable to absorb American exports? Restoring the economies of those partners, including those of the defeated nations, was a matter of vital importance for the American people.

Truman's adoption of the policy of containment, then the subsequent cold war, gave a political slant to these economic considerations that eventually came to dominate them entirely. War and poverty provide fuel for the class conflict, whereas prosperity damps it down. A rapid return to prosperity in western Europe was the best way of preventing it from going over to communism, which already had strong roots in France and Italy.

France sought to obtain American aid all through 1945 and 1946.

The liquidation of its lend-lease stocks at a rate very advantageous to the French and the sale of "American surplus" at minimal prices proved insufficient. At various times the Export-Import Bank granted France substantial loans, amounting to more than two billion dollars. Trade agreements, often very stringent ones, were also signed, such as the Blum-Byrnes agreement of December 1946, which obliged France to screen a considerable number of American films.

On 6 December 1945, the United States made a proposal to expand world trade by means of a progressive lowering of tariffs, thereby putting an end to the absolute protectionism of the interwar years. This system was to be buttressed by two newly created institutions: the International Monetary Fund and the International Bank for Reconstruction and Development (or World Bank). But on the other hand the loans agreed to by the United States in practice produced difficult problems for France. Since each was an ad hoc affair, requiring long and arduous negotiations, they created great uncertainty over the future. Truman's advisers and General Marshall consequently came to the conclusion that they must provide Europe with systematic and continuing aid over a four-year period (1948 to 1952). This was the reasoning behind the Marshall Plan of 5 June 1947. What the Americans must not do, Marshall said, was to be miserly in their aid, to hand out grants only when a crisis occurred. It was quite simply a matter of logic that the United States must do all it could to help restore world economic health, he pointed out, since otherwise political stability and peace would be impossible to maintain. American policy was not directed against any country or doctrine but against famine, poverty, despair, and chaos.

This program could not have arrived at a better time to consolidate the new "third force" governments taking power in France. When, quite predictably, the Russians rejected the Marshall Plan, which in their eyes was a manifestation of American imperialism, and accused the countries accepting it of being "the lackeys of imperialism," the French communists hurled themselves into the struggle with all guns blazing. Their arguments were somewhat difficult to sustain, however, since what they tried to prove was that the Americans were aiding Europe only in order to stunt its economic growth. Nevertheless, the situation was an uncertain one. By late summer the government had only $240 million, the remnant of previous loans, to cover a trade deficit estimated at $450 million. The excessive imports producing this situation would clearly have to be stopped, at a time when social unrest was at its peak—the rash of strikes was to culminate in a general strike in November, plus the growing strength of the Rassemblement du Peuple Français (a Gaullist and ultranationalist movement) at the expense of the "third force." Georges Bidault immediately asked the United States for interim aid. President Truman and his advisers realized that the juncture was a critical one and that it would be unwise to wait for the ratification of their European Recovery Program (ERP), which, because of the leisurely American political machinery, was not to occur until April 1948. As far as Truman was concerned, the hungry peoples of the world were appealing to the United States, and the United States must not disappoint them. Congress voted interim aid of $580 million, and France was allotted three-fifths of it. There are few occasions in history when a decision so purely technical on the surface has produced such tremendous consequences.

The system on which the Marshall Plan worked was extremely ingenious. The American aid, shared out more or less by mutual agreement among the European nations, consisted partly of loans but mainly of outright grants. The greater part of it was made over in kind, in other words in the form of American goods consigned to the French state. The latter then sold them for francs to such public or private enterprises as required them. This exchange value in francs of the aid consignments was used in part—about 10 percent of it—to finance the administration of the Economic Cooperation Administration (ECA), whose agents, quite separate from the diplomatic corps, were to play a large role in Franco-American relations alongside Jean Monnet, the high commissioner of the French Economic Development Plan, to whom I shall return later. The other 90 percent of the exchange value was used by the French state, subject to ECA approval, for investment in all branches of economic activity.

Between 1948 and 1952 Marshall aid amounted to a total of $13.8 billion, $2.7 billion of which went to France. The boost this gave to the French economy was undeniable, and the Marshall Plan became extremely popular in France, despite the rearguard action put up by the communists.

It was less successful than in Germany, however. Little by little, as a result of the Korean War, launched in June 1950, economic aid was increasingly replaced by military aid. Deeply involved in their own war in Indochina, the French, instead of making an all-out effort to expand their exports, began relying on this military aid to fill their dollar gap. One may justifiably say that of the Marshall Plan's three fundamental aims (restoring the economy, resolving the dollar-gap problem, and establishing European harmony), only the first was really achieved; and also, in consequence, the political end apparent behind America's aspiration to restore world prosperity was achieved as well: the Marshall Plan, as the communists had feared, marked the beginning of a real decline in communist influence in France. As for European harmony, we shall see that this theme was to play an essential role in Franco-American relations after 1950. Only the dollar-gap problem still yawned as wide as ever.

4. France, the cold war, and the Atlantic Pact

We have just seen how close the links were between France's economic recovery and its political regime. Equally close links were soon established between the maintenance of that regime and the military situation.

The French and the Americans, although they had been allies before, in the eighteenth century, had different conceptions of what such an alliance meant. The French had a long tradition of alliances, and for more than fifty years these had been directed against Germany. General de Gaulle had continued that tradition, and France had concluded an alliance with the Soviet Union in December 1944. After the general's resignation, an alliance was also signed with Britain, in February 1947. Both these treaties specifically named Germany as the potential aggressor. One might almost have been back in the days of 1914 and the Triple Entente! In 1947–48, however, such a treaty structure had begun to seem meaningless to the majority of French people. Germany, ruined and disarmed, clearly presented no immediate threat, especially since there was very good reason to hope that the Germans had had their fill of militarism. Since there seemed to be collusion between the "internal threat" of communist sub-version and the "external threat" of a Russian invasion, it was against the Soviet Union that precautions clearly needed to be taken—all this to the great indignation of the militant communists, who were totally

dedicated to the cause of Stalinist Russia. As a result of constant war
rumors, fueled by the growing Soviet-American dissension, and of the
Prague coup (when the communists seized power in Czechoslovakia by
means of a *coup d'état*), Georges Bidault, the French foreign minister,
signed a pact of alliance on 17 March 1948 with the United Kingdom,
Belgium, Holland, and Luxembourg. This was the moment at which
the quadripartite organizations in Germany fell apart and the Soviet
Berlin blockade began. It is true that the Russians did not yet have the
atomic bomb, but they were nevertheless maintaining an enormous
army in a state of full mobilization, and throughout the West there
reigned a veritable war psychosis, an ever-present fear of a third world
war in which Europe would finally disappear forever.

Bidault and his British colleague, Ernest Bevin, knew perfectly well
that the five Brussels allies stood absolutely no chance whatever of
standing up to a Russian invasion. Naturally enough, therefore, they
very soon addressed themselves to General Marshall, requesting the
adhesion of the United States to enlarge and strengthen their alliance.

The American tradition, however, quite the opposite of that in
France, was Jefferson's policy of nonentanglement, endorsed by
George Washington in his 1796 Farewell Address. Even during the
two world wars the Americans had always refused the official term of
"ally." The United States had been an "associate" in 1917–18 and a
member of the United Nations in 1941–45. But now the war had
made them into a superpower, and isolationism had given way to a
feeling of global responsibility. In order for it to work, "containment" could not be confined to economic measures. There had to be a
military underpinning to the concept. Of this, some Americans, such
as James Forrestal, by then secretary of defense, and General Lucius D.
Clay, the United States commander-in-chief in Germany, were utterly
convinced. As they saw it, there was already a grave crisis, a clear threat
that the United States, its atomic monopoly apart, was at the time
inadequately equipped to counter. The construction of an alliance was
becoming essential. It alone would preserve western Europe from
"satellization" by the Russians.

As we know, the United States Senate gave its assent in advance,
with the famous Vandenberg Declaration of 7 June 1948. Long and
detailed negotiations were begun. Robert Schuman, who succeeded
Georges Bidault as foreign minister in July 1948, was even more

attracted than his predecessor by the prospect of an alliance with the United States. Eventually twelve countries, including France, signed this alliance—the North Atlantic Treaty—on 4 April 1949. As the French premier of the day, Henri Queuille, told United Press International on the previous 25 February: "The United States must never permit France and Western Europe to be invaded by Russia as they were by Germany. [But] France, in her position as Europe's advance guard, cannot hold the fort alone.... If, for example, we could count on a force sufficient to prevent the Russian army from crossing the Elbe, then European civilization could breathe again.... Even a mere two weeks after the invasion would be too late."

The North Atlantic Treaty is not an alliance that conforms with French traditions. In the first place it is essentially an unequal one, since United States strikepower is considerably greater than that of all its allies put together. Second, it is not entirely automatic in its operation. Article five merely says that, in the event of aggression in Europe, North America, Algeria (inserted at the request of France), or the Atlantic north of the Tropic of Cancer, each member, both individually and in association with the other members, will assist the country attacked "by such action as it deems necessary," including the use of armed force. There were weighty debates on this point in France. The philosopher Etienne Gilson wrote a series of pessimistic articles in 1949 for *Le Monde* upholding the thesis that the United States had not in fact entered into any real commitment. This belief does not appear to have been shared by the Russians, who with the aid of the various national communist parties, particularly in France, kept up an unrelenting attack on "American imperialism." This was a line they found very easy to maintain, since imperialism, according to their Leninist definition, is the final stage of capitalism, and this means that the Soviet Union, being the destroyer of capitalism, is *ipso facto* incapable of being imperialist, even if it conquers the entire world against the wishes of its inhabitants.

As far as the European nations were concerned, a certain feeling of relief prevailed, albeit still tinged with unease. What would happen if some future American government, one more swayed by warlike emotions, should one day drag the whole alliance into total war? The French were acutely aware of such arguments and were also very

disturbed at the realization that the path to final victory, from the
American viewpoint, might well take the form of an occupation of
Europe by the enemy, as in 1940, followed by another liberation. But
what is the good of "final" victory when you are dead?

This explains why the Atlantic pact has never enjoyed wholehearted
popularity in France. The neutralist tendency retained its strength—
though how exactly does one remain neutral in a global conflict?—
while the idea that France had become a satellite, continually
expounded by the communists, then later by the Gaullists, became
widespread in many circles, especially among intellectuals. Under the
shelter of the "American umbrella," the French sat and pondered
these problems. From the countless polls dealing with the Atlantic
pact, here is one spanning the period between September 1952 and
September 1957. In the event of war between the Soviet Union and
the United States, it asked, should France support:

	USA	USSR	Neither
September 1952	36%	04%	55%
September 1957	15	03	62

This does not mean that French sympathies became equally divided
between the two camps. If we average out nine polls taken between
1952 and 1957, the results are as follows:

Opinion of countries	USA	USSR
Very good	04%	03%
Good	23	08
Average	37	22
Bad	13	24
Very bad	02	16
No opinion	21	27
	100	100

In other words, only 11 percent of public opinion was clearly
favorable to the Soviet Union (at a time when 25 percent of French
votes were being cast in favor of the Communist party) and 40 percent
clearly unfavorable. As against this, 27 percent of public opinion was
clearly favorable and only 15 percent clearly unfavorable to the United
States.

There remains the all-important question for any evaluation of the Atlantic pact's value in France: In the event of war, can France count on the help of the United States?

To a large extent	38%
Up to a certain point	37
Not at all	08
No opinion	17

The French, humiliated by their subordinate position, preferred the United States to the Soviet Union, believed to a large extent in the likelihood of American support, but aspired wholeheartedly to neutrality, despite an awareness that such a course was extremely problematical.

WITH ECONOMIC RECOVERY set in motion by the Marshall Plan and now accelerating under the power of France's own efforts, with the country enjoying a certain degree of security, thanks to the Atlantic alliance, with the peaceful intentions of the United States becoming steadily more evident (despite the clamor of the communists and their fellow travelers), the problem that began to take center stage was that of France's true place in the world.

The regime of the Fourth Republic, however absurd its internal instability, did at least strive to bestow a certain continuity, even luster, on its foreign policy. With Robert Schuman, and to a lesser degree his successors in the French foreign office, the French centered enthusiastically on a policy of European integration, albeit not without setbacks and contradictions. For one thing, the colonial tradition was still so deeply ingrained in France that it was impossible to prevent a great deal of the country's energies from being squandered in a vain attempt to preserve its former empire. The Americans were not content to follow the development of these conflicting French policies from a distance. They intervened continually, sometimes with tact and sometimes crassly, often with no effort to conceal the small regard they felt for this erstwhile great power in decline. American newspapers, the *New York Times* particularly, were forever making comparisons between France and Germany, invariably to the detriment of the former.

Since France was also dotted with American bases, since the North Atlantic Treaty was further strengthened in December 1950 by the creation of a permanent organization (NATO) and a Supreme Headquarters of Allied Powers in Europe (SHAPE), under American command, and since the physical headquarters of these organizations were in France, at the Porte Dauphine and at Rocquencourt, people in France did have a very real feeling of "satellization," less harsh, no doubt, than that imposed by Stalin on eastern Europe, but rather humiliating all the same. Their streets were full of American servicemen in handsome uniforms, making the French troops look like poor relations. In the vicinity of their bases the Americans generally "forgot" to translate their various signs and notices into French. The rights of Allied aircraft to use French airspace were granted en bloc annually, and the U.S. air force frequently "forgot" to consult the French authorities on flight plans.

Naturally, a great many French people felt uneasy and upset. There were occasional outbursts of protest. Since the Americans, unlike the Russians, respected the principle of national sovereignty, they did not use force to impose their policies. But they were nevertheless outraged by such protests. Germany was a "good ally" (having become party to the Atlantic pact in 1955). The British had the advantage of their "special relationship," which they cultivated assiduously, and which for a while masked the fact that they were falling behind their partners in the economic field. France was the capricious, unreliable, recalcitrant ally, whose behavior was sometimes excellent, at other times execrable.

1. Jean Monnet, Europe, and America

One man did succeed during this period in convincing the Americans that France was still a vital force, a man who shares first place with General de Gaulle in France's gallery of great men, even though he offers an almost total contrast with him: Jean Monnet.

We have already met him several times before: as the originator of the Allied Maritime Transport Council in 1917–18; as an organizer of the American program for manufacturing aircraft on France's behalf in 1938; as mediator between General de Gaulle and the American-backed French leader Giraud in Algeria in 1943.

He was born in Cognac in 1888 and was thus almost an exact contemporary of the general, who was born in Lille in 1890. Both belonged to families of some consequence. But whereas Jean Monnet's father came from an upper-middle-class business family that produced and sold cognac, de Gaulle's father, a member of the lesser nobility, was a teacher and headmaster of a Catholic school. Jean Monnet did not attend a university. Prior to 1914 he traveled the world selling his father's brandy, especially in the English-speaking countries, thereby acquiring a perfect knowledge of English and also the naturally cosmopolitan attitude that was so much a part of his character. Charles de Gaulle's education, on the other hand, led him from the first in the direction of the most ardent nationalism. He became a cadet at Saint-Cyr, France's West Point, then an officer in the infantry.

In 1914, being unfit for active service on account of his weak health, Monnet decided not to enter the service but instead to employ his intelligence and energies in helping to organize Franco-British economic cooperation, and he was to spend the entire war in London. De Gaulle proved a brave soldier, was wounded, then taken prisoner. As a result of the war, Monnet came to the conclusion that Europe's frontiers were absurd and that its people must be made to unite if they were to survive. De Gaulle was meanwhile forming "a certain idea" of France. Emotionally he was to devote all his fervor to that idea; rationally he came to the conclusion that only "vast undertakings" could dispel the "ferments of dispersion" that the French nation contains within itself. Between the two wars neither of the two men succeeded in imposing his ideas to any extent, so that, though they gained the respect of certain restricted circles, they remained unknown to the country at large.

The general's great fame stemmed from his decision on 18 June 1940 that France would continue the war and from the fact that during the next four years he successfully rallied the majority of French people to that cause. In 1945 he decided to make use of Jean Monnet by entrusting him with the post of high commissioner for France's Economic Development Plan, a flexible organization formed for the purpose of setting France on the path to ultramodern, ultradynamic growth, a goal dear to the hearts of both men, even though they were aiming at different end results: in de Gaulle's case, national greatness; in Monnet's, social progress and international collaboration.

Jean Monnet's appointment as head of this plan had an overriding importance as far as Franco-American relations were concerned. In practice, from 1948 onward the renewal of France's industrial plant, and some of its investment, was carried out in close liaison with the Marshall Plan organization. As administrators of this latter, Washington had sent over to Europe, and to Paris in particular, a great many agents, drawn mostly from sources other than the diplomatic corps: young academics, economists, brilliant experts in their fields. Almost at once a kind of friendly camaraderie developed between Jean Monnet, his French colleagues, and these Americans, the majority of whom later went on to fill important posts in the United States. Young officials like Harold Van Cleveland, Theodore Geiger, and John Hulley were to convert their chief, Paul Hoffman, administrator of the ECA, to the idea of European integration. First, Congress, with the conversion of such men as Democratic Senator J. William Fulbright and Republican Senator John Foster Dulles (later secretary of state), then the State Department itself became enthusiastic supporters of European unity. The same was true of Robert Bowie, future head of the State Department's policy planning staff, and of George Ball, the future undersecretary of state. A total harmony was achieved between these men and Jean Monnet's team: Pierre Uri, Etienne Hirsch, and Paul Reuter. Around this nucleus many politicians in France also embraced the cause, as well as a great many other Europeans, the most important among them being German Chancellor Konrad Adenauer and Italian Premier Alcide de Gasperi.

There is therefore nothing surprising in the fact that the Americans very quickly came to see Jean Monnet's initiatives in favor of European integration as a means of strengthening the Atlantic pact. On 9 May 1950 there came the Schuman Plan, a scheme to promote the creation of a supranational high authority that would regulate the production and marketing of coal and steel in France, Germany, and any other western European countries wishing to take part in such a project. The British refused membership, but the Benelux countries and Italy accepted, thereby enabling the foundation to be laid for the European Economic Community. The American press as a whole, and the various levels of American government, did not conceal their enthusiasm. At last Europe was on the right path, strengthening the Atlantic community by creating an integrated Europe favorable to the United States. The European Coal and Steel Community (known by the abbreviation CECA in France), which was to result from the Schuman Plan, had the great advantage of consolidating Europe on the political level against the "communist peril." It also laid down solid foundations for a solution to the German problem by encouraging West Germany's reintegration into the community of civilized nations. No amount of "denazification" or "democratization" measures could ever have produced such a result. And this idea had come from France. Robert Schuman and Jean Monnet were proving to the somewhat startled Americans that French creative genius was not dead.

Unfortunately, however, the Americans and the French "Europeans" tried to push ahead too fast. After the start of the Korean War on 25 June 1950, the idea of maintaining German disarmament faded in the United States. A parallel was drawn between the two Koreas and the two Germanys. What would happen if East Germany, spurred on by the Russians, were to attack West Germany? The conclusion drawn was that the latter must be rearmed. This was proposed by the Americans in August 1950.

France, so recently occupied and ravaged by these defenseless Germans, opposed any such move with all its strength and used its power of veto in the Atlantic alliance to prevent the admission of Germany as a thirteenth member. This attitude was an extremely negative one, however. Jean Monnet—again—suggested to René Pleven, the French prime minister, a further plan, modeled on the Schuman Plan. This Pleven Plan of 24 October 1950 proposed the amalgamation of all the European armed forces of the Six (that is, all the future members of CECA) at battalion level, so as to constitute a "European army." This would bring two simultaneous advantages: first, the recruitment of German troops, whose military ability was rated very high, without the necessity for a German army, and second, further progress in the direction of European integration.

This idea threw some Americans into great alarm at first, in particular the United States high commissioner in Germany, John McCloy. On the other hand, it proved very attractive to the famous man chosen by the Atlantic Council in December 1950 to become commander-in-chief of SHAPE, General Dwight D. Eisenhower. During a tour of Europe in January 1951, despite the fact that he had by then begun a peaceful retirement as president of Columbia University, Eisenhower announced that he was prepared to accept this new command, and persuaded the Truman government to adopt a policy favorable to the idea of a European army. Long negotiations ensued, resulting on 27 May 1952 in the signing of a treaty in Paris setting up among the Six a European Defense Community (EDC) that was to be a military counterpart to the Coal and Steel Community. That same year, in November, Eisenhower was elected president of the United States, and John Foster Dulles became his secretary of state. This meant that the EDC had become the darling of Washington as far as its policy in western Europe was concerned, and once again it was France that had come up with this "inspired" idea.

At this point, however, the idyll soured into pseudotragedy. Coal and steel are material *things*. Armies are collections of *men*. Worse still, armies are the very essence of the modern states—France, England, Spain—that made their appearance in Europe during the fifteenth century only with the simultaneous appearance of permanent taxation and permanent armies. Logically—though it was a logic that the Korean War had suddenly obscured—the integration of national armies ought to have been envisaged not as one of the first, but as one of the final, stages of integration.

Apart from the communist opposition to everything that looked as though it might reinforce a coalition of the West against the Soviet Union, the EDC found itself confronted with hostility from many other sources as well. It was true that the German army was not to be reestablished (even though the Paris treaty had raised the level of integration from that of the battalion to that of the division), but, on the other hand, the French army would vanish. The elite of the French armed forces was at that time fighting in Indochina. How much of her colonial armed strength would France be allowed to retain? There was also another factor that aroused suspicion: how was it that the British, such apparently ardent supporters of the European army and the EDC, were jealously maintaining the national character of their own forces and refusing to participate? Why was this idea good for France and bad for Britain? Lastly, the extremely complicated EDC pact clearly placed the future "European" army under American command, within the framework of SHAPE. In the eyes of many Frenchmen, this was clearly a plot on the part of the "Anglo-Saxons," a way of ensuring that they became the sole possessors of independent armed forces, while bringing the "continental" European powers under their control, thereby depriving the latter of all autonomy. Thus the antagonism of the communists and a section of the socialists (hostile to any form of German rearmament) was now reinforced by that of General de Gaulle (opposed to any commitment to war not required by "national defense"), Maréchal Juin, National Assembly President Edouard Herriot, and—as everyone was aware, despite his discreet silence—President of the Republic Vincent Auriol.

All the French cabinets between March 1952 and June 1954 were in favor of the EDC. But being only too aware that assent from the Assembly was extremely problematical, they did not dare propose its ratification. Time was slipping by. France—or at least its establishment—was split into two camps. Irritation was steadily growing in the United States, where Dulles was making it plain that it was "all or nothing," that there could be no question of redrafting the treaty in order to break the deadlock. Then, after long reflection, on 14 December 1953, he decided that it would be an astute move to attempt what amounted to blackmail. If France did not ratify the EDC —in his eyes the only means of eliminating the possibility of future war between France and Germany—there would be "an agonizing reappraisal" of American policy. Did this mean that Germany would take France's place as favored ally? Hardly, since the facts of geography were against it. Or that the United States would cease defending the European continent and switch to a "peripheral" defense? But that would mean punishing the "well-behaved" Germans too, as well as the Benelux countries, all of whom had already ratified the EDC. Besides all this, purely on the level of self-interest, it was of capital importance to the United States that France not swing over to the communist camp.

However carefully considered it may have been, Dulles's statement must be ranked among the greatest diplomatic blunders of history. It angered and outraged the French—even those who were EDC supporters—who took it as a violent affront to their national independence. The same reaction followed the statement put out by Eisenhower in July 1954, threatening to cut off all aid to countries that had not ratified the EDC treaty (France and Italy).

In June 1954, Pierre Mendès-France became prime minister. That summer was to see a serious crisis in Franco-American relations. Not only did the new premier sign the Geneva armistice ending the Indochinese War on 20 July, a document the Americans considered unacceptable, but on 30 August he allowed the National Assembly to reject ratification of the EDC, on the viability of which he himself had the gravest doubts. John Foster Dulles expressed his fury by refusing to visit Paris during a European visit. Clearly France was a totally frivolous nation if it could produce such imaginative plans, tempting one to believe in the resurrection of its genius, then reject them as soon as they threatened to become political reality.

General gloom descended on pro-European and pro-American circles in France. Jean Monnet, president of the CECA High Authority since 1951, decided to give up that post in order to work at injecting new vigor into the European movement. It was not his intention to launch a propaganda campaign. Unlike General de Gaulle, he was neither an orator nor a writer. What he did have was an extraordinary gift for influencing individuals, and an equally extraordinary capacity for attracting the friendship of important men. I have already mentioned several of his American friends, and there were a great many others. Since, in the words of one of his supporters, Guy de Carmoy, "the idea of an integrated Europe, driven back by a rising tide of nationalist feeling, was then at its lowest ebb in France," it had become essential to convince the leaders of all the European political parties and unions—apart from the immovably hostile communists and Gaullists—of the necessity for renewed efforts.

In 1955, the foreign ministers of the Six met at Messina. They were presented with a series of projects, once more inspired by Jean Monnet, and decided on a "relaunching" of European unity aimed at the integration of the continent's economies (the Common Market) and cooperation in the production of nuclear energy for peaceful purposes (Euratom). Shortly afterward, Jean Monnet founded an Action Committee for a United States of Europe.

At first sight it might seem that Franco-American relations, excellent at the time of the Schuman Plan, then eroded by French rejection of the EDC, were about to improve appreciably, at least in the European context, for had the United States not loudly proclaimed its approval of *any* form of European unification?

The problem was much more subtle and complex, however. In practice, obsessed by their enormous responsibility as defenders of the free world, the Americans were clearly becoming increasingly opposed to two possibilities: a European free-trade area encircled by tariff barriers, and a Europe possessing autonomy in nuclear matters, particularly in the military sphere.

Of the Common Market and the future Euratom (both set up by the Treaty of Rome 1957 and coming into force on 1 January 1959), the more important in the eyes of Jean Monnet and his friends was the second. This was also the attitude of Louis Armand, a friend of Jean Monnet and former head of the French railways, who during the 1950s had realized the need for an over-all European energy policy.

As far as Euratom was concerned, what was essential was a growing supply of weakly enriched uranium (highly enriched uranium being necessary only for military uses). At that time the Americans still had what amounted to a monopoly of uranium in the West (apart from a small plant in Britain). In France, the Commission on Atomic Energy was extremely anxious to achieve a position of autonomy. Whereas the Americans would sell enriched uranium only with an extremely strict proviso forbidding any kind of military use, the large European isotopic separation plant contemplated by Euratom would be less restrictive in its attitude. This worried the Americans, who promptly lighted on a simple but effective way of scuttling the plans for a European plant. They announced that they were lowering the price of weakly enriched U-235 by 20 percent, or from twenty-five dollars per kilogram to sixteen dollars. The construction of a European plant immediately ceased to be cost-effective.

Here I shall quote the opinion of Pierre Melandri, the author of the best, though still unpublished, work on this subject. "At a price, the United States had succeeded in controlling the political and technical orientation of the Euratom program. But their policy was a short-sighted one, for they were at the same time opening a rift within the Community from which it was never to recover" (Melandri, *Les Etats-Unis et le "défi" européen*). In the eyes of France's rulers the situation was made even worse by the institution of a new "special relationship" between the United States and Britain, who alone of all the smaller powers possessed atomic military capability. The first British hydrogen bomb was in fact detonated in 1957, and it was felt in Washington that the best way of maintaining control over Britain's tiny nuclear strikepower was to hand over certain technological secrets, in particular that of the atomic submarine. This meant that the British military atomic capability was automatically bound by the American MacMahon Act and thus no longer really independent. This was the purpose of the agreement signed in Bermuda on 24 March 1957, on the very eve of the signing of the Treaty of Rome setting up Euratom and the European Economic Community. "Great Britain was to enjoy American support ensuring its atomic progress, and it was understood that Great Britain was to enjoy that support alone. . . . France very soon realized that she had been put in her place once again. . . . The atomic club had been difficult to get into before: in 1957 it had apparently become a totally closed caste" (Melandri, *Les Etats-Unis et le "défi" européen*, pp. 132–35).

The Six received compensation in another direction, however. The British, extremely uneasy at the imminent prospect of a Common Market that they were refusing to join, proposed the parallel forma- tion of a "free-trade area" that would include the Six as well as the other western countries. From the American point of view, such an association would mean abandonment of the European tariff barrier they were so fearful of. From the British point of view it would mean creating a very favorable trading position for themselves. Since they would then belong to two quasi-free-trade areas, the Commonwealth and Europe, they would be able to attract massive injections of American capital and might eventually succeed in solving the problem vitiating their entire economic life, the balance-of-payments problem. In 1958, both before and after General de Gaulle's return to power, France, with German support, fought tooth and nail against the British plan. The Americans were placed in an embarrassing position, since their allies were urging contradictory proposals. Despite reserva- tions over the European Trade Barrier (to be set up by the Six at the end of five years and arrived at by averaging out their individual tariffs for each product), Washington decided for political reasons to come down on the side of France and Germany—that is, of the Common Market—against the British, just as in atomic matters the British were receiving American favors to the detriment of the other European countries. The British plans for a European Free Trade Association covering the whole of Europe therefore failed. American businessmen began to take an interest in the Common Market and to invest massively in its member countries as a way of insuring themselves, until finally a hope was born in America that it might be possible to combine the Common Market, the seven countries of the European Free Trade Association, and North America into one vast Atlantic community. We shall see what became of this idea during General de Gaulle's years in power.

2. Four kinds of anti-Americanism in France

There existed in France a compact group of "pro-Americans," some of them motivated by emotion, others by reason. With the benefit of hindsight, it seems fair to say that their true leader was Jean Monnet. A man of outstanding liberalism, an antichauvinist, and a realist, committed to the construction of an integrated Europe because of his aspirations to a united mankind, hostile to all dictatorship on Soviet lines, involved all his life in the English-speaking world, where he found innumerable friends and admirers, Jean Monnet had always thought that nothing could be achieved, on the political or on the economic level, without an understanding with the Americans. True, his attitude was far from unconditional, and he expected the Americans to recognize European interests. But opposing them seemed to him to be essentially unrealistic. He was, as we shall see in the next chapter, the outstanding advocate of Atlantic "partnership".

Around him, besides his own Action Committee for a United States of Europe, we find a number of similarly minded politicians, all with their own circles of influence: almost all the MRP Christian Democrats, such as Robert Schuman, Pierre Henri Teitgen, Jean Lecanuet (though some, like Georges Bidault, have been more concerned with colonial policy, while others, like Maurice Schumann, became supporters of Gaullism); a great many *SFIO** socialists, notably Guy Mollet, the party's general secretary after 1946; men of the center, like René Pleven, Jean-Jacques Servan-Schreiber, General Paul Stehlin, and Maurice Faure; and men of the classical and liberal right, like Antoine Pinay. "Only the French and Italian communists, plus the RFP [Rassemblement du peuple français, founded by de Gaulle in 1947] under the Fourth Republic ... have denied [Monnet's] independence of spirit, his authority, and have rejected his ideas totally" (Fontaine, *Le Comité d'action pours les Etats-Unis d'Europe*, p. 62).

---

* Section française de l'internationale ouvrière.

Nevertheless, there were also strong anti-American currents of opinion in France.

We must not neglect the emotional aspect of this question, linked as it is with a phenomenon we have already seen in action during 1918 to 1919 and which recurred with even greater intensity after 1944: the effect of "mass contacts." The eight million American soldiers who landed in Europe were undoubtedly and before all else liberators. The French admired these well-clothed, good-natured, dynamic, magnificently equipped, well-fed fellows who had come such a long way to crush Nazism. But soldiers aren't diplomats. American army discipline, however excellent during duty hours, leaves something to be desired off base. In addition, the Americans were bound by international law to give their German prisoners the same rations as their own men, while the scarcity of shipping space was at the same time preventing them from providing France's forty million civilians with equivalent fare. Psychologically this was damaging, since, when hungry French civilians saw German prisoners eating luxuries like oranges, chocolate, and so on, unknown in France for four years, they became extremely indignant, and a rumor began to go around, cleverly fostered by communist propaganda, that the Americans "preferred the Germans to the French."

The Americans did certainly provide the French with a certain amount of food supplies in the form of gifts. But the winter of 1944–45 was a bad one. Bread rationing had been abandoned too soon and had to be reintroduced. The Americans sent over shipments of flour. But probably as the result of an error on the part of a French official, who used the word "corn" instead of "wheat" to translate the French blé, this flour turned out on arrival to be whole-maize flour, which meant that, for much of that winter, the French were fed on bright yellow loaves that tasted dreadful, turned rock-hard overnight, and were well-nigh indigestible.

This mass contact with the American forces was followed by another form, that with American tourists. This influx was certainly helpful in balancing France's budgets. In 1946, 600,000 civilians crossed the North Atlantic; in 1959 the figure was 2,400,000, of whom 900,000 came by sea and 1,500,000 by plane—in other words almost two-thirds of the total (as against 4 percent in 1938). The number of tourists visiting France was by that time approaching the million mark. The crossing by air took twenty and a half hours in 1946 and six and a half hours in 1960. True, the flow was very irregular. It varied a good deal according to the amount of advertising (France spent $800,000 publicizing itself in 1962; see Jean Ginier, *Les Touristes étrangers, passim*), the political situation, and price levels—French prices being generally considered excessively high. These tourists were generally well-off middle-aged people with no language other than English. They found a country in the throes of recovery, tense, often snappy, in which hotel accommodations were very much inferior to what they had grown accustomed to at home. The French, expecting to win all hearts with the excellence of their food, were staggered to find that it didn't suit the tastes of these tiresome visitors at all. American businessmen loathed the famous French "business lunch," which does admittedly have a slightly deleterious effect on one's afternoon work. And since French families traditionally keep very much to themselves, no real contacts were established. Only the student exchange programs (in particular the one launched by Congress in 1955 at the instigation of Senator Fulbright), the industrial and technical missions that brought over visiting experts and officials, and teacher exchanges created any really beneficial, far-reaching results. Mass tourism, on the contrary, resulted in unpleasant relations and a legacy of unfavorable comment on both sides.

This wider context must not be forgotten when one turns to the political scene, which produced various types of anti-Americanism. For the sake of clarity I shall deal with these under four headings.

1. First, there was the *entrenched anti-Americanism of the French Communist party*. This was an inherent element of the cold war. The French Communist party was pro-Stalin in the Stalin era, pro-Khrushchev in the Khrushchev era, and pro-Brezhnev thereafter. It was very far indeed from displaying the flexibility of opinion to be found in the Italian Communist party. At the height of the cold war, its militants were resolute supporters of the Soviet Union and equally resolutely hostile to the United States, a position to which they clung all the more doggedly as a result of the fact that most French people—including many communist voters—had opted for the Western democratic way of life. The party's basic argument was that only the Soviet Union and its allies were working for peace, since the Americans were by definition imperialists. Lenin had defined imperialism as "the final stage of capitalism." This meant that the Soviet Union, having abolished capitalism, could therefore not be imperialist

even when it sent its tanks into Hungary (1956) or into Czechoslovakia (1968). It followed that the American camp consisted of nothing but warmongers. It was the South Koreans who had started the Korean War, the communists said, not the North Koreans. The Americans were also accused of practicing "germ warfare" in Korea. Hence the demonstrations organized by the French Communist party in 1953 against General Matthew Ridgway, the American general they dubbed "Ridgway the Plague." The party's secretary-general, Maurice Thorez, openly declared that the communists would oppose any war against the Soviet Union, a statement that naturally diminished the credibility of the French forces in the Atlantic alliance.

2. Parallel with this pro-Russian anti-Americanism on the part of the communists, there also existed *a vast current of neutralist feeling*, which swelled still further after the death of Stalin, when the probability of a third world war seemed to be receding. The neutralists were recruited mainly from the intelligentsia. Guided more by instinct, it seems, than anything else, they drew a parallel between the Americans and the Russians and declared them to be equally dangerous. Apparently ignoring France's geographical situation, which makes the preservation of neutrality extremely difficult (unlike Sweden's in the two world wars), they nevertheless aspired to that status and condemned the Atlantic alliance. Some of the neutralists, those nearest to the communists, signed the Stockholm peace appeal (March 1950). Others made it clear that they had no faith in the reality of American protection. In October 1957, when the Russians put up their first *sputnik*, thereby making it clear that before long even the United States itself would be open to nuclear attack, the neutralists began dreaming up plans for a neutral Europe, involving the departure of all its American garrison troops, completely ignoring the fact that the Russians, whatever anyone did, were always going to remain an immovable European presence. Neutrality is certainly a wonderful ideal. As far as the French neutralists were concerned, it was also an attainable one. Only the Americans and their "unconditional" supporters were standing in the way of its realization, it was felt. Thus French neutralism always included a sharply anti-American element. It waxed indignant over all American "intervention" anywhere in the world (such as United States support of the Caribbean dictators) while politely ignoring the assaults on freedom launched by the Russians.

When Victor Kravchenko defected to the West and published a
sensational book, *I Chose Freedom*, describing Stalin's purges and the
Russian concentration camps, they expressed virtuous indignation at
these slurs—until the moment came when Khrushchev himself confirmed the sad reality of the accusations.

3. The third kind of anti-Americanism was to be found in a totally
different milieu: the colonialist right. Many officers in the armed
forces, many French colonists in North Africa, and even a great
number of people in metropolitan France were united in condemning
American anticolonialism, which has a solid emotional foundation: one
may justly claim that the United States was the first country in the
world to be "decolonized." The arguments used by this colonialist
right were equivocal. Either the Americans were stupid to encourage a
decolonization process that could only benefit their communist
adversaries (wasn't it American secret service agents who in 1945
encouraged the communist Ho Chi Minh to declare independence in
Indochina?) or, on the other hand, the Americans were cunning and
cynical. Under a cloak of noble ideals they were surreptitiously
maneuvering to oust the poor French and take their place. It is
certainly a fact that after the Geneva armistice (20 July 1954), which
brought the French Indochinese War to an end, the Americans did give
their wholehearted support in South Vietnam to the government of
Ngo Dinh Diem, which was strongly anti-French, and that many
American agents and businessmen did use the full weight of the vast
resources backing them to eliminate all French political, economic,
and cultural influence in order to replace it with their own. When a
succession of blunders finally resulted in a further war there, the
Vietnam War, there were very few French people who did not feel that
the whirligig of time was bringing in his revenges.

Nevertheless, in order to obtain American support in what was in
fact a colonial war, these champions of empire had only one path open
to them: to convince the United States that the struggle against Algerian independence was in reality an anticommunist war. They had succeeded earlier, in the case of Indochina; but all their efforts proved
vain when it came to the war in Algeria, to which I shall return later.
That failure led them to adopt an attitude of aggressive hostility to the
Americans.

4. The fourth group of anti-Americans, and eventually the most

important, consisted of the *Gaullists*. During the Fourth French
Republic this group tended to merge with that previously described, as
witness the fact that the *coup d'etat* in Algiers on 13 May 1958—
which brought General de Gaulle back to power and led to the
setting up of the Fifth Republic—was instigated by army officers and
French colonists. In fact, they were very soon to find that the general
had by then reasoned himself into accepting the inevitability of
Algerian independence, with the result that he proceeded to present
decolonization to the French people as one of his "vast undertakings." After that, de Gaulle was to have no worse enemies than the
colonialists. General de Gaulle's anti-Americanism, based on his experiences between 1940 and 1945 or, more precisely, on the subjective
convictions he had formed of American intentions during those years,
was characterized by its insistence on national independence and on
France's return to "greatness." France must not be integrated into
vague constructions, such as the European Community or an Atlantic
Community, that would denationalize her. The Americans, however,
supported that policy of integration. They were outraged, for example, by France's resistance to joining the European Defense
Community, yet expressed no objections to Britain's remaining
outside it. France, a nation-state quite as old as Britain—and much
older than the United States—had the right to the same independence, a right that *les Anglo-Saxons* were trying to wrest from her in
order to achieve their own ends, which included forcing France to obey
their orders. I shall devote the whole of my next chapter to the France
of General de Gaulle, and we shall see then how, and with what
resolute obstinacy, Gaullist anti-Americanism expressed itself.

   In sum, the sheer might of the United States was now the single
most important political factor in Europe. France, not divided like
Germany, without Britain's "special relationship" with Washington,
possessing a great many communists and Gaullists among its population, was in American eyes the most baffling and most irritating of
allies. It was in France that people believed least in an American world
"mission," and there was something shocking about such skepticism
to the United States.

3. The bitterness of decolonization

As a matter of fact, one has to admit that the whole postwar situation
was somewhat baffling for the Americans. Their allies consisted
mainly of the western European nations, almost all of which still
possessed colonies. It was true that the Germans had been relieved of
theirs by the Treaty of Versailles and that Italy's had all been
relinquished by 1949. But that still left Denmark (with Greenland),
Holland, Belgium, Portugal, and of course the two greatest colonial
powers of all, Britain and France. Meanwhile the world had moved
into an era when power had become concentrated, even hypertro-
phied, in just two gigantic states, whose eventual preponderance had
long ago been predicted by Tocqueville, Michel Chevalier, and many
others: the United States and Russia. Though divided by the cold war,
these two giants did have at least one trait in common, hostility to
colonialism, even though the Americans were given to accusing the
Soviets of possessing what amounted to colonies in Transcaucasia and
central Asia. Since each wished to undermine its rival's power, each
began competing for the support of the colonized areas.

Until 1955 the bidding was largely verbal. The Russians gave real
support only to nationalist communists and declared their hostility to
all the *bourgeois* of the dependent countries. They were gambling on
the advent of the great cyclic economic crisis that was supposed to
shake the capitalist world to its foundations and provide "socialism"
with new zones of influence. But the crisis took a long time to
materialize, and the notion began to develop, even before Stalin's
death, that it might be possible to weaken the "colonialists" by
encouraging independent revolutions. Increasingly the distinction
began to be made in colonial countries between the *compradore
bourgeoisie*, supporting the rulers out of self-interest, and the national
bourgeoisie, with which the proletariat must ally itself in order to win
political independence. These theories were eventually to be acclaimed at the Twentieth Congress of the Communist Party of the
Soviet Union in 1956.

On the American side the problem was considerably thornier.
Public opinion was clearly anticolonialist, and, in addition, it would
be folly to let the Russians reap all the benefits of the world
independence movement. But at the same time, America's allies
needed to be handled with some care. The British, by granting

independence successively to India and their possessions in Southeast Asia (the last being Malaysia in 1957), posed less of a problem in this respect than the French. Once again France appeared in the light of America's least comfortable ally.

The French Indochina War is a case apart. There the nationalists were also communists, and eventually the Americans came round to supporting the French against the Viet Minh and supplying them with considerable military aid, thus providing France with a useful source of dollars. Like the French leaders themselves, albeit with much greater sincerity, the Americans were advocating the creation of an independent anticommunist state in what had been French Indochina. Hence they took part in the Bao Dai experiment. But Bao Dai, the former emperor of Annam, was soon discredited, and, once the French had left, the Americans switched their support to the Roman Catholic and Gallophobe Ngo Dinh Diem. Moreover, as we noted earlier, they were hostile to the Geneva agreement of 1954 that put an end to the Indochina hostilities, as least for France.

Indochina apart, however, there still remained a vast French colonial empire, most of which was in Africa. American policy with regard to these colonies took two successive forms, one operative until 1955, the other after that date. In the earlier period, despite American public opinion, which wanted action and often failed to understand its own government's attitude, Washington came down overtly on the side of independence only if troubles broke out, because such troubles tended to engender communism. If the situation remained calm, then Washington was not going to display open opposition to the policy of its colonialist ally in Paris. True, in 1949 the American representative at the United Nations did stand out against the setting up of a trusteeship in Libya, involving the handing over of Fezzan to France, and supported Libyan independence instead, a state of affairs that was to hasten independence in neighboring Tunisia, France's politically most advanced protectorate. But in that same year, 1949, Washington agreed to treat the whole of Algeria as an integral part of France and to include it in the protected zone specified in the Atlantic Pact. Every year, the Arab states in the United Nations General Assembly regularly attempted to have a motion adopted condemning France for her policy with regard to Tunisia, Morocco, and Algeria, where a long war of independence finally broke out in 1954. The American

delegate Philip Jessup consistently made conciliatory speeches in an
effort to pour oil on the troubled waters, but without ever managing
to satisfy either the French colonialists or the Arab nationalists
entirely.

In 1955, American policy changed, abruptly and almost simultaneously with that of the Russians. This was the result of an event that
had taken place in the spring of that year at Bandung in Indonesia: the
first conference of underdeveloped countries, the group of nations
soon to become known as the Third World. The first sign of change
was that both the Americans and the Russians decided to withdraw the
veto they had been imposing on the entry of newly independent states
to the United Nations Organization. From then on, with rare
exceptions, any state acquiring independence was automatically admitted to the United Nations, thus beginning the rapid increase in the
number of member nations that in the 1960s was to give the new
countries a majority in the General Assembly, thus in turn accelerating
the emancipation process. This "package deal," as the massive
increase in membership in 1955 came to be called, led the Americans
to take a much more intransigent attitude in the matter of decolonization. The Atlantic Pact, unlike the old pre-1914 Franco-Russian
alliance, was not an *entente* entailing global solidarity. The Americans
were continually reminding the French after 1955 that defending
oneself against the Soviet threat was one thing, but that extending
U.S. support to cover their allies' colonial policies was quite another.
As far as Washington was concerned, the Atlantic alliance was exactly
that, not a global one. In passing, I might add that this American
attitude, maintained throughout the late 1950s, was to be reversed in
the 1960s. Disturbed by the events in Vietnam, the Americans were to
seek to persuade their allies that the Atlantic Pact should in fact be
extended to the rest of the world, and it was the allies, France chief
among them, who were to refuse. Thus may apparently lofty principles derive essentially from pressures of the moment.

It was from this new and militantly anticolonial viewpoint that the
Americans approached the Suez episode. I need hardly go over this
affair here in all its detail. In brief, on 26 July 1956, Colonel Gamal
Abdel Nasser announced that he intended to nationalize the Suez
Canal Company and that Egypt, having regained her sovereignty,
would henceforward control all transit through the great waterway

opened in 1869. There followed a summer of feverish discussions, during which Britain and France, supported without much vigor by John Foster Dulles, sought to reimpose "internationalization" of the canal in a new form. Then, in the face of Nasser's obdurate opposition to their suggestions, they decided to enlist the aid of Israel and resort to force. The crucial dates were: 29–30 October, invasion of the Egyptian Sinai by Israel; 30 October, Franco-British ultimatum to Israel and Egypt, demanding that each should evacuate a ten-mile strip on its side of the canal (Israel, their accomplice, accepted the ultimatum, the terms of which enabled the Israelis to continue their occupation of almost the entire Sinai area); 5 November, Franco-British landings; 6 November, after a threat of action from the Soviet Union, implying the possible use of atomic weapons, an abrupt cease-fire before the French and British had advanced more than fifteen miles from Port Said. In the weeks that followed, the French, the British, and the Israelis were forced to accept a resolution passed by the United Nations requiring them to evacuate all the territory they had occupied. A United Nations peace-keeping force was created and posted along the Israel-Egypt border inside Egyptian territory. The only advantage for Israel was that this force occupied Sharm al Sheikh, thus protecting Israeli shipping in the Gulf of Akaba, even though the Suez Canal itself (in any case temporarily blocked as a result of the war) remained closed to Israeli vessels. For Nasser, despite his military defeat, it proved a resounding political victory.

The Suez affair produced a lasting deterioration in Franco-American relations, and the reason for this requires examination. Looking at the events with hindsight, in their historical perspective, it is quite obvious that the American position was both more moral and more realistic than that of the French and the British. Where the latter are concerned, it is fair to say that the method resorted to—the use of force against a weaker power—was the dying kick of the old colonial tradition, a tradition of immediate armed intervention whenever one's interests are threatened. In other works, Suez was a classic case of "gunboat diplomacy." Had it any hope of success in the mid-twentieth century, at the height of the decolonization era, at a time when the world's two superpowers were both hostile to empires? The answer, strictly speaking, is yes, perhaps, if like Hitler—a dubious model—the British and French had struck like lightning. In fact, so

poor was the coordination of the civil and military decisions involved
that the troops were not ready to go into action until 5 November.
Needless to say, a whole week was quite enough for the mobilization
of world opinion, and mobilized it was—against Britain and France.
Although both countries were technically in a position to use their
right of veto on the United Nations Security Council, they found
themselves in the doghouse, as it were, in the General Assembly. The
all-important vote of 2 November, on the resolution demanding an
immediate cease-fire, produced 64 members in favor (including the
United States and the Soviet Union), 5 against (Britain, France, Israel,
Australia, and New Zealand), and 6 abstentions (including Belgium
and Canada).

Apart from violations of international morality, Washington had
other matters of complaint against its allies.

1. Eisenhower was running for a second term as president at the
time, and the election actually took place on 6 November 1956. In the
1952 elections he had included in his platform a pledge to replace the
"containment" policy of the Democrats with a policy of "rollback,"
the aim of which was to win back territories that had fallen into
communist hands. The attempt naturally failed, and in April 1954 it
had even been necessary to refuse France's urgent request for United
States Air Force intervention in Indochina to rescue the French
garrison trapped in Dien Bien Phu. In the 1956 election Eisenhower
had been running on a quite different platform. He was now the
champion of peace: armistice in Korea in July 1953; armistice in
Indochina in July 1954; relaxation of the cold war. Now, threatening
the very foundations of this beautiful construction, violence had once
more exploded in the world, violence detonated by two of America's
own allies, who, to make matters even worse, hadn't so much as
consulted her. In Eisenhower's eyes Suez was a piece of flagrant
disloyalty, a fatal blow to the United Nations, and a hole torn in the
fabric of Atlantic unity.

2. Much more serious was the adverse effect of the Franco-British
initiative on the vast tide of disquiet that had been rising, ever since
the Twentieth Congress of the Communist Party of the Soviet Union,
in eastern Europe, a tide that in Poland and Hungary would even lead
to attempts at self-emancipation. At the very moment when the
United States, as champion of the "free world," was almost in a

position to offer clear proof of its adversary's imperialism to world public opinion, its two principal allies, with utmost stupidity, had provided the Soviet Union with a means of counterattack, of broadcasting to the world, and particularly to the black nations, the persistence of "Western imperialism."

3. Eisenhower and Dulles were haunted by the danger of nuclear war. Since they seemed to be withdrawing their protection from their faithless allies, Marshal Nikolai Bulganin felt able to issue vague threats against those allies. In the ultrasensitive area of nuclear deterrence a vague threat was quite sufficient to trigger an alert, to force Eisenhower—on the very day of his reelection—to take military measures and telephone Anthony Eden, the British prime minister, urging him to stop the Suez operation immediately.

4. In sum, Eisenhower's whole foreign policy, which involved holding the Americans up as models of international morality in contrast to the innumerable proofs of Russian expansionism, had been brought crashing to the ground, since the third-world countries could not help but believe that the French and the British had received secret encouragement from Washington.

In the Suez invasion, the British, who were the principal users of the canal, since it was the main trade artery of the Commonwealth, had been seeking above all to ensure continued use of it for their shipping. The Americans, who used the canal much less, were not much concerned on that score, nor were the French. What needs to be understood, then, is why a French government, headed by the socialist Guy Mollet, should ever have involved itself in a gamble of this nature when its failure was so predictable. It was certainly not because the majority of the Suez Canal Company shares were in French hands. The company had made such enormous profits since the opening in 1869, had reinvested so much capital, that, even if the Egyptian indemnities had proved insufficient, the company's future was still assured. The French government's real motivation lay in the Algerian War. Guy Mollet and his ministers knew that Nasser's Egypt was aiding the Algerian "rebels." They imagined that, if Nasser were to fall from power, then the "foreign plot" that, according to them, was spurring on a minority of Algerians to wage war against France would collapse of its own accord and that they could then return to normalcy—in

other words, cease to maintain a French army of half a million men in
Algeria. Guy Mollet compared Nasser to Hitler. Acceptance of his
"strong-arm tactics" over Suez would be tantamount to another
Munich.

A great many French people, beginning with Guy Mollet himself,
reproached the Americans bitterly and believed that everything that
went wrong was the result of Washington's "stupid" policies. (1) The
fact that the Suez Canal was nationalized in the first place was due to
the recently announced American refusal to finance Egypt's huge
Aswan Dam project. (2) At the very outset, ignoring the most
elementary rules of diplomatic tactical procedure, Dulles had publicly
announced that he excluded all use of force, thereby encouraging
Nasser to harden his position. (3) At the height of the operation,
instead of aiding their allies, who were fighting for the rights of the
West as a whole, the Americans had acted as accomplices of Russia,
against their own clear interests.

Even though, tactically speaking, there were some telling points in
this French official reasoning, the essential facts remain unchanged.
The Fourth French Republic, discredited at home by its inability to
govern, had now finally discredited itself in the sphere of foreign
affairs as well by a retrograde and, one may add, an immoral act.
Why? Because the Algerian War was poisoning everything. It had
already infected the Fourth Republic with the fatal disease that was to
destroy it. Its side effects were to harm Franco-American relations for a
long time to come.

The fact was that the majority of French people—opposed, it is
true, by an active and vigorous minority of communists and left-
wingers—felt a strong bond with the million French-speakers of
European origin living in Algeria. Algeria, so habit made them
believe, was French. France stretched "from Dunkirk to Tamanrasset"
(in the heart of the Sahara). As for the nine million "French
Moslems" (French citizens with a special civil status allowing them
fewer rights than the European French), they, it was believed, were for
the most part loyal to France. Hadn't they fought magnificently for
her from 1943 to 1945, in Tunisia, in Italy, in Provence, in Alsace, in
Germany? The Front de Liberation Nationale (FLN) in Algeria could
therefore be nothing but a plot of foreign inspiration, in which the

French variously discerned the hand of Nasser, the Russians, and even the big American corporations, greedy to get their hands on the oil being discovered in the Sahara.

Such arguments, needless to say, carried no weight with the Americans. In the United States it was becoming daily more clear that Algeria would have to be granted its independence. The argument already used to such good effect during the war in Indochina, that the conflict France was engaged in was no longer a colonial war but one more episode in the anticommunist struggle, was, to be sure, put forward by many leading figures in France. But this time it met with great skepticism on the other side of the Atlantic. President Habib Bourguiba of Tunisia and the king of Morocco were both supporting the Algerian revolution. Were they communists? Generally speaking, what better rampart against communism cound there be than an independent Islamic state?

I shall give only one example of this American attitude, but it is an all-important one, since it provoked considerable emotional reaction in France. On 2 July 1957, John Fitzgerald Kennedy, already emerging as one of the Democratic Party's greatest hopes, made a speech of some length to the Senate on the Algerian question. "The most powerful single force in the world today is neither communism nor capitalism, neither the H-bomb nor the guided missile—it is man's eternal desire to be free and independent." It was therefore necessary to combat both Russian imperialism and Western imperialism with equal vigor, since it was on that criterion that America would be judged by millions of people in Asia, in Africa, and behind the Iron Curtain. Algeria was a test case in this respect. "I am ... reluctant to appear critical of our oldest and first ally, whose assistance in our own war for independence will never be forgotten, and whose role in the course of world events has traditionally been one of constructive leadership and co-operation. I do not want our policy to be anti-French." But the war in Algeria, which was weakening French participation in NATO and compromising the French economy, was "no longer a problem for the French alone." It was affecting American prestige in the eyes of the free world and, in consequence, American security. The policy of the Republican government, Kennedy went on, was too favorable to France. The principles of independence and anticolonialism had to be placed before all other considerations. It was therefore essential "that the President and Secretary of State be strongly encouraged to place the influence of the United States behind efforts ... to achieve a solution which will recognize the independent personality of Algeria and establish the basis for a settlement with France and the neighboring nations" (Kennedy, *Strategy of Peace*, pp. 97 ff.).

It is true that Kennedy was speaking in his own name and that Eisenhower's government refused to the very end to adopt a policy so extreme. But it is nonetheless true that the young senator from Massachusetts had put his finger on the crucial spot: only Algerian independence could reestablish the good relations between France and the United States so gravely affected by the Suez affair. In the event, it was on the French side that the great shift occurred. The Algerian War in fact dealt the Fourth Republic its death blow, brought General de Gaulle back to power, and established in the Fifth Republic a regime better equipped, should it prove necessary, to defend France's "independence."

IN EARLY 1958 France's situation was gloomy. On the economic level the dollar-gap problem had still not been really resolved, largely for want of a systematic export policy. The United States had to be summoned to the rescue, and in the early part of the year the French government sent Jean Monnet over to America to head a mission. But, above all, the problem of the Algerian War seemed to be increasingly insoluble. Was it possible, as was hoped by the socialist leader Guy Mollet (whose government had been brought down in 1957), "to obtain a cease-fire in order to organize free elections in the presence of observers from the democratic countries"? The strength of the "rebels" lay precisely in the fact that their "rebellion" was armed. Would they agree to laying down those arms? Then, in February 1958, the French air force, claiming that it was a reprisal raid, bombed the Tunisian frontier village of Sakhiet-Sidi-Youssef. This act of violence aroused a tremendous storm of outrage all over the world, including the United States. The French government, led by the young Radical, Felix Gaillard, clearly lacked the necessary grasp and experience to cope with the resulting situation. The Americans attempted to offer their good offices and had already dispatched a mission to Tunisia headed by Robert Murphy, who earlier, it will be remembered, had represented Roosevelt in Algeria during the war. Would the French government accept this American offer, which, according to the supporters of *Algérie française*, would lead to a "biased mediation" and "the total liquidation of the French position in North Africa"?

It was this drift toward an "American solution" of the Algerian War that on 13 May 1958 triggered a veritable *coup d'état* by the Algerian colonists and armed services. A "committee of public safety" was set

up, under General Jacques Massu, which demanded the "creation in
Paris of a government of public safety, such a government alone being
capable of preserving Algeria as an integral part of the metropolis." It
was a rebellion of Algiers against Paris, in other words against the
state, a total rift in the nation's unity. Over the next two weeks a rising
tide of public opinion began to flow in favor of the only man who was
seen as capable of reestablishing that unity: General de Gaulle, who
had been living aloof from the centers of power for eleven years.

Summoned by the president of the Republic to form a government,
with the agreement of all parties except the communists, General de
Gaulle accepted, but only on condition that he be empowered to draw
up a new constitution to be submitted to a national referendum. Thus
on 1 June the general became the last prime minister of the Fourth
Republic, and on 28 September, with an almost 80 percent "yes"
vote, the French adopted the constitution of the Fifth Republic, the
essential characteristic of which was to ensure governmental stability
by handing over the main executive power to the president. De Gaulle
was elected to the presidency later that year. He was to be reelected in
December 1965 by a national ballot, a practice introduced in 1962 as
the result of a further referendum.

It must not be supposed, however, that the new republic was a
presidential regime of the American type. France remained cen-
tralized. The cabinet was still answerable to the National Assembly.
Lastly, it was a democratic but at the same time authoritarian regime,
exactly tailored to fit General de Gaulle, yet also capable of surviving
him, for, as numerous polls have shown, the French still remain
attached to it.

1. The general's cautious first steps

The Americans greeted de Gaulle's return to power with little
enthusiasm. True, his relations with Eisenhower were reasonably
good. But he had stepped back into the arena with the reputation of
being a champion of *Algérie française*—a totally erroneous notion
also held by the French colonists in Algeria itself—who would bring
all the attempts at European integration to nothing and whose relations with the United States were likely to be just as prickly as they had
been during the war.

Yet everything began very well. De Gaulle had a meeting with Adenauer, and together they rescued the Common Market from the threat of dissolution into the British-backed European Free Trade Area. Then he made it clear that he was going to concentrate all his attention on the war in Algeria. On this point the course he took proved amazingly congenial to Washington. During his visit to Algeria in June 1958 he had only once mentioned *Algérie française*. He also made a great point of expressing his respect for the FLN, the liberation movement that had now become the Algerian Provisional Government. What he would have liked, of course, was an immediate cease-fire ("knives left in the cloakroom"); but he realized very quickly—much more quickly than French opinion in general—that peace in Algeria was not going to be possible until an agreement had been reached with the new provisional government and that the latter would never abandon its struggle prior to such an agreement, since its sole negotiating weapon was precisely the continuation of the war. With equal speed he announced that it was the right of the Algerians to determine their own future. If it was to be a "French Algeria," clearly de Gaulle could have no objections. But a "Moslem Algeria"? A total break with France? That solution appeared to him absurd. He allowed it to become plain, without making any specific statement, that his own preference was for an "Algerian Algeria," in which the million or so European French inhabitants would retain a special status. In other words he wanted an independent but pro-Western Algeria. And wasn't that exactly what the Americans were hoping for?

It was certainly not what the colonists had been hoping for, however. Having supported the first Algerian coup, aimed at keeping Algeria French, then having backed de Gaulle in the belief that he would champion that aim, they now discovered to their consternation, then their fury, that the general, a ruthless realist, had become an advocate of decolonization. This realization led to two more attempted coups, one civilian (the "Algiers barricades" in January 1960), the other military (the "generals' *coup d'état*" in April 1961). Both of them failed, mainly as a result of energetic action on de Gaulle's part; but they were accompanied by the creation of an underground resistance movement, the OAS (Organisation de l'Armée Secrète), which continued the hopeless and desperate fight to prevent Algerian independence. Nevertheless, after long negotiations, several times interrupted and resumed, de Gaulle did eventually achieve his aims. In March 1962 there came the signing of the Evian agreement with the Algerian Provisional Government promising Algeria self-determination. In April, a referendum in France expressed approval of independence for Algeria with a 90 percent "yes" vote— clearly an amazing result, attesting to a total reversal of French opinion on the subject of decolonization. After a plebiscite in Algeria itself, the country finally became independent on 1 July 1962, by which time the backlash produced by the activities of the OAS had forced the majority of French colonists to leave the country altogether.

This outcome could hardly fail to please the Americans. The same was true as well of de Gaulle's offers of independence to the Black African colonies. Guinea became independent in September 1958 as the result of a referendum in which the population rejected the proposed new constitution. All the other former French territories in Black Africa (except Djibouti, the subject of a dispute between Somalia and Abyssinia) acquired independence in 1960, thus creating a sizable group of French-speaking nations in the United Nations.

De Gaulle's popularity was very high in the United States at this time, especially since the economic reforms of 1958, accompanied by a devaluation of the franc, had solved the dollar-gap problem (eight years behind Germany!), stimulated an economic expansion that was to continue through the 1960s and early 1970s, and gave the Americans the impression that their old ally, with the miasma of past defeat, colonial wars, and recent indecisiveness now left behind, was once more about to play its true role in the world. De Gaulle's policy of "cooperation," as it was called, with regard to Algeria and Black Africa, and later with Morocco and Tunisia, also seemed to them a healthy one, insofar as it tended to prevent those countries from "swinging over" into the Soviet camp and possibly providing military bases for America's great communist rival.

In addition, as is plain from the texts of his press conferences printed in the annual *L'Année politique*, the general never ceased proclaiming the necessity of the Atlantic alliance, the keystone of American world strategy. Here is one example: "Supposing that the Atlantic alliance did not exist, there would be nothing to prevent the Soviet dictatorship from expanding across the whole of Europe and the whole of Africa, and subsequently from spreading over the entire world. Well! France prefers to maintain the Atlantic alliance until the day when the reign of peace has been truly assured'' (25 March 1959). Whenever there was any appearance of threat, de Gaulle consistently declared his active support for the Americans and rejected the compromise positions sometimes suggested by the British. "The recent test," he said on 31 May 1960, referring to the Berlin crisis created by Khrushchev, "has demonstrated the profound solidarity of the Western powers. No doubt President Eisenhower, Mr. Macmillan, and myself all have our own problems and our own temperament. But faced with this eventuality, we three friends, for such we are, experienced no difficulty in reaching a wise and firm agreement. Our alliance emerged as a living reality" (31 May 1960). The general was to display the same firmness in his support for the United States during the Cuban missile crisis of October 1962.

Moreover, however great his desire for détente between East and West, he never held back from public expression of the low esteem in which he held the communist regimes. Commenting on the setting up of the Berlin Wall, he had no hesitation in attributing this move to the Russians' own difficulties:

> Despite the constraints, the isolation, and the acts of force used by the communist regime to hold down the countries under its yoke, and despite certain collective successes it has achieved by making free with the substance of its subjects, in reality its deficiencies, its weaknesses, its internal failures, and above all its crushing inhumanity are becoming increasingly apparent to elites and masses that it is becoming more and more difficult to dupe and curb. And then too, the satellites the Soviet regime maintains under its jurisdiction are also, as nations, becoming increasingly aware of the cruelty inherent in the annexation to which they have been subjected (5 September 1961).

His vision of China was equally pessimistic and grandiloquent: "China, multitudinous and wretched, indestructible and ambitious, building up by dint of successive ordeals an immeasurable power, and gazing around her at the vast expanses into which she must someday spread" (10 November 1959). It was in this future territorial rivalry between China and Russia that he perceived the forces that might one day bring about a *rapprochement* between Russia ("a white European nation") and the Western powers, together with an internal liberal-

ization of the Soviet Union. It was from this notion that he derived his
curious concept of a "Europe stretching from the Urals to the
Atlantic."

Such a philosophy of the world could not but appeal to American
opinion. The visit de Gaulle paid to the United States in April 1960
took on the character of a triumphal procession. He achieved a
prodigious success with the address he delivered to both houses of
Congress:

> Since the United States first appeared on the world stage, France
> has fought at its side three times, and for three great causes. The
> first time it was for American independence. The second time it was
> for that of others. The third time it was for France's own. Our
> common past is heavy with struggle and sacrifice. It is a great past,
> because together we have never, at any time, served any cause but
> that of liberty. . . . Despite changes of fortune, the Americans and
> the French feel for one another a friendship now two centuries old,
> and still as much alive as ever. . . . France, for her part, has made
> her choice. She has chosen to be on the side of the free peoples.
> She has chosen to be on that side with you (25 April 1960).

Congress acclaimed him. American opinion was inclined to regard
him, as John Foster Dulles had done when he met him in Paris during
July 1958, as "one of the great men of our time."

Nevertheless, even during this relatively euphoric phase, the well-
informed were less optimistic. De Gaulle did not have the support of
the French intelligentsia, or of many high-ranking civil servants, or of
the "Europeans" grouped around Jean Monnet. A large sector of the
French establishment, in contact with American friends, maintained a
subdued and slightly aloof skepticism. But most important, there were
already some disquieting signs. The Americans were hostile to the
dissemination of nuclear armaments and convinced that they must
retain their leadership in the atomic field. Yet already, in 1958,
de Gaulle had told Dulles that, whatever happened, France intended
to develop its own atomic weapons—the decision to make an experi-
mental bomb having already been taken during the Fourth Republic.
The only question was how far the Americans were prepared to help
France, as they had Britain, with the technology. But American
reluctance on this score was to produce no modification in the French
decision to develop the bomb. After all, even with a ten-year

handicap, even with the necessity of rediscovering all the technical processes on her own, France was still perfectly capable of developing such a weapon. The first French atomic bomb was in fact detonated in the Sahara during February 1960. The Americans consoled themselves by reading the unending stream of sarcastic articles in the anti–de Gaulle French press pouring scorn on the general's *bombinette*. It was to take a good dozen years before American opinion came to realize that France had developed what was in fact a very considerable nuclear armory. Moreover, since they had never passed on any of their secrets to the French, the Americans had no way of exerting pressure on them. This remains a crucial problem, to which we shall return.

Another disquieting sign had occurred as early as September 1958. De Gaulle sent President Eisenhower a handwritten (!) letter proposing changes in the organization of NATO. The general suggested that the present leadership exercised by the Americans, aided by their "brilliant second-in-command," Britain, should be replaced by a three-nation directorship provided by the United States, the United Kingdom, and France. The purport of this letter, albeit not its actual contents, was revealed by the German newspaper *Der Mittag*. It aroused protests from the British, who had no wish to relinquish the advantages of their "special relationship" with Washington, from the Germans, from the Italians, who did not wish to see France playing such a dominant role, and also from many Americans, who in view of their country's great power wished to see it retain its role as leader. President Eisenhower replied in friendly terms but remained evasive. For a long while de Gaulle contented himself with merely referring periodically to the desirability of NATO reforms, without anyone's being quite sure what he meant by the term.

In May 1961, when the new president of the United States, John Fitzgerald Kennedy, made an official visit to Paris, the relationship he developed with the general proved extremely interesting. De Gaulle had certainly felt very warm toward Eisenhower, but it was a fact that his own intensely historical and philosophical culture and cast of mind had awakened very little response in his American colleague. Kennedy, on the contrary, a former student at Harvard, was, like de Gaulle himself, a great reader and thinker. To the general that was very important. "Despite [their] differences," writes Theodore Sorensen, "the two men retained a consistent admiration for each other. De Gaulle in 1961 toasted Kennedy's 'intelligence and courage' with unaccustomed warmth. . . . 'I have more confidence in your country now,' said de Gaulle when Kennedy departed Paris.'' As for Kennedy, "he was fascinated by de Gaulle's role in previous history and his focus on future history. . . . he did not share the view that the General was merely a nineteenth century romantic with nostalgic yearnings for the past." But even though, in Kennedy's words, these conversations "could not have been more cordial," no progress was made toward a reform of NATO (Sorensen, *Kennedy*, p. 562).

The final suspicious sign from the viewpoint of informed American observers was the general's contempt for the United Nations. Not only did he refuse to pay the French contribution toward the dispatch of U.N. troops to the Congo, he also had no hesitation in describing what he referred to as "these united or disunited nations" in terms calculated to outrage the large sectors of American opinion with great faith in the organization. "The meetings of the United Nations have ceased to be anything but rowdy and scandalous sessions in which there is no possibility of organizing an objective debate, filled with constant diatribes and insults emanating particularly from the communists and those allied with them against the Western nations" (11 April 1961).

All these things, however, were still largely masked by the initial blaze of cooperation. It was in 1963 that the storm was to break.

2. De Gaulle scuttles Kennedy's Grand Design (1963–65)

When one analyzes de Gaulle's actions in the light of his own writings, his speeches, and above all his behavior, one is confronted by several dilemmas. First, did de Gaulle have a "theory," a "plan," whose various aspects he gradually revealed to the world, or was he an opportunist of genius, always ready to extract whatever profit he could from every situation as it occurred? The opportunist hypothesis has been expounded on the American side by John Newhouse in his book *De Gaulle and the Anglo-Saxons* (1970). George Ball, undersecretary of state under President Lyndon B. Johnson, although he spoke of the general's flexible tactics, was on the contrary a believer in the existence of a "strategic plan," already more or less worked out as early as 1945.

According to Ball, there was a remarkable conformity between de Gaulle the writer of the *Mémoires* and de Gaulle the man of political action. Stanley Hoffmann likewise thought that de Gaulle had a "scenario," or rather that his approach to the ever-shifting world of action was governed by a number of clearly defined principles and an ultimate vision, and that he was totally inflexible where those principles and that vision were concerned. Having had numerous conversations with him, Ball also said that he was invariably courteous, warm, and categorical.

I myself took part, between 1963 and 1967, in about ten discussions, organized and financed by the Ford Foundation, on the theme "Europe and the United States," in Chicago, New York, Washington, Paris, Bellaggio, and so on. These discussions among academics, politicians, and top civil servants invariably ended up revolving around the central question: "What will General de Gaulle be up to next?" I remember once, in 1965, during a morning of discussion devoted to Germany, counting the number of times each leading political figure was mentioned. The score was Chancellor Ludwig Erhard twice, President Johnson three times, General de Gaulle nineteen times. In those circles, on the whole unfavorable to Gaullism, its founder had become an obsession. Irritation with him had produced what amounted to a new and bizarre branch of learning, what one might term "Gaullology." This irritation was essentially a product of the general's anti-Americanism.

The great drama may be said to have begun in July 1962. This was the month of Algerian independence, which, far from weakening the French, as both the Soviet leaders and the supporters of *Algérie française* had expected, restored them to a position of total independence in their foreign policy. It was at the very same time, on the Fourth of July 1962, that President Kennedy launched his Grand Design. Strongly influenced by Jean Monnet, who was a friend of his "special assistant," McGeorge Bundy, as well as of the president himself, Kennedy took advantage of the anniversary of the Declaration of Independence to make a speech in Philadelphia's Independence Hall putting forward a "Declaration of Interdependence." He offered "a concrete Atlantic Partnership, a mutually beneficial Partnership between the new union now emerging in Europe and the old American Union founded here 175 years ago.'' This was what later came to be known as the ''two pillars'' doctrine.

In what did it consist? First, of course, in a soon-to-be-created United States of Europe, which was to include the United Kingdom, already (since 1961) a candidate for entry into the Common Market. Then, that first step accomplished, the two groups of United States would become equals and would cooperate in political, economic, and cultural plans. From the economic view they would reap the benefits of a bill that Kennedy put before Congress in October 1962, which resulted in the Reciprocal Trade Act. This was to create what amounted to free trade between the United States of America and the enlarged Common Market—an admirable means of calming American fears over the effects of the European Economic Community's common external tariff. The president was to receive the right, over a five-year period, to lower American tariff barriers by 50 percent, on condition that analogous measures were taken by the Common Market. He could even suppress import tariffs altogether on all products of which at least 80 percent were manufactured within the combined United States–western European area. The list of such products would be a very long one should Britain enter the Common Market.

On one point, however, equality was not to exist: nuclear armament. Why should the Europeans go to the bother of developing nuclear weaponry, since the United States already possessed sufficient deterrent power and could therefore protect its allies? This part of the Grand Design was linked with the new and more subtle American strategic policy known as the McNamara Doctrine (after the then secretary of defense), or ''doctrine of flexible response.'' It was brought in, at the very height of the Berlin crisis, to replace the previous ''doctrine of massive retaliation.'' Instead of a declaration of all-out nuclear war in the event of any aggressive act, the new doctrine allowed for a graduated form of retaliation, one that would bring increasingly destructive weapons into play in succession. The complexity of the decisions to be made, and the urgency of their nature, made it more than ever imperative that they should be left in the hands of one man—the president of the United States.

Thus Kennedy's Grand Design entailed the maintenance of the

American atomic monopoly. Europe, at that time protected by the American "umbrella," was to remain so indefinitely. The historic Cuban missile crisis in October 1962, the only occasion since 1945 when there was a real possibility of nuclear war, ended happily for the Americans. Kennedy—with the wholehearted support of de Gaulle, be it said, even though he was not consulted, or rather informed, until the last moment—had during those days amply demonstrated both his character and his ability. Was this not one more proof of the necessity for American monopoly and American supremacy?

At all events, buoyed up by his success, the young president announced that the moment had come to reinforce American leadership. This is one of those cases when politics can hinge on a semantic interpretation. In French there is no one word that provides an exact translation of "leader." The English word has been adopted by the French, but only in one of its meanings, that of "chief" or "head," and not in its other sense, common in America and much more modest, of "guide" or "inspirer" (though it is true that the German word for "guide" is *Führer*). As far as General de Gaulle was concerned, there was no doubt whatever: Kennedy was proclaiming the necessity for an American *hegemony*. He was seen as driven by the same covert ambitions that de Gaulle had once discerned in Roosevelt. Now it was clear why Eisenhower had not accepted his suggestion of a three-nation directorship of the alliance. Whatever the American president's own personality, he was ineluctably led to express the tendency inherent in his nation, and that was to establish its domination while cloaking that domination in fine speeches about equality. De Gaulle said nothing, but he set about preparing his answer.

That answer could only be *European independence*. And Europe could be independent only if, in the years ahead, she was able to undertake her own defense, which implied the possession of nuclear armaments. Let us ignore for the moment the general's personal conception of Europe. At that point, what he needed was the support of his principal European partners and that of the French people.

Did he in fact have the latter? Everything seemed to indicate that the French, in general, were behind him. Apart from a small minority they were then experiencing intense relief at the ending of the war in Algeria. It was true that de Gaulle had taken four years to achieve it, but by that very lack of speed he had avoided civil war and prepared people's minds for decolonization. The OAS had faded from existence, with the exception of a few tiny groups of activists (on 22 August 1962 de Gaulle miraculously escaped an attack on his life by one of them). On 28 October, despite strong opposition, he brought off a personal triumph with the referendum approving the election of the Republic's president by universal ballot (61.75 percent of the votes cast were in favor). In November, in the elections to the National Assembly, his supporters greatly increased their share of both votes and seats. The polls showed that his popularity was still very high. He could therefore ignore the strong opposition of the intelligentsia and those who supported Jean Monnet's concept of a united Europe.

As far as the other European nations were concerned, his relations with Adenauer (whom he visited in September) were excellent, and the two men had drawn up a treaty of friendship intended to reconcile their two peoples, until recently regarded as hereditary enemies. This treaty was to be signed in January 1963. What de Gaulle undoubtedly minimized was the opposition of many Germans to a policy of "independence" with regard to the United States. Nothing could alter the fact that West German security depended on the physical presence of American troops within their national territory. In the event of any major Franco-American dispute, West Germany ultimately had no choice but to align itself with the United States. Moreover, any bonds Germany had with France were not really those of friendship—it was too soon—but of trade. Thanks to the Common Market, France and Germany were becoming indissociable partners. Each was both the primary supplier and the primary customer of the other. Yet the fact remained that German security still came first.

That left the United Kingdom. De Gaulle was hoping that he would at last be able to dissolve the "special relationship" with the United States and, since Britain had applied for entry to the Common Market, to "swing" the British toward Europe. On 15 December 1962, General de Gaulle received a visit from the British prime minister, Harold Macmillan, at the Château de Rambouillet. Had de Gaulle already decided to oppose British entry into the Common Market, as has been suggested by his British biographer, Alexander Werth? Or was he hostile to the maintenance of British nuclear capability, as George Ball believes? The most generally accepted interpretation is that at the time of Rambouillet he genuinely thought that the British accepted his views, that they were going to support the creation of a "European Europe" that would maintain a firm distance in its relations with the United States, develop its own nuclear defense, and be more concerned with its own independence than with any Atlantic partnership. Several days later, on 18–21 December, Macmillan met Kennedy for talks in Nassau. At Nassau, as de Gaulle saw it, Macmillan gave way to the Americans all along the line. He agreed that the Americans should cease manufacture of the special air-ground missile Skybolt for British use. He agreed that the Skybolts should be replaced with the American Polaris missiles. But above all he agreed that the Polaris missiles should become part of a multilateral organization that would be under American command, except in the event that Her Majesty's Government should decide that its highest national interests were at stake. In short, far from handing in its resignation as America's "brilliant second-in-command," Britain had only proved eager to sign on for a further term. It was a reaffirmation of the "Anglo-Saxon" unity that had been arousing de Gaulle's passionate mistrust ever since the war. Britain in the Common Market would be the Americans' Trojan Horse. As de Gaulle remarked shortly afterward, during a conversation at the Elysée Palace, "Britain transferred all the meager nuclear forces in her possession to the United States. She could have handed them over to Europe. Well, that's the choice she made." The supreme insult came when Macmillan and Kennedy invited France to become a member of their "multinational" or "multilateral" force.

De Gaulle's answer to all this—that is, ultimately, to President Kennedy's Grand Design—came on 14 January 1963, during one of the most famous of his press conferences.

On that occasion he dissociated the two problems in fact so closely linked in his own mind: that of British membership in the Common Market and that of the proposed multilateral force. In vetoing British entry into the Market, he employed exclusively economic arguments. But his foreign minister, the former ambassador to the United States, Maurice Couve de Murville, who found himself saddled with the unpleasant task of announcing the veto to France's five partners in Brussels (who were furious at this unilateral decision) did not hesitate to make use of the political argument: Great Britain is a "satellite of

America.'' Britain's entry, the general himself said, would lead to ''the emergence of a colossal Atlantic Community that would be dependent upon and controlled by America, and would in no time at all swallow up the European Community.''

His rejection of the multilateral force was even more trenchant: ''I say again, as I have said many times before, that France intends to have her own national defense.... To pour our resources into a multilateral force, under foreign command, would be to run counter to that governing principle of our defense and our policy.'' The essential section of this statement merits quotation in full:

> It is wholly explicable that this French undertaking should not appear very satisfactory to certain circles in America. In politics and in strategy, as in the sphere of economics, monopoly quite naturally seems to him who holds it the best possible system. So we hear a massed choir of American officials, experts, and media men taking violent, extreme exception to our armament policy. The atomic capability France intends to develop for herself is, and must remain, they tell us, minute in comparison to that possessed by the United States and Russia. To develop it is therefore a great waste of effort and money for nothing. And besides, given the alliance, the United States possesses an overwhelming superiority, provided nobody goes ruining its strategy by doing things that don't fit in with it! It is perfectly true that the quantity of nuclear weapons we can produce for ourselves will not match, and by a long way, the massive stock-piles of those two titans of our day. But since when has it been proved that a people must remain without the most efficient available weapons simply because its principal possible adversary, and its principal friend, possess resources far superior to its own? (14 January 1963).

Thus, the scene dramatically set, free at last from the war in Algeria, General de Gaulle launched himself into the realms of high diplomacy. France could henceforth ''deal with problems, not in a constantly breathless way, never quite able to catch up with them, but in terms of ongoing designs and long-term decisions.'' Some weeks later he was to justify his decision to develop nuclear strikepower with an argument well calculated to appeal to the French.

> To turn us from this path we hear raised, as always, the simultaneous voices of immobilism and demagogy. 'It is futile!' says the

first. 'It is too expensive!' says the other. France has listened to these voices in the past, and sometimes to her misfortune, above all on the eve of both world wars. 'No heavy artillery!' they clamored in concert until 1914 was upon us. 'No tank regiments!', 'No strike aircraft!' they cried in unison before 1939, these same cretins and madmen. But this time we shall not permit the sluggards and the self-deluders to summon the invaders into our land (19 April 1963).

The press conference of January 1963 raised a storm of protest. France's five partners in the Common Market were particularly furious because they were all advocates of British membership and because the Europe they wanted, a Europe with increased supranational powers, had been loftily rejected by the general, who would not accept any form of "integration," be it Atlantic or European. Nevertheless, by insisting on the creation of a common agricultural policy within the Market, by issuing ultimatum after ultimatum, and even by leaving the community for several months in June 1965, France did get her way on many occasions. At the same time, however, this French policy contributed to a deterioration of the community spirit that had existed until then and to a tendency for the European meetings to become a forum for bitterly urged claims based on national interest. What de Gaulle would have liked was "cooperation," which in his mind presupposed the preservation of each member's sovereignty (the "Europe of states") but also support for the French policy of "independence" with regard to the United States. On this point he failed completely, and the replacement of his old friend Konrad Adenauer in October 1963 by a thoroughgoing pro-American, Ludwig Erhard, is one proof of this among many.

In both France and Europe the group headed by Jean Monnet, with his Action Committee for a United States of Europe, formed the spearhead of an opposition to Gaullism that might be described as both "European" and "Atlantic" in its outlook. True, Jean Monnet was something less than enthusiastic in his defense of the multilateral force, which according to one expert close to him, General Stehlin, was not "realistic" and which, in any case, the American government was to abandon. "We have come to a time of patience," Jean Monnet himself wrote on 26 February 1963. "Nothing has changed, but everything has been delayed" (quoted by Fontaine, *Le Comité d'action pour les Etats-Unis d'Europe*, p. 147). Jean Monnet was never

a man for recriminations. But his position was nonetheless radically
opposed to that of de Gaulle. What was needed, according to him,
was British membership in the Common Market, a genuine European
political authority, and "a European military organization in association with the United States." In short, Jean Monnet, together with
many supporters, was continuing Kennedy's Grand Design. Un-
happily, Kennedy himself was assassinated in November 1963, and his
successor, Lyndon Johnson, preoccupied by his country's growing
participation in the Vietnam War, was to turn his attention away from
Europe and concern himself very little with the idea of NATO
reforms.

Is it possible to measure the influence of this "Atlantic" group on
French opinion? Unfortunately, what data we have are rather too
general in nature. The percentage of those describing themselves as
"satisfied" with the general as president of the Republic immediately
before the press conference was 62 percent. Immediately after the
conference the figure rose to 64 percent. Then it experienced a swift
decline—down to 42 percent in March—and did not rise above 50
percent again until November. It remained at about that figure all
through 1964, rose as high as 66 percent in September 1965, then
declined again to 52 percent at the time of the elections in December.
But it would be extremely arbitrary to link these fluctuations too
closely with de Gaulle's "anti-Atlantic" policy. In a poll taken in
March 1963 only 11 percent of French people thought that the most
important problem was that of foreign policy (as a whole). The
following table shows responses to the question: "What is your
opinion of the United States?"

	Good	Neither good nor bad	Bad	No opinion
1961	49%	32%	7%	12%
1963	46	34	10	10
1964	52	31	11	6
1967	22	46	18	14
1968	35	40	13	12

There is a clear increase in unfavorable opinions after 1964, obviously
connected with the war in Vietnam. But between 1961 and 1963 one
observes no significant change at all. The most interesting poll,

however, was one asking the following question: "Do you approve or disapprove of General de Gaulle's policy with regard to the United States?"

	May 1962	January 1963	September 1965	April 1966
Approve	32%	47%	46%	41%
Disapprove	15	17	21	29
No opinion	53	36	33	30

This indicates that, while General de Gaulle enjoyed fairly widespread approval in this respect, the percentage of those disapproving was steadily increasing at the expense of the no-opinion group. Finally, in the presidential election of December 1965, one fact is certain: Jean Lecanuet, the "Atlantist" par excellence, supported by Jean Monnet, succeeded in preventing the general's election on the first ballot by winning almost 16 percent of the votes cast—which did not prevent the general from being reelected on the second ballot.

In America, reaction to the press conference of 14 January 1963 was very sharp. The general, never inclined to attribute much importance to "press bombardment," as he thought of it, found it in this instance rather exaggerated. "I confess that for some time now both its tone and its refrains where France is concerned have seemed to me excessive." He added: "These flurries in the press, in political circles, in the various more or less official organizations that so abound over the Atlantic, and that are naturally echoed eagerly over here by various kinds of entrenched opponents, all this flurry and fuss, I repeat, can never affect the fundamental things in France as far as America is concerned . . . our friendship and our alliance." This "moral capital," he said, could never be eaten away by "journalistic backbiting" (29 July 1963).

In some sections of American opinion, and especially in government circles within the Democratic Party, all France's actions were henceforth analyzed with suspicion: the continuation of French trade with Cuba, the recognition of the People's Republic of China in January 1964, reluctance in the tariff negotiations between the United States and the Six during the Kennedy Round, and the general's visit to Mexico in March 1964, which was viewed with particular mistrust. Ex-president Truman roundly stated his opinion that General de

Gaulle was trying to compete with the United States in Latin America
and that he would be well advised not to poke his nose into American
affairs, because he was likely to have it cut off. At home, Gaston
Defferre, a socialist opponent, wondered whether the visit had been
made "in order to achieve a *rapproachement* between France and
Mexico, or just to annoy the Americans."

Psychologically, the most serious gesture of all was the general's
refusal to take part personally in the ceremonies on the twentieth
anniversary of the Normandy landings. Had they not been the
indispensable first step in France's liberation? What the general
remembered, however, was that he hadn't been consulted and that
Roosevelt had done his utmost to restrict the powers of the provisional
government within the liberated areas. A petty incident, no doubt,
but indicative of the general's elephantine memory with regard to past
affronts. Then finally, in 1965, there came the start of the Gaullist
offensive against the dollar. But I won't go into that fully until later,
in the last section of this chapter, when dealing with de Gaulle's final
years in power and the big crunch that eventually came.

The question some people were asking themselves in 1965 was
whether the moments of doubt over General de Gaulle's reelection in
December of that year would lead him to adopt a more conciliatory
policy, particularly in his relations with the Americans. Such speculation suggested a singular misunderstanding of that obdurate man.

3. The challenge to the Americans

Once reelected, the general wasted very little time in resuming the
offensive where he had left off and even in intensifying it. Despite a
slight deceleration connected with the "stabilization plan" (a package
of antiinflationary measures introduced by the finance minister,
Valéry Giscard d'Estaing), France's rate of economic growth in the
1960s was magnificent: faster than Germany's, and in 1968 overtaking
that of Italy (which had started from a point much lower on the scale).
In the late 1960s France's gross national product first equaled that of
Britain, then exceeded it. French industrial production moved up neck
and neck with that of the British, and France's foreign trade actually
surpassed Britain's. France had become the fifth-largest industrial
power in the world and the third-largest trading nation, even

outclassing Japan in this latter respect. A closer examination of the facts, and particularly of the social aspects of this phenomenon, undoubtedly shows that things were far from perfect, but in the general's eyes this expansion was a justification of his labors. Had he not named economic expansion as one of the "vast undertakings" he had proposed to the nation? Meanwhile, the development of France's nuclear strikepower was moving doggedly ahead. The first French hydrogen bomb was detonated in 1968, eight years after the first French atomic bomb (and one year after China's). The first nuclear submarines were launched. In the Pentagon, and among American political experts, wry amusement gave way to a certain respect, particularly since France had achieved all this entirely on her own, without any American technological aid. Indeed, in 1967 the Washington government had actively discouraged exportation to France of the giant "control data" computers that would have facilitated certain necessary calculations for the hydrogen bomb.

In 1967, an extremely brilliant journalist and businessman, the founder of *L'Express*, Jean-Jacques Servan-Schreiber, published a book called *Le Défi américain* (*The American Challenge*) that was to sell hundreds of thousands of copies. An admirer of the United States' gigantic industrial capacity, its predominance in almost all the "advanced" industries, its superiority in the management field, and its lead in cybernetics and the space race, he believed that the efforts of isolated countries like France to imitate the Americans in certain spheres were ludicrous. As he saw it, only a united Europe could hope to rival them. The entire nationalistic, "call to arms" side of Gaullism seemed to him absurd.

I am not concerned here with whether Servan-Schreiber was right or wrong, only with making it plain how wrong he was in the eyes of General de Gaulle. The general believed that it was in fact possible to take up this "American challenge." Of course he was quite aware that French power was minimal beside that of America. But he had already achieved "successes"—for example, preventing the realization of Kennedy's Grand Design. And preoccupied as he was with foreign policy above all else, he had the art of acquiring supporters abroad who would increase France's political influence. At first, he had tried to elicit support for his policies from the European countries, and during the Adenauer era had met with some success. But from 1963

onward, open as they all were to the influence of Jean Monnet, these
European partners became increasingly exasperated by de Gaulle's
anti-Atlantism, his anti-integrationism, his stubborn refusal to permit
British entry into the Market, and his continual use of ultimatums over
the common agricultural policy. Well, never mind, the general would
find supporters elsewhere, among the two billion inhabitants of the
third world. He had already made a start with the French-speaking
African nations. In March 1964 he visited Mexico, then ten other
Latin American countries in the autumn. We shall also see how he set
about creating sympathy in Southeast Asia—where the Americans had
by then entangled themselves in the Vietnam War—and in the Arab
countries, by withdrawing French support from Israel.

This policy of courting the support of the third world necessarily
entailed an understanding attitude toward its problems. France was in
fact the country allotting the largest percentage of its GNP to foreign
aid. At the World Trade Conference in Geneva, France put forward a
plan for stabilizing the prices of raw materials that was welcomed by
many poorer countries but was rejected, on the grounds of technical
nonfeasibility, by the Americans. But above all, in order to attract the
good will of the third world it was essential to display opposition to
foreign military bases, to encourage nonalignment, and consequently
to practice in one's own case a policy of relative impartiality between
the Soviet Union and the United States, which meant, if one was an
ally of the United States, disengaging oneself to some extent from that
alliance and moving closer to Moscow.

Seen in this light, de Gaulle's successive moves, perhaps incoherent
at first glance, acquire an admirable unity. It would be absurd to
believe that the unity of his attitude consisted simply in an emotional
anti-Americanism. What the general was after was national independence, as he conceived it, with regard to the United States; and in
order to take the appropriate high tone, he had to have support. In
order to acquire that support, at a time when the popularity of the
United States had declined considerably in the third world, he had to
be seen to make a few steps in the direction of nonalignment, a move
that was inevitably going to hurt feelings in America. But contrary to
what some infuriated Americans imagined, he hadn't the slightest
intention of taking France out of the Atlantic Pact. There was no
chance of that, because he knew that all his maneuvers could only be

carried out under the protection of the United States. After all, without that protection, how could France possibly have continued calmly building up an atomic arsenal? The slightest frown from the Soviet Union would have put a stop to it immediately.

It will be enough at this point to list the general's main policy moves in their chronological order.

First, at a press conference on 21 February 1966, having been unsuccessful in obtaining the modification in NATO's structure he had been demanding since 1958—even though he had never put forward a clear statement of what he envisaged—the general announced that France, without abandoning the Atlantic alliance, was withdrawing from the military side of NATO and in particular from SHAPE, its European headquarters. The United States ambassador, Charles Bohlen, was handed a letter from President de Gaulle to President Johnson. In it, apart from confirming the withdrawal from NATO, the general added a further demand: "France proposes to resume the entire exercise of her sovereignty over her territory, a sovereignty at present breached by the permanent presence of allied military forces and by the use made of her skies; to cease participation in the joint command; and no longer to place her forces at the disposal of the Atlantic Organization" (7 March 1966). President Johnson expressed his concern, remarking that the action proposed would gravely affect the security and the well-being of the citizens of all the allied states. But what could he do? The United States, unlike the Soviet Union, is not given to imposing its views on its allies with tanks. On 1 July 1966, France did in fact withdraw from NATO's military organizations (which moved their headquarters to Brussels), while still remaining a member of the North Atlantic Council. By 1 April 1967, all American and Canadian bases on French territory had been evacuated. A serious problem then arose: if the use of French airspace was forbidden to NATO aircraft, then the organization would be cut completely in two by a vast swath of unusable sky, running west-east over France, Switzerland, and Austria. But because France still needed to make use of NATO's early-warning radar facilities, things did not come to that, and a system of overflight authorization was arranged on a monthly, as opposed to the previous annual, basis. (De Gaulle had protested very strongly when an American aircraft had flown over the Pierrelatte military atomic plant on 16 July 1965.)

Late in June 1966 there came another worrying sign for the
Americans: de Gaulle's dramatic visit to the Soviet Union. It was the
general's belief that détente could not be achieved by direct negotiations between the Americans and the Russians—as it in fact was
during the Nixon era—and in his eyes any *rapprochement* should
take place between the two halves of Europe. Hence the establishment
of an "understanding" with the Soviet Union, in the hope that other
European countries, notably Germany, would follow. Needless to say,
speculation in the United States ran high, and some people even
imagined that the general was contemplating a vast French reversal of
alliances.

Immediately after the Russian visit, General de Gaulle set off on his
travels yet again, this time to Southeast Asia. It was during this tour,
at Phnom penh, capital of the essentially nonaligned Cambodia, that
on 1 September 1966 the general made a speech that stirred up storms
of protest in the United States while at the same time being greeted
by most of the third world with extraordinary enthusiasm. He implied
quite clearly that the United States alone was responsible for the
Vietnam War, whereas the official Washington line was that the
American presence was a response to invasion of South Vietnam by
regular North Vietnamese troops. The general congratulated the
Cambodians on having opted, back in 1954, "courageously and clear-
sightedly for the policy of neutrality." Then he added: "While your
country was successfully preserving its body and its soul, by remaining
master within its own territory, we saw the political and military
authority of the United States arriving in its turn in South Vietnam,
and the war simultaneously blazing up afresh." He went even further.
France "condemned" these events. She intended to "keep her hands
free," and proposed to contribute toward the reestablishment of peace,
a peace "aimed at reestablishing and guaranteeing the neutrality of
the peoples of Indochina, as well as their right to self-determination."
But such a peace was dependent on the withdrawal of the American
forces.

It is impossible not to recognize today that the general was
fundamentally in the right as regards the necessary conditions for a
peace. But in the United States at the time the storm of protest was
almost unanimous. Was this not a blow below the belt, delivered to a
major ally in difficulties?

The next year, 1967, was marked by a further spate of activities and statements calculated to exasperate the Americans. Even the setback for the Gaullists in the March elections did nothing to mollify the general's anti-Americanism.

First of all, faced with a second bid by Britain for Common Market membership, the general remained as adamant as ever in rejecting an "England that is not continental, that because of its Commonwealth and its own insularity still retains distant overseas commitments, and that remains bound to the United States by all kinds of special agreements." True, Britain was beginning to "show signs" of *rapprochement* with Europe. But in the present state of things, "the English . . . envisage their participation as being automatically bound to lead the Community into becoming other than it is" (16 May 1967).

Then there came the Six-Day War (5–10 June) in the Middle East between Israel and the Arab countries. Totally disregarding the motives underlying the Israeli attack, the general promptly condemned the aggressor. On 24 May, at the height of the crisis that preceded the war, France had put forward the idea of a conference of the four great powers to examine the Arab-Israel problem, but there had been very little likelihood of this lead being followed. As one deputy remarked during a foreign policy debate, France's "policy exceeds her means." But above all, breaking with a fifteen-year tradition of pro-Israeli policy, General de Gaulle ordered an embargo on fifty Mirage aircraft ordered, and already paid for, by Israel. In January 1968, after an Israeli attack on the Beirut airport, he was to go further and forbid the exportation of all spare parts. He referred to the Israelis as "an overweening and aggressive" people. In the United States, where the Jewish vote is very sizable and where support for Israel is accepted policy, the French position was taken as a further insult.

Worse was to come. In late July the general traveled to Canada. On 20 July he broke his journey to visit the tiny French islands of Saint-Pierre and Miquelon, which, it will be remembered, he had rallied to the Free French movement in December 1941 against Roosevelt's wishes: a good opportunity of reasserting French independence. Later, with the reluctant agreement of the Canadian federal government, he also paid a visit to Quebec Province. On 24 July, in response to clamors from an enthusiastic crowd gathered below, he emerged onto the balcony of the Hôtel de Ville in Montreal and delivered a short impromptu speech. Was he carried away by his emotions, or was it a calculated act? At all events, he came out with some amazing things. "There is an atmosphere here," he said, "that reminds one of the Liberation." Instead of referring to "French-speaking Canadians," he used the term "the French in Canada." And he concluded with: "Long live free Quebec! Long live French Canada! Long live France!"

France had abandoned the French Canadians in 1763, when she signed the Treaty of Paris. That a cultural, economic, and emotional *rapprochement* would have been welcome was not in doubt. But the phrase *"Vive le Québec libre,"* which he had used, was the slogan of the Quebec separatists, the declared enemies of the very federal government that had invited the general to the country in the first place and had then agreed to his touring Quebec before even visiting Ottawa, the Canadian capital. There was a tremendous outcry. The Canadian prime minister, Lester Pearson, issued a statement on 25 July describing the general's phrase as "unacceptable." The latter, taking this as an insult, immediately canceled the rest of his tour and returned to France.

There can be no doubt that a large number of French Canadians approved of what de Gaulle had done. His speech later forced the federal government to bring in a great many measures favorable to the French language and the interests of Quebec. On the other hand, all the world's English-speakers, Canadian, British, and American—the latter near neighbors of Quebec and heavy investors in the province— were extremely indignant. Surely, considering that he was the guest of a country with an English-speaking majority, his behavior had been extremely ill-mannered? But the general expressed no contrition. For him it had simply been one more opportunity to oppose what he called "United States encroachment."

One may justifiably say that it was during the summer of 1967 and the following few months that Franco-American tension reached its climax.

4. Gold, the crisis in France, and the general's fall

As if to underline these innumerable French moves, which were characterized by what Alfred Grosser has called the general's

"American obsession," changes in the world's economy were at the same time focusing attention on the problem of gold and the dollar. De Gaulle, himself no economist but anxious to use every means at his disposal to restore French "national independence," became influenced very early on by the great economist and financier Jacques Rueff. Although Rueff had been de Gaulle's adviser for some time, he did not come into particular prominence until the very early days of the Fifth Republic, from September to December 1958, when he presided over the committee of experts formed to look into the question of economic and financial reforms. It was Rueff more than anyone who was the inspiration behind de Gaulle's long campaign against the privileged role of the dollar (and to a lesser extent the pound sterling) as the gold exchange standard. Because its exchange rate was unshakable (thirty-five dollars to the gold ounce), the currency of the United States was universally accepted as the global medium of exchange. This system had worked perfectly well as long as America's vast gold reserves had continued to increase, that is, up to and including 1957. But since 1958 there had been an undeniable erosion of those reserves.

This erosion was linked, needless to say, with America's enormous expenses abroad: occupation forces, economic and military aid, and then the Vietnam War. But it derived also from the accelerating rate of private American investment throughout the world and particularly in Western Europe. For many years such investments had been welcomed. But in the early 1960s fears began to emerge that the Americans were in the process of gradually taking over certain essential industries, in particular the "advanced" industries, which require a great deal of research money and into which France herself, at some risk to her economy, had now begun to venture.

Now the fact that the dollar was accepted as a medium of exchange equal to gold clearly presented the Americans with a temptation: that of issuing dollars for the purpose of investing them. When Kennedy decreased the rate of taxation paid by American firms, a measure taken in order to stimulate economic recovery, he made it possible for those firms to use the resulting liquid assets for foreign investment. At a press conference on 4 February 1965, General de Gaulle made public his feelings on this subject—feelings inspired, I repeat, by Jacques Rueff: "The convention conferring a transcendent value on the dollar as an international currency no longer rests upon its initial foundation, which was the possession by America of the largest part of the world's gold.'' The United States, he went on, was running up debts abroad "at no expense to itself.'' "In practice, what it owes it pays, partly at least, in dollars, over the issuing of which it alone has control, instead of paying those debts wholly in gold, the value of which is real, and which one comes to possess only by earning it. . . . This unilateral facility conferred upon America helps to create a vague notion that the dollar is an impartial and international token of exchange, whereas it is an instrument of credit appertaining to a particular state.'' The result was all manner of abuses amounting to a "sort of expropriation of certain enterprises to the benefit of American firms.''

From then on, scarcely a press conference went by without de Gaulle resuming his campaign against the dollar in one form or another. In addition, suiting his actions to his words, he saw to it that France converted a large proportion of its currency reserves into gold. This accelerated the erosion of American gold reserves and had tremendous repercussions. Many Americans saw the move as a challenge from the general, the most serious of all. At the same time, as a result of the takeover of the computer industry in France by an American company, General Electric, the French government from 1962 to 1966 instituted a policy of absolute restriction with regard to American investments. After 1966, however, because all such investment capital was finding its way into the other Common Market countries, France switched to a less rigorous selective policy, made easier by the fact that its partners, as well as Britain, had all become equally concerned, as Britain's Labour prime minister, Harold Wilson, put it, to prevent domination of the European economy by American investments.

General de Gaulle's motives were undoubtedly more political than economic. Taking a long view, and leaving aside the question of whether it is actually possible to replace the gold exchange standard with gold itself as the basis for international exchange, it is reasonable to claim, with Stanley Hoffmann, that "the dramatic crisis of the world currency system in 1971–73 demonstrated the soundness of his criticisms.''

In the short term, however, the gold war was to end in the general's defeat.

That defeat was linked with the extraordinary upheaval that shook

France in May and June 1968. The upheaval itself had very little to do with Franco-American relations, so there is no necessity to describe it in detail here. There had already been a number of serious student uprisings in the United States, Germany, and other countries of the Western world. These revolts, occurring in periods of great prosperity, but also of frustrations and worries over career opportunities, testify above all to a crisis of our civilization itself, bound up with the emergence of both a great but unequally divided affluence and what is in human terms a frightening technological expansion. What made the wave of protest so much more dramatic in France than elsewhere was the fact that the student crisis was overlaid by a general strike and that in combination these two phenomena seemed briefly on the verge of leading to a dissolution of the state.

It is noteworthy that although the student and worker "movements"—there was no real solidarity between them—certainly attacked de Gaulle as the holder of power ("Ten years is enough!"), no criticism was ever made of his anti-Americanism. On the contrary, the leftists, the communists, and the various other protesters of all sorts themselves displayed the most violent anti-American feelings and clearly saw the Vietnam War as the very symbol of "imperialism."

On the surface, it looked as though de Gaulle had carried the day. He ordered the dissolution of the National Assembly, and the French people, as though terrified by what they had done, elected 355 Gaullist deputies out of a total of 490. In fact, however, this victory was due less to the general than to his prime minister, the shrewd Georges Pompidou, who managed with some difficulty to persuade him that calling a general election would be a wiser move than the vague referendum scheme that de Gaulle himself had been pondering. After the crisis, the general felt obliged to replace Pompidou with his faithful foreign minister Maurice Couve de Murville, a man some American weeklies had compared to Talleyrand but who, like Talleyrand himself, fatally lacked the power to arouse the enthusiasm of the masses. This was to become plain in April 1969, when a complicated referendum on the "regionalization" of France produced a majority of "noes" and led to the immediate resignation of the great and thereafter silent man.

It was during the intervening months, however, that his defeat on the gold front had occurred. The franc, considered until May 1968 as a safe currency, fell victim in that month to an immediate and total

crisis of confidence. Twice, in July and November 1968, the "flight
from the franc" reached such proportions that its exchange value shot
down dramatically. Nevertheless, de Gaulle refused to devalue. In
order to restore the franc's value, larger amounts of money were
needed than France had available in gold and foreign-exchange
reserves. In other words, the Bank of France needed support from the
central foreign banks and, in particular, *American support*.

In the United States, the immediate and superficial reaction to the
May–June crisis had been to smile: America's indefatigable adversary
and critic was suddenly powerless in the face of an incomprehensible
revolt on the part of his own people. But irony soon gave way to
disquiet. What would happen if France "swung over" to the left or
even into the camp of the communists? On 30 May, when a short
speech from the general, accompanied by a million-strong Gaullist
demonstration in the Champs-Elysées, made it clear that the old lion
was not dead, there was a huge sigh of relief in the United States, and
the Gaullist triumph in the subsequent elections brought further
welcome reassurance. As a result, on 24 November 1968, when the
general refused to devalue the franc, President Johnson conveyed his
congratulations and promised United States support. The franc, for a
time at least, had been saved (though later, in August 1969 under
Pompidou, it was to undergo a moderate devaluation of 12.5 percent).

During his last months in power de Gaulle ceased all manifestations
of anti-Americanism. One interesting detail: he was delighted by the
election of the Republican Richard Nixon to the presidency in
November 1968. De Gaulle considered Nixon a man of great ability
and had told him so back in the late 1950s. For de Gaulle, Nixon's
accession to power signified a return in the United States to a healthy
realism. When Nixon visited Paris, in late February 1969, de Gaulle
showered him with demonstrations of friendship.

This era comes to an end with a gesture that, for all that it was quite
silent and in a way passive, nevertheless had profound significance.
Exactly twenty-three days before the referendum of 27 April that was
to carry him from power, on 4 April 1969, by a tacit agreement of
renewal, General de Gaulle confirmed France's adherence to the
Atlantic alliance, thus putting an end to the anguished speculations of
all those Americans, and there were many, who had thought they
discerned in his resolutely hostile attitude the ominous signs of a great
reversal of alliances.

Conclusion

1. "Back to normalcy"

During the whole of the period when General de Gaulle was governing France, and especially after 1962, Franco-American relations had acquired a certain sensational character. For seven years the American press had kept the full blaze of its spotlight on this figure, who was seen simultaneously as the last great surviving "historical character" from the war years, an unexpected obstacle to American ambitions, an inspired prophet, a Jove hurling *banderillas* rather than thunderbolts, and lastly as an incomprehensible and intolerable man. Almost every day he could command the front page of the great east-coast newspapers, the *New York Times* and the *Washington Post*.

The extreme ease with which his successor, Georges Pompidou, was elected in the face of a divided left was greeted with relief. That things were returning to normal again was apparent from one unmistakable sign: France vanished from the front page and found herself relegated to the modest supporting role that she ought logically to have been playing all along. The irritation faded as if by magic. The general's arrogance was forgotten across the Atlantic, and when he was mentioned, which was rarely, he was seen as a vast, silent shadow, or later, after his death on 9 November 1970, as a historical figure purged of all power to harm.

Better still, the relations established between Georges Pompidou and Richard Nixon proved much easier than those between de Gaulle and Johnson. The dazzling emergence of Henry Kissinger at the head of foreign policy, first operating under the aegis of the National Security Council, then as secretary of state, contributed very largely to this "detente." In the first place, during the years before his rise to stardom, Kissinger had never concealed the fact that he was far from disapproving of all de Gaulle's activities. Unlike McNamara, he was not opposed to French possession of nuclear arms and, instead of following the American fashion of the 1960s, which was to scorn those arms as insignificant, he was perfectly well aware that France, on her own smaller scale but by her own unaided efforts, was acquiring a by no means negligible deterrent. Kissinger and Nixon were not unconditional supporters of the 35-dollar gold ounce either, as was made evident when the dollar was in practice detached from gold in August 1971. Neither of them, moreover, was a supporter of the "Atlantic partnership" theory in the form favored by Jean Monnet, that of the "two pillars." Neither the construction of a united Europe nor the admission of Britain into the Common Market (to which Pompidou in fact finally consented) was seen by them as a sacred dogma outside which lay certain damnation. Lastly, *rapprochement* with the Soviet Union, and even with China—already set on foot by de Gaulle—was in their eyes a prime necessity. They also encouraged the German Federal Republic to follow a similar path toward détente and the recognition of East Germany.

In his book *The Troubled Partnership*, published in 1965, Kissinger castigated the gift that certain Americans have for self-delusion. De Gaulle prevented them from realizing certain plans. For many Americans, being deprived of something they ardently desire is a tragedy. But as Kissinger suggested, there is something that can be just as tragic and perhaps more poignant: achieving one's desires and realizing that they are hollow. In the America–de Gaulle quarrel, Kissinger also remarked, the Americans sometimes allowed themselves to be guided by Jean Monnet and Robert Schuman, while de Gaulle made the mistake of being too rational, of having excessively long-term aims. The irony of the Franco-American rivalry was that de Gaulle's conceptions tended to outrun his means, while the power of the United States was superior to its conceptions. Kissinger also believed, despite a less than wholehearted admiration of de Gaulle's style, that history would prove his conceptions to have been superior to those of most of his critics. Fundamentally he was comparable to Churchill but much more uncompromising in his language, which infuriated the Americans. But then, as Kissinger also pointed out, outraged pride is not a good guide in political matters.

While Pompidou found himself reduced, as it were, to France's own resources, hesitating between a "fresh start" policy (initiated by his first foreign minister, Maurice Schumann) and one of Gaullist "continuity" (pursued ardently by the second, Michel Jobert), the United States, with Kissinger, boldly resumed its "leadership." By organizing Nixon's visit to China, by succeeding through negotiation, through sheer realism, through persuasion, in securing the withdrawal of all American troops from Vietnam, by resolutely stepping in before the Russians to call a halt to the Yom Kippur War, then setting up peace talks in Geneva between the Israelis and the Arabs, by applying with apparently inexhaustible energy his conviction that diplomacy is a matter of persuasion and not constraint, Kissinger was leaving a lasting mark on world politics during the very time when Nixon, for internal reasons—the Watergate scandal—was being steadily forced toward resignation by the reactions of a fundamentally democratic public opinion. France, meanwhile, could only look on; for want of the weight carried by only a really great power, none of the initiatives she attempted, in Vietnam or in the Middle East, bore any real fruit.

Thus on the whole everything remained "formal." True, at a conference at the Hague in 1969 the French veto against British entry to the Common Market was lifted, but, at the same time, Europe was being fragmented by economic disputes of every kind. True, France continued the general's pro-Arab, anti-Israeli policy, but much more from a desire to sell arms to Libya than as the result of any long-term strategic concept. Georges Pompidou visited the United States in February 1970, but the reception given him by the American Jews was violent in the extreme, and Nixon was obliged to make a polite gesture—an unplanned appearance at the farewell banquet—as a demonstration of American friendship. The interest of the next Nixon-Pompidou meeting, in the Azores on 13–14 December 1971, centered mainly on a new American devaluation and the French president's arrival in a Concorde. But the Concorde wasn't selling in the United States, and there was no certainty that it would even be allowed to land there.

The formation of a new government, after the April 1973 French general elections, was to introduce a little more piquancy into French foreign policy for a year or so, albeit without producing any greater results. A personal adviser to President Pompidou, Michel Jobert, not previously even remotely familiar to the general public, was appointed as foreign minister. For a year, until Georges Pompidou's death on 2 April 1974, France's attitude to the United States recovered some of its acerbity. Apprehensive that the remarkable improvement in Soviet-American relations might eventually lead to a veritable "condominium" of the world by the two superpowers, Michel Jobert began to adopt an increasingly sharp tone with regard to all American moves. But his stay at the Quai d'Orsay was too short, and his language somewhat too esoteric, for it to be possible to judge whether what underlay his behavior was a new grand design, a resumption on a smaller scale of de Gaulle's anti-Americanism, or simply a total incompatibility of temperament between him and Henry Kissinger.

2. Indifference, incomprehension, affection

At the time the United States became independent, the new nation had a population of about 2.5 million and France one of 25 million. Two centuries later, in 1976, the figures are 210 million and 52 million. At first glance those figures tend to inspire one with rather obvious thoughts about the pendulum of power. But as far as the relations between the two peoples are concerned, mention of those "millions" ought to conjure up one central impression: their mutual indifference. Workers in the mass, restricted to their own narrow environments, whether agricultural or industrial, pay little attention to the rest of the world, except in the case of some exceptional occurrence, and the degree of their ignorance in the matter of international relations, a subject much studied by sociologists and political scientists, is sometimes fantastic. Besides, it is only too well known that major elections are almost never fought on foreign policy platforms.

So if we are to speak of relations between two peoples, what we have to concentrate on above all are the relations between their two governments, between their administrators, traders, navigators, businessmen, missionaries, and, over and above those categories, between their cultured classes, who alone possess the groundwork of knowledge necessary for curiosity to emerge; such knowledge presupposes leisure, reading, and travel. Let us not forget that, until the middle of the twentieth century, factory workers, peasants, and small traders did not know what vacations were. The men, because of their period of compulsory military service (which exists in France but not in the United States) did travel rather more than the women. But travel for which one is culturally unprepared, especially when narrowly circumscribed by the unit to which one is attached, does little to educate one in foreign ways of life and thought.

The only "mass contacts" possible are of three types: military expeditions, immigration, and tourism. It has to be admitted that, as far as Franco-American relations are concerned, these three factors have had a very limited incidence, at least until very recently. The expeditionary force sent out in 1780 under Rochambeau consisted of 6,000 men, a figure later increased to 10,000 by reinforcements. A century and a half later, 2,000,000 "Sammies" came over to France, but most of them stayed no more than a few months. In 1944–45, almost 8,000,000 American soldiers were ferried across to Europe. Many of them merely passed through France, although it is true that there were to be American bases in the country until the spring of 1967.

Emigration from France to the United States has been even less significant. Of 40 million Europeans who left their own continent for good between 1800 and 1930, 18 million were British, 6 million German, 9 million Italian, and less than 1 million French (and the majority of those settled in North Africa). Whereas there were almost 7 million people in the United States in 1930 either born in Germany or born in the United States of German parents, the number of those born in France or of French parents cannot have exceeded 200,000 (not, of course, counting the French-speaking Canadians). Thus France has never had in the United States those natural spokesmen for the mother country provided by other American citizens of recent foreign origin. There have been German, Irish, and Italian sectors of the electorate that have on occasion greatly affected Washington policy and have played their part at all times in major national electoral choices. The French, mostly individual, scattered immigrants, insignificant in number, have never played such a role.

As for tourism, before the First World War that remained something restricted to a chosen few. The "travelers," those who wrote about their visits, were not really tourists. Between 1830 and 1840, F. C. Bowen has calculated, the east-west voyage took an average of thirty-three days (minimum twenty-five, maximum forty-four). "The passengers thank heaven when they escape with no more than a month at sea" (Rémond, *Les Etats-Unis devant l'opinion française*, p. 21). As a result, in the nineteenth century the annual number of tourists in both directions has to be counted in hundreds rather than thousands, though one ought also to add those making the crossing with a view to a longer stay, the "diplomats, traders, and millionaires," as René Rémond puts it. Between the two world wars, when the new giant liners had shortened the crossing to a mere five or six days, the numbers increased. There were several tens of thousands of Americans each year coming to Europe (300,000 in 1929), and several thousand French people crossing to the United States. But it was still "millionaire" tourism: the 1929 slump reduced the numbers by 55 percent. Only since the end of World War II have the airplane and American affluence made real mass travel possible to Europe—and to France in particular, since it is the main transit area. Always very sensitive to economic and political fluctuations, American tourism in France did not move beyond the million mark (arrivals in France) until 1967. Since 1945, moreover, America has moved down from first place. In 1968, only one out of every eleven visitors was American, whereas one out of every five was British and one out of every six was German. These modern-day tourists are to a large extent middle class.

But what sort of tourism is it? Taine, in his *Voyage aux Pyrénées*, listed six types of tourists: the walkers, the gastronomes, the scientists, the sedentary conformists, the curious, and the family parties. Jean Ginier, in a recent thesis, distinguishes "family tourists," "addicts of group travel," "solitary tourists," "sedentary tourists," and "businessmen tourists." Let us say that walking and gastronomy would be atypical American motivations.

One final point: such mass contacts never do anything to improve the image that two peoples form of one another. They merely reinforce existing stereotypes. But those stereotypes are not the creation of the masses, who are always completely indifferent to one another. It is the educated, cultured classes that invent and then add to them. Here we reach the phenomena that lie at the heart of our subject: *incomprehension* and *affection*.

"France," André Siegfried wrote,

occupies a place apart in the United States. No other country, at certain times, is more passionately loved. On the other hand, no other nation is more disparaged or more harshly condemned. It seems that there is always an excess in either direction, that either illusion or deep disappointment is alternately dominant. With England, there is no sentimentality but a sense of security: the British are family. With France, it seems to be a passionate love relationship, in which antipathy, never completely eliminated, sometimes gains the upper hand (*Les Etats-Unis d'aujourd'hui*, p. 313).

Antipathy? Certainly incomprehension, at any rate. The quarrels have left their mark across two centuries of history. They began in 1782 with the peace negotiations, grew under France's National Convention, of which President Washington was decidedly not an admirer, reached a climax with the "undeclared war," and continued from Jefferson to Jackson over the indemnities relating to the privateer war. They flared up again under Napoleon III over his Mexican adventure, then again early in the Third Republic over the Spanish-American War. The Dreyfus affair triggered off a campaign of censure in the American press. Then, after the friendly intermission of 1917–18, the conflict became more intense than ever, first over the treaty, in which Wilson was seen as being dominated by the "cynical" Clemenceau, and then over the war-debt problem. After the fall of France in 1940 we find an amused contempt for de Gaulle the "prima donna" and later for the defects of the Fourth Republic, plus a certain disgruntlement over France's 25 percent communist vote. Then, finally, under de Gaulle, there came the American exasperation at his "ingratitude." Meanwhile, on the French side, there were all those who formed the currents of anti-American feeling I attempted to classify earlier: communists, neutralists, colonialists, and Gaullists.

It is this phenomenon that one must attempt to explain for, after all, the two countries that together symbolized the "Western revolution" at the end of the eighteenth century still preserve a common ideal: that of democracy, liberty, and equality.

One can, of course, like André Siegfried, find underlying moral causes: "Our scale of values is totally different: Cartesian rationalism, which has left its mark on ten generations of Frenchmen, is diametrically opposed to Bostonian puritanism and Wesleyan sentimentalism; our moral system, based on the rule of the family and the classical respect for moderation, evokes no echo in the moral system preached by Anglo-Saxon Protestantism.'' In consequence, the Americans look upon the French as immoral. ''The very realism of the French mind, one essential virtue of which is not to mince words when uttering its judgments, is not seen as a desirable form of intelligence but as a shocking expression of cynicism: they talk of the 'cynical Frenchman.' ... In the United States, as in England, they know how to be realists when it comes to deeds, but it is 'not done' for one's mind to take cognizance of the fact'' (*Les Etats-Unis d'aujourd'hui*, p. 315).

Important though these observations may be, there is no doubt that we need to look further back, to the roots in both countries' pasts that still feed the trunks and branches visible today.

First, there is the unending conflict between the French and the English. Though such close neighbors, the two peoples have never understood each other. And the essence of the United States, despite the wars of independence and the republican system, is profoundly British. Not only the original settlers but almost all the immigrants until 1850 were British. Those who came later (the Irish, Germans, Scandinavians, and Dutch) never put up much resistance—especially after the second generation—to assimilation by the American ''melting pot.'' The Italians, Slavs, Greeks, and Jews of the ''new immigration'' presented more of a problem. But their arrival in such numbers triggered a protective reflex, and the immigration laws brought in during 1921 and 1924 succeeded in preserving the Anglo-Saxon character of the United States just in time. Whether one looks at the educational system, particularly the universities—at the very architecture of the buildings where higher learning is dispensed, so obviously Oxford- and Cambridge-inspired—at the style of cooking or serving meals, at table manners, at the way households are run, at social life generally, the British imprint is still indelibly there. A certain francophile snobbery does admittedly exist, manifested in the names of many smart stores or the attribution to France of dubious culinary processes, such as ''French-fried potatoes'' or the ''French dressing'' used on salad. But the real snobbery, the most authentic, is that of an artificial return to British pronunciation in speech and the use of upper-class British slang.

This impregnation by the British ethos, whatever the exceptions, also left its mark indelibly imprinted on the American concept of the state. The English, having got their revolutions over with in the seventeenth century, progressed toward democracy by means of a gradual, reformist development. Violence played only a secondary role in the process. Respect for the state, represented by the sovereign, and for the written and unwritten law remains very much alive to this day. In a sense, it was in the name of that very law that the Americans used force to achieve their independence. But that done, they settled down again to the more congenial prospect of progress by reform. Moreover, they were extremely fortunate in that historical chance had provided them with a small group of exceptional men to plan and draft their Constitution.

To the French, on the contrary, the state in 1789 represented the enemy. The new principles were introduced by violence. Since the Cartesian cast of mind has a constant tendency to prefer logic to life, those principles were carried to their absolute—and wildly absurd—conclusions, as in Saint-Just's "No liberty for the enemies of liberty!" Thus, thanks to the Terror, the new state became almost as hated as the old. There followed a reaction against the new abuses, then reaction against that reaction. There was the Terror under the Convention, but also the White Terror of 1815. If we take May 1789 as the date of France's first *coup d'état*, then there have been at least fourteen others since: 10 August 1792; 18 Fructidor, year V (September 1797); Germinal; Prairial; 18 Brumaire (November 1799); 1814; Napoleon's return, 1815; July 1830; February 1848; December 1851; 4 September 1870; 10 July 1940; the liberation; 13 May 1958. While the Americans piously retained the same Constitution and changed it gradually by successive amendments (even the seceding South carried over its essentials in 1861), the French, always enemies of the state, have experienced a score or so regimes during the same period, some provisional, some "permanent."

If the state is the enemy, then it is basically lawful to evade the taxes it imposes. If the state inspires general respect, then such things as avoiding taxes, black marketeering, and so on, indeed everything unlawful, are seen as indistinguishable from sin or, at any rate, as cynical and disgraceful. The Frenchman pays just as much tax to the state as the American, although the distribution between direct and indirect taxes is not the same. Yet the American is often convinced that the Frenchman pays none at all, simply because the Frenchman is so ready to proclaim from the rooftop that not to pay taxes is his dearest wish.

Another source of incomprehension is the different degree of attachment to the land in the two countries.

As a result of historical chance, France, which like all other countries in the eighteenth century was a peasant nation, possessed a very large number of small peasant landowners. The Revolution, by freeing them from feudal rights and bringing the possessions of the clergy and the *émigrés* onto the market, increased this tendency without carrying it to its ultimate conclusion. In other words, besides all the peasant properties, there was also an enormous quantity of aristocratic or middle-class land. With a growing rural population until the mid-nineteenth century, "land hunger" became acute, especially since the physical area of the country remained more or less the same. One of the Frenchman's characteristics is therefore a love of the land. Not of just any land: of his. Even if he is a member of the middle class, or if he has succumbed to the pull of industry and moved into the city, the possession of a plot of land, of a house, haunts him all his life. He does not emigrate, or if by chance he does—to Algeria, for example—he takes this passionate love of the soil with him. He is infinitely stable, rooted to one spot.

Although excessive generalizations should always be avoided, one can say with some justification that the American has never felt this passion to possess his own piece of land. During the first two-thirds of the nineteenth century he saw immense and apparently inexhaustible territories being opened up to him. The mobility that is the very essence of immigration was maintained within the new national territory, encouraged by the pull of a constantly advancing frontier. Although the famous historian Frederick Jackson Turner went too far in seeing the frontier as one of the origins of democracy, he was certainly correct in regarding it as one of the most important constituents in the formation of the American psyche. For the newly arrived immigrant, attachment to his own small plot no longer has the same meaning. He has already taken the risk of abandoning the one where he grew up. Why should he not keep on moving, keep searching for ever broader, more beautiful, more abundant lands elsewhere?

In line with these two mentalities there are probably two correspondingly different attitudes to economics in general. The Frenchman saves in order to acquire land or enlarge his holding. Even today, moving a working-class population inevitably results in high drama.

The American prefers taking risks, searching for wider horizons. These attitudes lead to two contradictory work methods. The Frenchman, says André Siegfried, "does not really excel except in individual effort, freed from strict disciplines and standardized cooperative processes. But in American eyes such a system is outdated, it leads nowhere, and is worthy of indifference and contempt" (*Les Etats-Unis d'aujourd'hui*, p. 315). Naturally this is another stereotype, since a deeper examination shows that the French, once freed from the constraints imposed by the "family" firm, become eager "Saint-Simonians," ready to spread their wings in the vastest of undertakings. They constructed the Suez Canal, secured themselves through their banks a dominant place in world economic imperialism, and, after 1945, their economy expanded proportionately much faster than that of the United States, faster even than that of Germany. Never mind! The stereotype is still there. The English and the Germans are "serious," the French aren't. French brandy, France's two hundred cheeses, and the Folies Bergères can still make people forget Concorde, the SECAM color television system, France's lead in the superconductor field, and her atomic industry. At least the American experts at the Hudson Institute are not taken in, thank goodness.

The French have equally false and unjust notions about the Americans. Since every human collectivity has its occasional defects and localized diseases, the vast number of French people who have never been to the United States, and who know it only through articles written by journalists either avid for sensational stories or enslaved by the fashion of denigration for denigration's sake, see America by turns as a hive of gangsters or mafiosi, as the country they see in westerns, where every argument is settled with a gun, as a den of hippies, long-haired students, and the like, or as a permanent battlefield between blacks and whites. They criticize American visitors to Europe for their moralizing tone or their arrogance. They remain totally ignorant of the vast middle stratum of people that dominates the United States, of its hard work, its discipline, its virtues, and its civic sense, and also of the formidable pressure it exerts. An individualist, the Frenchman builds a wall around his little house, often knows nothing about his neighbors, and is jealously secretive about how much he earns, how much he spends, and often even about which way he votes. The American has no fence around his yard and cannot buy a piece of furniture without all his neighbors expressing their interest. For the French, that would be intolerable interference, while to an American the French are undisciplined egoists.

In addition, even when they practice no religion, Americans rarely describe themselves openly as atheists. Since the separation of church from state in the United States has also preserved them from clerical-anticlerical controversies, they are inclined to be very harsh in their verdicts on the skeptical French, who still, from time to time, pass laicizing and antireligious laws. The American Irish and the French Canadians have also made their contribution to the blanket of suspicion that hangs over the land of the Folies Bergères—where the audiences consist almost wholly of foreign tourists.

Among all these multifaceted distorting mirrors, is there any chink left for *affection*? Oddly, it does exist, and it is strong. In the United States it is to be found above all on the East Coast, in the South, in Louisiana, in the big cities of the West, and in the universities. In those places you will still find the myth of Lafayette, and his name, devoid as it is of any particular political resonance, always makes a good effect in speeches. But what you find above all is a very great and sympathetic curiosity with regard to French affairs. The Society for French Historical Studies has hundreds of members. Some of the best American political scientists and sociologists, such as Lawrence Wylie and Stanley Hoffmann at Harvard and Nicolas Wahl at Princeton, and many excellent historians, such as Norman Palmer, Louis Gottschalk, Arno Mayer, Stewart Hughes, David Pinckney, Gordon Wright, and many more, are devoting all or a large part of their labors to France. Certain anthologies, such as Donald McKay's *The United States and France* (1951), *Modern France* (1953), edited by Edward Mead Earle, and *In Search of France* (1962), edited by Robert Bowie, count among the most reliable available analyses of the transformations France is undergoing. At moments there are brief explosions of enthusiasm, proving that France, the former great nation, now less than a major world power, still retains its essential power of attraction in the eyes of America, the great nation of the twentieth century.

As for the French, the torrents of antiimperialist, anticapitalist propaganda continually being pumped out (from the obvious sources) seem to have almost no effect on American popularity. Since about 1950, all the polls taken to determine the French order of preference for foreign nations have placed the United States first. The Vietnam War, passionately exploited by the French left, sometimes led to incidents and certainly soured the atmosphere considerably. Its conclusion, with the withdrawal of American troops, then the victory of the communist North, cleared the air only slowly.

But beyond the incomprehension that is normal between all peoples, however close, beyond the indifference of the masses, the disputes over specific issues, the simplistic and stereotyped judgments, there remains, where the United States is concerned, one special factor: its power. The world's foremost economic power, its foremost military power alongside the Soviet Union, and beyond doubt its leader as regards the average living standard of its population, the United States draws the eyes of the whole world—which is to a very large extent dependent on its decisions and its behavior—and, in particular, the eyes of France. The same is true of the Soviet Union. The United States is the symbol of "capitalism" just as the Soviet Union is the symbol of "communism." Once that situation became established, reality flew out the window, and purely emotional propaganda shunted aside any deeper analysis of what was in fact an extraordinarily complex reality. For there is less difference between the American capitalism of 1978 and the capitalism of socialist Sweden than there is between the American capitalism of 1978 and the capitalism of Herbert Hoover of the 1920s, the era of big business and unrestricted, almost limitless "free enterprise." It was the word "capitalism" itself that became the sacred or reviled monster (just as the word "communism" did in the case of the Soviet Union). The opponents of capitalism were to stress the alienation of the wage earner and the existence of the "poor" in the United States. The opponents of communism pointed out that alienation of the wage earner can occur just as easily in the case of an all-powerful state governed by a minority party, and that the poverty threshold officially laid down in America would leave millions of Russian workers below it in quantitative terms. While these two countries remain the only two superpowers, they will continue to draw upon themselves the world's polarized admiration and hate.

None of this detracts from the old fund of affection, however vague it may be, that still outweighs everything else, because it has the weight of history behind it, because that history has in general been one of peace between the two peoples, and because, whenever violence did occur, both found themselves naturally, as it were, on the same side.

Ought we to speak of a "special relationship" between the French and the Americans during these two centuries of history? If we are speaking of diplomacy, of strategy, of economics, or even of intellectual influence, then the answer must surely be no. But if we turn aside from those essential realities, if we move onto the intangible yet fundamental plane of sentiment and the attraction it can exert, then yes! In the last quarter of the twentieth century I do not hesitate to assert it: Franco-American relations have never lost the mysterious charm that assures them a place apart in the history of mankind.

Selected Bibliography

THE SUBJECT OF THIS BOOK is so vast, covering as it does more than two centuries of history, that an *exhaustive* bibliography would take up several volumes and require a lifetime of labor. It has therefore been judged wiser to provide simply a working bibliography of more practical dimensions, since researchers and students should be in a position to trace essential sources by indirect means.

A conscious choice has therefore been made not to list either archive material (which fills hundreds of miles of shelfspace in Washington, Paris, and even London) or much other printed material in the form of documents, correspondence, memoirs, and so on.

What has been provided is a list of works written from firsthand knowledge, in other words, books written by good historians after consulting the appropriate sources and carrying out extensive research.

Since there exist thousands of works, some on French history, some on American, in which information relevant to our subject may be found, it has been decided to list only books that deal directly with one or more of the episodes that have directly involved the relations between the two countries.

There then follows a list of "great classics," meaning basic books written by authors from one of the two countries about the other.

1. Scholarly works dealing with Franco-American relations

The listing is alphabetical in subsections. Insofar as possible, the divisions follow the chronology of the historical events.

RELATIONS BEFORE 1776

Bolton, H. E., and Marshall, T. M. *The Colonization of North America, 1492-1783*. New York, 1920.

Chesnel, P. *Histoire de Cavelier de la Salle: Exploration et conquête du bassin du Mississipi*. Paris, 1904.

Giraud, Marcel. *Histoire de la Louisiane*. Paris, 1957.

Jaray, G. L. *L'Empire français d'Amérique, 1534-1803*. Paris, 1938.

La Roncière, Charles, Tramond, J., and Lauvrière, E. *L'Amérique*. Paris, 1932. (Vol. 1 of *L'Histoire des colonies françaises*, edited by G. Hanotaux and J. Martineau.)

Mauro, Frédéric. *L'Expansion européenne (1600-1870)*. Paris, 1964.

IN THE PEROD OF INDEPENDENCE AND REVOLUTIONS

Bonnel, Ulane. *La France, les Etats-Unis et la guerre de course, 1797-1815*. Paris, 1961.

Castries, Duc René de. *La France et l'indépendance américaine*. Paris, 1975.

Childs, Frances S. *French Refugee Life in the United States, 1790-1800: An American Chapter of the French Revolution*. Baltimore, 1940.

Corwin, Edward S. *French Policy and the American Alliance of 1778*. Princeton, 1916.

De Conde, Alexander. *Entangling Alliance: Politics and Diplomacy under George Washington*. Durham, N.C., 1958.

————. *The Quasi War: The Politics and Diplomacy of the Undeclared War with France, 1797-1901*. New York, 1966.

Fay, Bernard. *The Revolutionary Spirit in France and America*. New York, 1927. (Translated from the French.)

Godechot, Jacques. *L'Europe et l'Amérique à l'époque napoléonienne*. Paris, 1967.

Gottschalk, Louis. *Lafayette and the Close of the American Revolution*. Chicago, 1942.

Lyon, E. Wilson. *Louisiana in French Diplomacy, 1759-1804*. Norman, Okla., 1934.

Mahan, Alfred Thayer. *The Influence of Sea Power upon the French Revolution and Empire, 1793-1812*. 2 vols. 4th ed. Boston, 1894.

Minnigerode, Meade. *Jefferson, Friend of France: The Career of Edmond-Charles Genêt*. New York, 1928.

Morris, Richard B. *The Peacemakers: The Great Powers and American Independence.* New York, 1965.

Palmer, Robert R. *The Age of Democratic Revolution: A Political History of Europe and America, 1760-1800.* Princeton, 1964.

IN THE PERIOD 1815-1914

Bibliothèque France-Amérique. *Les Etats-Unis et la France: Leurs rapports historiques, artistiques et sociaux.* Paris, 1914.

Blumenthal, Henry. *A Reappraisal of Franco-American Relations, 1830-1871.* Chapel Hill, N.C., 1959.

Case, Lynn M., and Spencer, Warren F. *The United States and France: Civil War Diplomacy.* Philadelphia, 1970.

Casper, H. W. *American Attitudes toward Napoleon III.* New York, 1947.

Gavronsky, Serge. *The French Liberal Opposition and the American Civil War.* New York, 1968.

Willson, Beckles. *America's Ambassadors to France, 1777-1927: A Narrative of Franco-American Diplomatic Relations.* London, 1928.

IN THE PERIOD 1914-45

Artaud, Denise. *La France et le problème des dettes de guerre, 1917-1929.* In press.

Gottschalk, Louis. "Our Vichy Fumble," *Journal of Modern History* 20 (March 1948): 47-56.

Harbord, James G. *The American Army in France, 1917-1919.* Boston, 1936.

Kaspi, André. *Le Temps des Américains: Le Concours américain à la France en 1917-1918.* Paris, 1976. (Abridgment of Kaspi's thesis, *La France et le concours américain, 1917-1918.* 1974.)

———. *La Mission de Jean Monnet à Alger, mars-octobre 1943.* Paris, 1971.

Langer, William L. *Our Vichy Gamble.* New York, 1948.

Lemaigre-Dubreuil. *Les Relations franco-américaines et la politique des généraux: Alger 1940-1943.* Paris, 1949.

Nouailhat, Yves-Henri. *Les Américains à Nantes et à Saint-Nazaire, 1917-1919.* Paris, 1972.

———. *Les Relations franco-américaines de 1914 à 1917.* 2 vols. Lille, 1977.

Ornano, Henri d'. *L'Action gaulliste aux Etats-Unis*. Paris, 1948.

Pendar, Kenneth W. *Adventure in Diplomacy: Our French Dilemma*. New York, 1945.

Vigneras, Marcel. *Rearming the French*. Washington, D.C., 1957.

Viorst, Milton. *Hostile Allies: FDR and Charles de Gaulle*. New York, 1965.

IN THE PERIOD FROM 1945 TO THE PRESENT

Haviland, H. Field, Jr. *The United States and the Western Community*. Haverford, Pa., 1957.

Humphrey, Don Dougan. *The United States and the Common Market: A Background Study*. New York, 1964.

Melandri, Pierre. *Les Etats-Unis et l'Europe (1945–1955)*. In press.

――――. *Les Etats-Unis et le "Défi" européen, 1955–1958*. Paris, 1975.

Moore, Ben Tilman. *NATO and the Future of Europe*. New York, 1958.

Newhouse, John. *De Gaulle and the Anglo-Saxons*. New York, 1970.

Northrop, F. S. C. *European Union and United States Foreign Policy*. New York, 1954.

Osgood, Robert E. *NATO, the Entangling Alliance*. Chicago, 1958.

Steel, Ronald. *The End of Alliance: America and the Future of Europe*. New York, 1964.

Zurcher, Arnold. *The Struggle to Unite Europe, 1940–1958*. New York, 1958.

THE TWO COUNTRIES' IMAGES OF EACH OTHER

The early period

Chinard, Gilbert. *L'Exotisme américain dans la littérature française du XVIe siècle*. Paris, 1911.

――――. *L'Amérique et le rêve exotique dans la littérature française aux XVIIe et XVIIIe siècles*. Paris, 1913.

――――. *Les Réfugiés huguenots en Amérique*. Paris, 1925.

(Gilbert Chinard, a French-born scholar whose whole working life was spent in the United States, devoted his entire output to Franco-American relations.)

The period of independence and revolutions

Echeverria, Durand. *Mirage in the West: A History of the French Image of American Society to 1815*. Princeton, 1957.

Villard, Léonie. *La France et les Etats-Unis: Echanges et rencontres (1524-1800)*. Lyon, 1952.

The period 1815-1914

Copans, Simon. *French Opinion of the United States under the Second Empire*. Dissertation, Brown University, 1942.

Demolins, Edmond. *A quoi tient la supériorité des Anglo-Saxons?* Paris, 1897.

Jeune, Simon. *De F. T. Graindorge à A. O. Barnabooth: Les types américains dans le roman et le théâtre français (1861-1917)*. Paris, 1963.

Jones, Howard Mumford. *America and French Culture, 1750-1848*. Chapel Hill, N.C., 1927.

Klein, Abbé Félix. *Au pays de la vie intense*. Paris, 1904.

Rémond, René. *Les Etats-Unis devant l'opinion française, 1815-1852*. 2 vols. Paris, 1962.

Rousiers, Paul de. *Universités transatlantiques*. Paris, 1890.

West, W. Reed. *Contemporary French Opinion on the American Civil War*. Baltimore, 1924.

White, Elizabeth Brett. *American Opinion of France: From Lafayette to Poincaré*. New York, 1927.

The period 1914-45

Duhamel, Georges. *Scènes de la vie future*. Paris, 1928.

Lettres d'un vieil Americain à un Français, traduites de l'anglais par J. L. Duplan. Paris, 1918.

Pomaret, Charles. *L'Amérique à la conquête de l'Europe*. Paris, 1931.

Romains, Jules. *Salsette découvre l'Amérique*. New York, 1942.

After 1945

"Les Etats-Unis, les Américains et la France: 1945-1953." *Sondages*, no. 2 (1953), pp. 1-78.

Of the vast number of French works on American society and attitudes there are a few books (often critical in tone) that merit attention:

Alphandery, Claude. *L'Amérique est-elle trop riche?* Paris, 1960.
Gaument, Eric. *Le Mythe américain.* Paris, 1970.

Americans, since 1945 especially, have not in fact written a great deal
about what they think of France, which they scarcely ever distinguish
from Europe as a whole. They have been extremely preoccupied, on
the other hand, with what other nations think of them.

There is a very fine large-format book, only recently published,
that contains a vast amount of material reproduced from newspapers
in both countries:

Albert, Pierre, ed. *La France, les Etats-Unis et leurs presses, 1632–
1976.* Paris, 1977.

2. The Great Classics

FRENCH WORKS ON THE UNITED STATES

Aron, Raymond. *République Impériale: Les Etats-Unis dans le
monde, 1945–1972.* Paris, 1973.
Beaumont, Gustave de. *Lettres d'Amérique, 1831–1832.* Reprint,
edited by A. Jardin and G. W. Pierson. Paris, 1973.
———. *Marie ou l'esclavage aux Etats-Unis.* Paris, 1835.
Brissot de Warville, Jacques-Pierre, and Clavière. *De la France et des
Etats-Unis, ou de l'importance de la Révolution de l'Amérique
pour le bonheur de la France.* London, 1787.
Chevalier, Michel. *Lettres sur l'Amérique du Nord.* 2 vols. Paris,
1837.
Clemenceau, Georges. *Grandeurs et misères d'une victoire.* Paris,
1930.
Duvergier de Hauranne, Ernest. *Les Etats-Unis pendant la guerre de
Sécession.* Reprint, edited by Albert Krebs. Paris, 1966.
Jusserand, Jules-Joseph. *Le Sentiment américain pendant la guerre.*
Paris, 1931.
Lanson, Gustave. *Trois mois d'enseignement aux Etats-Unis.* Paris,
1912.
Leroy-Beaulieu, Pierre. *Les Etats-Unis au XIXe siècle.* Paris, 1910.
Murat, Achille. *Esquisse morale et politique des Etats-Unis de
l'Amérique du Nord.* Paris, 1830.

Servan-Schreiber, Jean-Jacques. *Le Défi américain*. Paris, 1967.

Siegfried, André. *Les Etats-Unis d'aujourd'hui*. Paris, 1927.

_____. *Tableau des Etats-Unis*. Paris, 1954.

Tardieu, André. *Notes sur les Etats-Unis*. Paris, 1908.

_____. *L'Amérique en armes*. Paris, 1919.

_____. *Devant l'obstacle: l'Amérique et nous*. Paris, 1927.

Tocqueville, Alexis de. *De la Démocratie en Amérique*. 2 vols. Paris, 1835, 1840.

AMERICAN WORKS ON FRANCE

The disparity in volume here is very striking. There are very few books about France by great American writers. The exceptions occur in the early years: Benjamin Franklin and Thomas Jefferson were unforgettable observers of the French scene.

After that, there was no American de Tocqueville, Michel Chevalier, or André Siegfried for France. Nor is there much of interest in the work of the essayists. They concern themselves much more with Europe as a whole than with France in particular.

Since the 1930s, however, it is true that interest in French *history* has increased markedly in the United States. There exists a Society for French Historical Studies with a brilliant array of members, and only space prevents mention of all the works by Louis Gottschalk, R. Palmer, Beatrice Hyslop, Frances Childs, and others, on the French Revolution; of David Pinckney, Lynn Case, Gordon Wright, and others, on the French history of the nineteenth century; and a great number of monographs, some of them excellent, dealing with France in the twentieth century. Of those dealing with the years after 1945 the most notable are:

Bowie, Robert, ed. *In Search of France*. Cambridge, Mass., 1962.

Earle, Edward Mead, ed. *Modern France*. Princeton, 1953.

McKay, Donald. *The United States and France*. New York, 1951.

Lastly, there is the quite exceptional case of Stanley Hoffmann. After pursuing the whole of his studies in France, up to and including his doctorate, at the age of twenty-seven he settled in the United States and is now a professor at Harvard. He alone is in a position to describe both countries from both inside and outside, and the result so far has been two very remarkable books published in both languages:

Hoffmann, Stanley. *Gulliver's Troubles, or the Setting of American Foreign Policy*. New York, 1968.
_____. *Decline or Renewal? France since the 1930s*. New York, 1974.

3. Miscellaneous works cited in the text

Alden, John Richard. *The American Revolution, 1775-1783*. New York, 1965.
Ball, George. *The Discipline of Power*. Washington, D.C., 1968.
Beaumont, Gustave de, and de Tocqueville, Alexis. *Du système pénitentiaire aux Etats-Unis et de son application en France*. Paris, 1883.
Carmoy, Guy de. *Les Politiques étrangères de la France, 1944-1966*. Paris, 1969.
Chinard, Gabriel. *Thomas Jefferson, the Apostle of Americanism*. Boston, 1929.
Conte, Arthur. *Yalta ou le partage du monde*. Paris, 1964.
Cunliffe, Marcus. *George Washington: Man and Monument*. Boston, 1958.
Duroselle, Jean-Baptiste. "Michel Chevalier Saint-Simonien," *Revue Historique* (April-June).
_____. *From Wilson to Roosevelt: American Foreign Policy, 1913-1945*. Cambridge, Mass., 1963.
Fischer, Fritz. *Griff nach der Weltmacht*. Hamburg, 1961.
Fohlen, Claude. *L'Industrie textile en France au temps du Second Empire*. Paris, 1956.
Fontaine, Pascal. *Le Comité d'action pour les Etats-Unis d'Europe*. Lausanne, 1974.
de Gaulle, Charles. *Mémoires de guerre*. 3 vols. Paris.
Ginier, Jean. *Les touristes étrangers en France pendant l'été*. Paris, 1969.
Kennedy, John F. *Strategy of Peace*. New York, 1960.
Keynes, John Maynard. *The Economic Consequences of the Peace*. London, 1919.

Kindleberger, Charles. *Economic Growth in France and Britain, 1851-1950.* Cambridge, Mass., 1964.

Kissinger, Henry. *Troubled Partnership.* New York, 1965.

Lefebvre, Georges. *La Révolution française.* Paris, 1930.

Lerner, Max. *America as a Civilization.* New York, 1957.

de Mandat-Grancey, Baron. *Dans les Montagnes Rocheuses.* Paris, 1884.

————. *En visite chez l'Oncle Sam, New-York et Chicago.* Paris, 1885.

Mantoux, Paul. *Les Délibérations du Conseil des Quatre.* 2 vols. Paris.

Mignet, François. *Vie de Franklin.* Paris, 1848.

Ministère des Affaires étrangères. *Documents diplomatiques français.* Paris, 1871————.

Murphy, Robert. *Diplomat among Warriors.* New York, 1964.

Padover, Saul K. *Jefferson.* New York, 1942.

de Pauw, Abbé Cornelius. *Recherches sur les Américains.* Berlin, 1768.

Raynal, Abbé. *Histoire philosophique et politique des établissements et du commerce des Européens dans les deux Indes.* Paris, 1770.

Sherwood, Robert. *Roosevelt and Hopkins, an Intimate Story.* New York, 1948.

Simonin, Louis. *Le Grand Ouest.* Paris, 1869.

Sorensen, Theodore. *Kennedy.* New York, 1965.

Stourzh, Gerald. *Benjamin Franklin and American Foreign Policy.* Chicago, 1954.

U.S. Department of State. *Foreign Relations of the United States.* Washington, D.C.

Index

Abraham, Plains of, 9
Acadia, 4-5, 7-8
Acheson, Dean, 172, 175
Action Committee for a United States of
    Europe, 194, 197, 226
Action Française, 106
Adam, Paul, 75
Adams, Brooks, 59
Adams, Charles Francis, 55
Adams, John, 25-28, 39-42
Adenauer, Konrad, 190, 214, 223, 226,
    230
Africa, 204, 210, 215; Black, 215; French
    Equatorial, 151, 162; North, 47, 153,
    155-56, 159-60, 212, 244; West, 161
Aguesseau, Henri-François d', 18
Air Force, U.S., 166, 207
Aix-la-Chapelle, Treaty of, 8
Alabama (ship), 56
Alden, John Richard, 27
Alembert, Jean d', 14
Algeciras Conference (1906), 59
Algeria, 153, 156, 159-60, 162, 184, 188,
    201, 204, 209-15, 222, 225, 249
Algerian Provisional Government, 214-15
Algerian War, 209, 211-12
Algérie française, 212-14, 220
Algiers, 153, 160-62, 170, 202
Algonquin (ship), 90
Alliance française, 75
Allied Maritime Transport Council, 95,
    188
Alsace, 47, 52, 58, 87-88, 103-5, 113,
    115-17, 166-67, 209
American Club of Paris, 80
American Committee for the Outlawry of
    War, 131

American Tariff League, 126
André, Major John, 22
Annapolis (Port-Royal), 7
Anschluss, 141
Antilles, 10, 12, 15-17, 21-24, 30, 32,
    41, 48, 153-54
Aranjuez, Treaty of, 26
Ardant, Michel, 76
Ardennes, 167
Arethusa (frigate), 20
Argonne, 101
Armand, Louis, 195
Arnold, Benedict, 22
Artaud, Denise, 123
Asia, 203-4, 210, 231, 233
Assembly of Notables, 31
Aswan Dam, 209
Atlantic alliance, 191, 197, 200, 205,
    215-16, 220, 224, 232, 241
Atlantic Community, 202, 225
Atlantic Council, 191, 232
Atlantic Organization, 232
Atlantic Pact, 182, 185-86, 188, 190,
    204-5, 231
Aubert, Louis, 92
Auriol, Vincent, 174, 193
Avranches, 165
Axis, Rome-Berlin, 138, 160, 163
Ayen, duc d', 18
Azores, Nixon-Pompidou meeting in, 242

Baker, Newton D., 97
Ball, George, 190, 219-20, 223
Bandung Conference, 205
Banque de France, 153, 239
Bao Dai, 204
Barnabooth, A. O., 76

Barrès, Maurice, 113
Barthou, Louis, 137
Bastille, 33, 35
Bayeux, 164
Bazaine, General Achille-François, 55, 57
Bazin, René, 75
Beach, Sylvia, 144
Beaumarchais, Pierre-Augustin Caron de,
    14–15, 29
Beaumont, Gustave de, 61–66, 68
Belgium, 36, 60, 137–38, 183, 203, 207
Belleau Wood, 99
Belle Poule, La (frigate), 20
Benelux, 190, 193
Bergson, Henri, 91
Berlin, 13, 118, 120, 127, 167, 177, 183,
    216, 221
Bermuda agreement (U.S. and Great
    Britain), 196
Bernstorff, count von, 89
Bethmann-Hollweg, Theobald von, 87
Bevin, Ernest, 183
Bidault, Georges, 174, 177–78, 181, 183,
    197
Bienville, Jean-Baptiste, 3
Bigelow, John, 57
Bir Hacheim (battle), 160
Bismarck, Otto von, 110–11
Bizerte, 152
Bliss, General Tasker, 97
Blum-Byrnes agreement, 180
Bohlen, Charles, 172, 175, 232
Boisson, Pierre, 161
Bonaparte, Joseph, 41
Bonaparte, Pauline, 44
Bonnel, Ulane, 38–39
Bonvouloir, Achard, 15
Borah, William, 127, 132, 134, 140
Boscawen, Admiral Edward, 8, 9
Boston, 5, 8, 20–21, 28, 50, 65, 69, 130
Bougainville, Louis Antoine de, 22
Bourbon family, 16, 45–46, 49, 64
Bourgeois, Léon , 113
Bourget, Paul, 75
Bourguiba, President Habib, 210
Boutroux, Emile, 75
Bowen, F. C., 244
Bowie, Robert, 190, 251
Braddock, General Edward, 8–9
Breda, Treaty of, 5

Brest, 20–21, 96, 110, 177
Brezhnev, Leonid, 199
Briand, Aristide, 87–88, 130–35
Broglie, duchesse de, 81
Brunetière, Ferdinand, 75
Bryan, William Jennings, 84, 87
Buck, Pearl, 145
Bulganin, Nikolai, 208
Bullitt, William, 141, 152
Bundy, McGeorge, 220
Burgoyne, General John, 17
Butler, Nicholas Murray, 130

Cabanis, Pierre, 14
Cabet, Etienne, 63
Cachin, Marcel, 119
Café Sélect, 144
Café Voltaire, 144
Caillaux, Joseph, 103
Caldwell, Taylor, 82
Cambodia, 233
Cambon, Jules, 59
Camus, Albert, 145
Canada, 1–2, 4, 9–10, 12, 15, 17, 25–26,
    49, 64, 112, 207, 234–35
Canadian Pacific Railway, 2
Canning, George, 49
Cantigny, 99
Cape Breton Island, 7
Carmoy, Guy de, 194
Carnegie, Andrew, 82
Carnegie Endowment for International
    Peace, 130
Carnot, Lazare, 34
Cartier, Jacques, 2
Case, Lynn M., 57
Castellane, Boni de, 82
Castries, Marquis Charles-Eugène Gabriel
    de, 22
Catroux, General Georges, 160
Cavelier de la Salle, Robert, 3
Chamberlain, Neville, 135, 142
Chamber of Deputies, 50, 107, 109, 120,
    129
Chambrun, René de, 150
Champagne, 101
Champlain, Samuel, 2–3
Champs-Elysées, 164, 239
Charles II, 5
Chasseloup-Laubat, Justin, 57

Chastellux, marquis de, 28, 32
Chateaubriand, Vicomte François René
    de, 62, 65, 76
Château-Thierry, 99
Chemin des Dames, 92, 99
Chesapeake Bay, 5, 22
Chevalier, Michel, 60, 63, 68–72, 75–76,
    203
Childe, Mrs. Frances, 81
China, 2, 59, 140, 170, 176, 216, 228,
    230, 241–42
Chinard, Gilbert, 27, 33, 39, 43
Choiseul, duc Etienne-François de, 14
Choiseul-Praslin family, 82
Churchill, Winston, 118, 147–48, 155–
    56, 161, 164, 167, 169–72, 175
Claudel, Paul, 132
Clausewitz, Karl von, 135
Clay, Lucius D., 183
Clemenceau, Georges: and American in-
    tervention in World War I, 99, 103;
    and Calvin Coolidge, 125; and the
    peace negotiations, 113–17; prestige of,
    in the United States, 150, 158–59;
    travels of, in the United States, 72, 89,
    97; and Woodrow Wilson, 104, 106–7,
    109–12, 118–20, 246. *See also* Tiger,
    the
Clémentel, Etienne, 112
Cleveland, Grover, 81
Cleveland, Harold Van, 190
Clinton, Henry, 19
Cobden, Richard, 72
Colbert, Jean-Baptiste, 7
Coli, François, 132
Collège de France, 72
Colonial Dames of America, 80
Columbia University, 75, 130, 191
Comité des Forges, 88
Comité Français de Libération Nationale
    (CFLN), 161–63
Comité France-Amérique, 75, 81
Comité National Français, 155
Commission on Atomic Energy, 195
Committee of Correspondence, 16
Committee of Public Safety, 34
Common Market, 194–97
Commonwealth, British, 196, 208, 234
Communist Party: French, 173, 185,
    199–200; Italian, 199

Concorde (aircraft), 242, 250
Congo, 219
Congress of the Communist Party of the
    Soviet Union, Twentieth, 203, 207
Conseil impérial, 156
Constant, Benjamin, 81
Constituent Assembly: of 1789–91, 34–
    35; of 1946, 174
Constitutionnel, Le (newspaper), 52
Conte, Arthur, 171
Coolidge, Calvin, 71, 125
Cooper, James Fenimore, 76, 81
Cordeliers (club), 34
Cornwallis, General Charles, 17
Corny, Mme de, 32
Coubertin, Baron Pierre de, 74
Coulet, François, 164
Council of Four, 114
Courrier des deux mondes, Le (news-
    paper), 73
Couve de Murville, Maurice, 224, 238
Cox, James M., 118
Cuba, 58, 77, 228
Cunliffe, Marcus, 19, 23
Czechoslovakia, 137–38, 141–42, 177,
    183, 200

Dakar, 152, 154, 161
Darlan, Admiral François, 152, 156
Daudet, Léon, 83, 106
Daughters of the American Revolution,
    80
Dawes Plan, 127
Deane, Silas, 16–17, 19–20
Decazes family, 82
Declaration of Independence, 13, 15–16,
    28, 220
Declaration of London, 85
Declaration of the Rights of Man and of
    the Citizen, 33
Declaration on Liberated Europe, 172
De Conde, Alexander, 41–42
Deffand, Mme Du, 14
Defferre, Gaston, 229
Degoutte, Jean, 98
Democratic Party, 210, 228
Demolins, Edmond, 74
Destutt de Tracy, Antoine-Louis, 32
Diderot, Denis, 14
Dien Bien Phu, 207

Directory, the, 34, 40-41
Djibouti, 215
Dollar gap, 178-79
Dos Passos, John, 144
Drake, Sir Francis, 22
Dreyfus affair, 246
Drouyn de Lhuys, Edouard, 54-55, 57
Duhamel, Georges, 144
Dulles, John Foster, 190, 192-94, 206, 208-9, 217
Dunkirk, 209
Du Pont de Nemours, Pierre-Samuel, 44
Duras, Mme de, 81

Earle, Edward Mead, 251
East Coast Society, 80
Ecole Polytechnique, 68
Economic Cooperation Administration (ECA), 181, 190
Eden, Anthony, 208
Edict of Nantes, 4
Egypt, 205-6, 208-9
Eisenhower, Dwight D., 159-64, 167, 191-93, 207-8, 211, 213, 216, 218, 222
Eliot, T. S., 144
Elysée Palace, 77, 224
Emancipation Proclamation, 54
Embargo Act (1807), 45
Emerson, Ralph Waldo, 81
Enfantin, Barthélémy, 68
Entente, the, 89-90, 95, 97, 99, 104-6, 118, 122
Erhard, Ludwig, 220, 226
Estaing, Admiral Jean Baptiste, comte d', 20-21
Estates-General, 29, 33
Euratom, 194-96
European Advisory Commission, 169
European Association for American Studies, 158
European Coal and Steel Community (CECA), 190-92, 194
European Community, 202
European Defense Community (EDC), 192-94, 202
European Economic Community, 190, 196, 221
European Free Trade Area, 214
European Free Trade Association, 196-97
European Recovery Program (ERP), 176, 181

European Trade Barrier, 196
Evarts, William, 80
Evian Agreement, 215
Export-Import Bank, 180
Express, L' (newspaper), 230

Fallières, President Armand, 77
Farewell Address, Washington's, 39, 48, 138, 183
Farrar, Marjorie, 86
Faulkner, William, 82, 144-45
Faure, Maurice, 197
Figaro, Le (newspaper), 75, 91
Fischer, Fritz, 87
Fitzgerald, F. Scott, 144
Flanders, 101
Florida, 4, 21, 24, 43-44, 49, 63
Foch, Marshal Ferdinand, 96-97, 99-101, 104-5, 107, 113-15, 117, 119, 150, 153
Focillon, Henri, 150
Folies Bergères, 250-51
Food Administration, 112
Ford Foundation, 220
Fordney-McCumber Tariff, 125
Forrestal, James, 172, 175, 183
Fort: Duquesne, 8-9; Necessity, 8; Saint-Louis, 3; Sumter, 52; Ticonderoga, 17; Vincennes, 7
Fourteen Points (peace program), 102-6
Fox, Charles James, 24
France, La: newspaper, 56; statue by Rodin, 81
France, Anatole, 107
France combattante, 151
France Libre, 151
Franco, General Francisco, 138
Franco-Soviet treaty (1944), 174
Frankfurter, Felix, 94
Franklin, Benjamin, 8, 14, 16, 18-19, 25-30, 32, 35, 90
Franklin-Bouillon, Henry, 120
Franz-Josef, Emperor, 54
Frederick II of Prussia, 9
Free French movement, 234
French and Indian War (Seven Years' War), 6
French Economic Development Plan, 181
French Forces of the Interior, 167
Front de Libération Nationale (FLN), 209, 214

Frontenac, Louis de, 3
Führer, 135-36. *See also* Hitler
Fulbright, Senator J. William, 190, 199

Gaillard, Felix, 212
Gallup, George-Horace, 143, 149
Gasperi, Alcide de, 190
Gates, Horatio, 18
Gaulle, General Charles de: and the
    Atlantic Alliance, 182, 237; and the
    Fifth Republic, 202, 211, 225-31, 233-
    36, 238-40; ideas of, 137, 150-53, 160,
    162, 164, 167-68, 170-71, 173-74,
    176, 188-89, 193-94, 196-97, 214-15,
    223-24, 246; memoirs of, 213, 216-22,
    232, 241, 243; and Roosevelt, 154-59,
    161, 163, 165, 169, 172
Gay-Lussac, Louis-Joseph, 62
Geiger, Theodore, 190
General Electric Company, 237
Genêt, Edmond, 36-38
Geneva, 134, 136, 193, 201, 204, 231,
    242
George II, 8
George III, 18, 24
George Washington (ship), 116
Gérard, comte de Munster, 20
Gérard, General, 99
German-Soviet Pact, 138
Germany, 46-47, 58-60, 78, 87, 90, 93-
    94, 104-6, 113-19, 121-23, 127-28,
    130, 137-38, 140-41, 143, 148-49,
    152-53, 155, 159, 165, 169-70, 177-
    78, 181-84, 187-88, 190-91, 193, 196,
    202, 209, 215, 220, 223, 229, 233, 238,
    241, 244, 250
Gerry, Elbridge, 40
Gershwin, George, 144
Gestapo, 165, 167
Ghent, Treaty of, 45-46
Gibbons, James Cardinal, 62
Gide, André, 145
Gilbert, Parker, 127
Gilson, Etienne, 184
Ginier, Jean, 245
Giraud, General Henri, 155-56, 159-62,
    188
Giscard d'Estaing, Valéry, 229
Gohier, Urbain, 75
Gottschalk, Louis, 251
Graindorge, Frederic Thomas, 76
Grant, Ulysses S., 56, 73, 91

Grasse, Admiral François Joseph Paul,
    comte de, 22-23
Graves, Admiral Thomas, 22
Gravier, Charles, 14
Great Lakes, 3-4, 17, 25, 45, 95
Greeley, Horace, 73
Greenwich Village, 72, 144
Grosser, Alfred, 235
Guadeloupe, 48
Guderian, General Heinz, 137
Guichen, comte Luc-Urbain de,
    22
Guinea, 215
Guines, comte de, 14

Hague Conference, 119, 242
Hahn, Michael, 55
Haig, Douglas, 105
Haiti, 10, 41, 46, 59
Hamilton, Alexander, 37, 42
Hanotaux, Gabriel, 58, 75
Harding, Warren G., 118, 125
Harvard University, 81, 176, 218,
    251
Helvetius, Mme, 14, 32
Hemingway, Ernest, 82, 144-45
Henry, Jules, 141
Herrick, Myron T., 127, 132
Herriot, Edouard, 129, 165, 193
High Commission of the French Republic,
    92
Himmler, Heinrich, 167
Hindenburg, President Paul von, 129-
    30
Hirsch, Etienne, 190
Hitler, Adolf, 121, 130, 135-38, 140,
    142, 206, 209
Hitler-Stalin Pact, 173
Ho Chi Minh, 170, 176, 201
Hoffman, Paul, 190
Hoffmann, Stanley, 220, 237, 251
Holland, 20, 27, 29, 86, 183, 203
Hood, Samuel, 22
Hoover, Herbert, 112, 125-26, 128-29,
    134, 252
Hopkins, Harry, 159
Houdetot, Mme d', 32
House, Colonel Edward Mandell, 87-88,
    91, 104, 106, 109, 113-14
Howe, Admiral Richard, 17, 19
Howe, General William, 18
Hudson Institute, 250

Hughes, Charles Evans, 126
Hughes, Stewart, 251
Hugo, Victor, 158
Huguenots, 4
Hull, Cordell, 153–55, 163
Hulley, John, 190
Humanité, L' (newspaper), 107, 119, 146
Huret, Jules, 75

Ile de France (ship), 133
Indochina, 150, 170, 176, 182, 192, 201,
    204, 207, 210, 233
Indochinese War, 193, 201, 204
Institut de France, 77
Interallied Council, 97
International Bank for Reconstruction and
    Development (World Bank), 180
International Monetary Fund, 180
Ireland, Archbishop John, 62
Iroquois Confederation, 6
Irving, Washington, 81
Israel, 206–7, 231, 234
Italy, 41, 87, 127, 138, 166, 174, 176,
    179, 190, 193, 203, 209, 229
Ivy League, 80

Jackson, Andrew, 45, 50–51, 65, 246
Jacobins (club), 34
James I, 5
Jamestown, 5
Japan, 134, 140, 230
Jardin, André, 65, 66
Jardin des Plantes, 63
Jaurès, Jean, 107
Jay, John, 25–26, 28
Jay Treaty, 38
Jecker debt, 54
Jefferson, Thomas, 16, 27–33, 35–45, 66,
    71, 80, 138, 183, 246
Jessup, Philip, 205
Jeune, Simon, 73, 76–78
Joan of Arc, 159
Jobert, Michel, 242–43
Joffre, Marshal Joseph, 88, 91–92, 94,
    97, 150
Johns Hopkins University, 75
Johnson, Andrew, 73
Johnson, Lyndon B., 219–20, 227, 232,
    239–40
Johnson, Robert Underwood, 84
Joliet, Louis, 3

Jones, Howard Mumford, 79
Journal des Débats, 68–69, 72
Juárez, Benito, 54–57
Juin, Maréchal, 193
Jumonville (French defender of Fort
    Duquesne), 8, 11
Jusserand, Jean-Jules, 59, 61, 86, 91, 108

Kalb, baron de, 19
Kant, Immanuel, 83
Kapp, Wolfgang, 120
Kaspi, André, 92–94, 97, 101, 107, 160
Kearsarge (ship), 56
Keitel, Fieldmarshal Wilhelm, 167
Kellogg, Frank, 132–34
Kellogg-Briand Pact, 121, 134
Kennan, George, 30, 172, 175
Kennedy, John Fitzgerald, 210–11, 218–
    22, 224, 227, 230
Kennedy Round of tariff negotiations,
    228
Keppel, Admiral Augustus, 20
Kermorvan, chevalier de, 18
Keynes, John Maynard, 110, 122
Khrushchev, Nikita, 199, 201, 216
Kindleberger, Charles, 178
King, Rufus, 43
Kissinger, Henry, 240–43
Klein, Abbé Félix, 61, 77
Korean War, 177, 191–92, 200, 207
Kravchenko, Victor, 201

Labiche, Eugène, 77
Lafayette, Gilbert du Motier, marquis de,
    2, 11, 18–22, 29, 32–33, 35, 64, 81,
    84, 86, 92–93, 150, 251
Lafayette, Mme de, 36
Lamotte-Picquet, Comte Toussaint de, 22
Langer, William, 153
Lansing, Robert, 87, 91, 106, 109
Lanson, Gustave, 75
Larbaud, Valéry, 76
La Salle. *See* Cavelier de la Salle, Robert
Latin America, 49, 229
Lattre de Tassigny, General Jean de,
    166–67
Lausanne reparations meeting (1932), 129
Lauzanne, Stéphane, 92
Laval, Pierre, 137–38, 150, 152–53, 165
La Vérendryes, father and son, 4
Lavigerie, Charles-Martial Cardinal, 61

Lavisse, Ernest, 88
League of Armed Neutrality, 20
League of Nations, 112–14, 116, 118, 121, 130, 132–34, 137, 139
Leahy, Admiral William, 153
Lecanuet, Jean, 197, 228
Leclerc, General Philippe, 44, 166
Lee, Robert E., 105
Lee, Richard Henry, 16
Lefebvre, George, 35
Lefebvre de Laboulaye, André, 140
Le Moyne d'Iberville, 3
Lend-Lease Act, 162
L'Enfant, Pierre, 80
Lenin, 107, 119, 199
Leo XIII, Pope, 62
Lerner, Max, 79
Lesseps, Ferdinand de, 81
Levinson, Salmon O., 131–33
Lévy-Bruhl, Lucien, 107
Lewis, Sinclair, 144–45
Libya, 204, 242
Liggett, General Hunter, 100
Lincoln, Abraham, 53–54, 56–57, 72
Lindbergh, Charles A., 131, 136
Livingstone, David, 44
Lloyd George, David, 86, 105, 111, 113–14, 116–18
Lodge, Henry Cabot, 59
London, 4, 14, 16, 25, 30, 36, 43, 46, 49, 55, 61, 69, 86, 111–12, 119, 136, 139, 144, 152, 159, 162, 164, 178, 189
Lorraine, 47, 58, 87–88, 103, 105, 113, 115–17, 166
Louis XIV, 4, 7, 11, 115
Louis XV, 12
Louis XVI, 12–15, 17, 19–20, 29, 36
Louis XVIII, 48
Louisbourg, 7–9
Louisiana, 3–4, 8–11, 24–25, 42–44, 50, 55, 251
Louis Philippe, 50, 64
Lowell, James Russell, 69–70
Ludendorff, General Erich, 95, 98–100
Ludlow, Louis, 139
Lusitania (ship), 86, 89
Luxembourg, 164, 183

MacMahon Act, 196
Macmillan, Harold, 216, 223–24
Madison, James, 35, 39, 45

Malmaison, 82
Mandat-Grancey, baron de, 74
Mangin, General Charles, 98, 100, 119
Mantoux, Paul, 114–15
Marie-Antoinette, Queen, 14, 16
Marne, 83, 91, 99, 150
Marquette, Jacques, 3
Marshall, General George, 99, 176, 180, 183
Marshall, John, 39, 40
Marshall Plan, 176, 178, 180–82, 187, 190
Martinique, 48
Mason, James, 53
Massu, General Jacques, 213
Maurepas, Comte Jean-Frédéric de, 14
Mauriac, François, 145
Maurras, Charles, 106–7, 152
Maximilian, Archduke, 54–57
May, Ernest, 86
Mayer, Arno, 251
Mayflower (ship), 5
McAdoo, William G., 123
McCloy, John, 191
McDougall, James A., 55
McKay, Donald, 251
McNamara, Robert, 221, 241
Melandri, Pierre, 195
Mellon, Andrew, 126
Mellon-Berenger Agreement, 127–28
Mendès-France, Pierre, 193
Mers-el-Kebir, 149, 151–52
Mexico, 54–57, 90, 228–29, 231
Michaux, F. A., 63
Mignet, François, 14
Milbert, Jacques, 63
Mill, John Stuart, 72
Miller, Henry, 82, 144
Mirabeau, 50
Mirage (aircraft), 234
Mississippi River, 3–5, 8–10, 18, 24–26, 29, 42, 65, 69, 72
Mitchell, Margaret, 145
Mittag, Der (newspaper), 218
Mollet, Guy, 197, 208–9, 212
Monde, Le (newspaper), 184
Monnet, Jean: and Algiers, 159–60; and European integration, 190–91, 194–95, 197, 217, 223, 226–28; in First World War, 95, 112; influence of, in United States, 181, 188–91, 212, 220, 231,

241; and Roosevelt, 142, 159
Monroe Doctrine, 49, 54
Monroe, James, 38-40, 44, 49
Montagnards, 34
Montcalm, Marquis Louis de, 9
Montesquieu, Charles de, 13
Montfaucon, 96, 101
Montmorin, Comte Armand-Marc de, 32
Montreal, 2, 4, 9, 65, 235
Morellet, Abbé André, 14, 32
Morgan, J. Pierpont, 82
Morgan bank, 90
Morgan and Company, J. P., 122, 126
Morgenthau, Hans, 30
Morgenthau, Henry, 142
Morny, Duc Auguste de, 54
Morocco, 59, 150, 153-54, 156, 204, 210, 215
Morris, Gouverneur, 12, 33, 35, 38
Moscow, 71, 171-72, 231
Motier, Gilbert du. See Lafayette
Mouvement républicain populaire (MRP), 173, 177
Munich accords, 141-42, 209
Munster, comte de, 20
Murat, Achille, 63
Murphy, Robert, 150-53, 160, 162, 212
Murray, William Vans, 41
Mussolini, Benito, 140, 142

Napoleon I, 10, 34, 41-45, 50, 72-73, 158, 248
Napoleon III, 51, 53-58, 68, 73, 246
Napoleon, Prince Jérome, 51-52
Nasser, Gamal Abdel, 205-6, 208-10
National Assembly, 193, 213, 223, 238
National Constituent Assembly, 33, 172
National Convention, 34, 36-38, 40, 246, 248
National Guard, 35, 50
National Resistance Council, 174
National Security Council, 240
Neuville, Hyde de, 61
New Deal, 139, 145-46
New Diplomacy, 30, 71, 104, 107
New England, 4, 6, 25-26, 69, 81
Newfoundland, 7, 10, 25, 154
New France, 3-4
Newhouse, John, 219
New Orleans, 3, 8, 11, 43-44, 54-55, 65, 69

New York, 5, 16, 19, 61, 64, 69, 72, 92, 150, 160, 220
New York Times, 92, 187, 240
New York Tribune, 73
Ngo Dinh Diem, 201, 204
Nicolet, Jean, 3
Nivelle, Henri, 88, 92
Nixon, Richard, 233, 239-42
Noailles, maréchal de, 18
Nobel: Peace Prize, 132; Prize for Literature, 145
Normandy, 52, 147, 165-66, 229
North Atlantic Treaty Organization (NATO), 187, 210, 218-19, 227, 232
North, Lord, 24
Notre Dame University, 61
Nouailhat, Yves-Henri, 58, 86, 107
Nungesser, Charles, 132
Nuremberg trials, 134

O'Hara, Scarlett, 145
Ohio Company, 7-8
Open Door policy, 59
Organisation de l'Armée Secrète (OAS), 214-15, 223
Orlando, Vittorio-Emmanuele, 114
Orléans, Louis-Philippe, duc d', 11, 50
Orvilliers, Admiral Louis d', 20-21
Oswald, Richard, 25-26
Owen, Robert, 62

Pact of Steel, 138
Padover, Saul K., 43-44
Palmer, Norman, 251
Panama Canal Company, French, 59
Paris, 14, 16, 28-29, 34-35, 38, 40-41, 44, 51-52, 54, 57, 59, 61, 63, 72, 75-77, 81-82, 86, 91, 93, 99-100, 104, 106, 114, 117, 130-31, 133, 144, 164-67, 169-70, 190, 192, 194, 204, 213, 217-20, 239
Paris Pact (1928), 133
Paris, Treaty of (1763), 1, 9-10, 15, 115, 235
Parlements, French, 12
Parliament, British, 12
Pasteur, Louis, 82
Patton, General George, 166
Patrie, La (newspaper), 52

Pauw, Abbé Cornelius de, 13
Pays, Le (newspaper), 52
Peace of Amiens, 42
Pearl Harbor, 154
Pearson, Lester, 235
Penn, William, 5
Perkins, Dexter, 30
Perse, Saint-John, 145
Pershing, General John J., 93, 97, 99,
   100-101, 105, 109, 153
Pétain, Marshal Philippe, 95, 97, 99,
   104-5, 150-53, 155
Philadelphia, 2, 12, 17-19, 22, 37, 65,
   69, 220
Phnom Penh, 233
Picpus Cemetery, Lafayette's grave in,
   93
Pierson, G. W., 66
Pinay, Antoine, 197
Pinckney, Charles Cotesworth, 40
Pinckney, David, 251
Pitt, William, 9-10
Pittsburgh, 8, 65, 69
Pleven Plan, 191
Pleven, René, 191, 197
Plummer, Mary, 73
Poe, Edgar Allan, 76, 82
Poincaré franc, 124
Poincaré, Raymond, 87, 99, 103-4, 124,
   127-28, 130
Poland, 137, 143, 148, 172
Polaris (missile), 224
Poli, Raymond, 158
Polignac, comte de, 49
Polignac family, 82
Pompidou, Georges, 238-43
Popular Front, 145-46
Portalis, Edouard, 73
Port-Royal. *See* Annapolis
Potasse, Eusèbe, 77
Potsdam Conference, 170
Pourtalès family, 82
Prague coup, 183

Quai d'Orsay, 243
Quebec, 3-4, 7, 9, 11, 65, 234-35
Queuille, Henri, 184

Raleigh, Sir Walter, 5
Rassemblement du Peuple Français (RFP),
   181, 197

Raynal, Abbé, 13
Rayneval, Joseph-Mathias Gérond de, 25
Reciprocal Trade Act (1962), 221
Red Army, 168, 172-73, 177
Rémond, René, 60, 66, 76-77
Republic: Third, 73, 165, 175, 246;
   Fourth, 174-75, 177, 187, 197, 202,
   209, 211, 213, 217, 246; Fifth, 202,
   211, 213, 236
Resistance, the, 165-66
Rethondes armistice (11 November
   1918), 102
Reuter, Paul, 190
Review of Reviews, 80
Revolution, French, 29, 33, 35-36, 39,
   49-50, 62-64, 67, 249
Revolution of October 1917, Bolshevik,
   95
Reynaud, Paul, 148
Rhineland, 113-14, 117, 119, 137-38,
   140, 143, 177
Ribot, Alexandre, 90
Richelieu (ship), 160
Ridgway, General Matthew, 200
Rives, William C., 50
Robert, Admiral, 153-54
Robespierre, Maximilien, 34
Rochambeau, Lieutenant General Jean-
   Baptiste Donatien de Vimeur, comte
   de, 21-23
Rockefeller, John D., 82
Rockingham, Lord, 24
Rodin, Auguste, 81
Rodney, Admiral George, 22
Roederer, Pierre-Louis, 42
Rohan-Chabot family, 82
Rolland, Romain, 107
Roman Catholic Church, 4
Rome, Treaty of (1957), 195-96
Roosevelt, Franklin Delano: and aid to
   France, 139-43, 146; and de Gaulle,
   154-65, 169-73; and defeat of France,
   148-51; and French debts, 129; ideas
   of, 58, 84, 118, 135; prestige of, 175,
   222, 229, 234; and Vichy, 151, 153, 212
Roosevelt, James, 58
Roosevelt, Theodore, 59, 77, 85, 91
Root, Elihu, 59
Rough Riders, 77, 85
Rousiers, Paul de, 74
Rousseau, Jean-Jacques, 13

Rueff, Jacques, 236
Russia, 45, 49, 54, 87, 95-96, 121, 135,
    173, 177, 183-84, 203, 209, 216, 225
Ryswick, Treaty of, 7

Saar, the, 115-16, 178
Saint-André, baron de, 61
Saint-Domingue, 41, 44, 46
Saint Ildefonso, Treaty of, 43
Saint-Just, Louis de, 248
Saint Lawrence River, 1-4, 7-9,
    26, 72
Saint-Mihiel, 100-101
Saint Nazaire, 93, 96, 108
Saint Pierre and Miquelon, 48, 154-55,
    234
Saint-Simon, comte de, 68
Salter, Arthur, 95
Sanford, Henry, 51
San Francisco Conference, 169
Saratoga, Battle of (1777), 17-18
Schuman Plan, 190-91, 194
Schuman, Robert, 183, 187, 191, 197, 241
Schumann, Maurice, 197, 242
Security Council, 170
Seicheprey, 99
Selective Service Act, 96
Senate Committee on Foreign Affairs,
    127, 132
Servan-Schreiber, Jean-Jacques, 197, 230
Seven Years' War, or French and
    Indian War, 6
Seward, William, 52-53, 55-56
Shakespeare and Company (bookstore),
    144
Sherman, General William Tecumseh,
    56, 145
Sherwood, Robert, 155
Shotwell, Professor James, 130-32
Siegfried, André, 144, 245-46, 250
Simonin, Louis, 74
Siney, Marion, 86
Six, the, 191-92, 194, 196, 228
Six-Day War, 234
Skybolt (missile), 224
Slidell, John, 53-54
Smith, Adam, 30
Smith, Cyrus, 76
Smoot-Hawley Tariff, 125
Society for French Historical Studies, 251
Somalia, 215

Somme, 99, 101
Sorbonne, vii, 77
Sorensen, Theodore, 218
Soviet Union, 2, 71, 133, 135, 137-38,
    162-63, 170-71, 173-74, 182, 184-86,
    192, 199-200, 203, 206-8, 217, 231-
    33, 241, 252
Spain, 9-10, 12, 17, 19-20, 24, 26, 29,
    43, 48-49, 54, 58-59, 138, 192
Spanish Florida, 5
Spencer, Herbert, 72
Spencer, Warren F., 57
Spirit of St. Louis (airplane), 131
Stalin, 136, 156, 169, 171-73, 175, 177,
    188, 199-201, 203
State Department, 102, 132, 155, 172,
    175, 190
Statue of Liberty, 80-81
Stehlin, General Paul, 197, 226
Stein, Gertrude, 82, 144
Steinbeck, John, 82, 145
Stendhal, 72
Stimson Doctrine, 134
Stimson, Henry, 129, 134, 143, 163
Stockholm peace appeal, 200
Stowe, Harriet Beecher, 51, 76
Sudetenland, 141-42
Suez Canal, 81, 205-11, 250
Suez Canal Company, 205, 208-9
Suffren, Pierre-André de, 22
Supreme Headquarters of Allied Powers
    in Europe (SHAPE), 187, 191-92, 232

Taine, Hippolyte, 76, 245
Talleyrand, Charles-Maurice de, 40-41,
    44, 81, 238
Tannenbaum, Frank, 30
Tardieu, André, 75, 92, 94, 116
Teitgen, Pierre Henri, 197
Temps, Le (newspaper), 72, 75
Terror, the, 34, 37, 248
Tessé, Mme de, 32
Thermidorian Convention, 34
Thiers, Adolphe, 58, 68
Third Republic, 58
Third World, 205
Thorez, Maurice, 200
Thouvenel, Edward, 51-54
Thureau-Dangin, Paul, 50
Tiger, the, 73, 103, 106, 109-10, 114.
    See also Clemenceau

Tocqueville, Alexis de, 60, 63–69, 71–72, 74–76, 81, 203
Track, William, 77
Trent (ship), 53
Triple Entente, 182
Truman Doctrine, 176
Truman, Harry, 159, 175–76, 179–81, 191, 228
Tuck, Edward, 82
Tuileries palace, 34, 41
Tunisia, 152–53, 160, 204, 209–10, 212, 215
Turgot, Anne Robert Jacques, 14–15
Turner, Frederick Jackson, 249
Twain, Mark, 82

Underwood Tariff, 125
United Nations, 155, 170, 204–7, 215, 219; General Assembly, 205, 207; Security Council, 207
Uri, Pierre, 190
Utrecht, Treaty of, 7, 154

Valley Forge, 2, 18–19
Valmy, 34, 36
Vandenberg Declaration, 183
Vanderbilt, Cornelius, 82
Vendée, 109–11
Verdun, 83, 86, 101, 150, 152
Vergennes, comte de, 14–17, 20, 24–26, 28, 32
Verne, Jules, 76
Verona, Congress of (1822), 48
Verrazano, Giovanni da, 4
Versailles, 4, 15–16, 23, 27–28, 64, 118
Versailles treaty, 110, 113, 118–19, 122–23, 130, 137, 140, 203
Vichy, 151–53, 156, 161, 164–65
Victoire, La (ship), 19
Viet Minh, 204
Vietnam, 205, 242; South, 201, 233
Vietnam War, 201, 227, 231, 233, 236, 238, 252
Villers-Cotterêts, 100, 150
Vimeur, Lieutenant General Jean Baptiste Donatien de, comte de Rochambeau. *See* Rochambeau
Virginia, 5, 7–8, 22–23, 30–31
Virginia Company, 5
Viviani, René, 91
Volney, comte de, 44

Voltaire, 10, 13–14

Wahl, Nicolas, 251
Wallace Fountains, 82
Wallace, Henry, 175
War Department, 96
War of the Austrian Succession, or King George's War, 6
War of 1812, 45
War of Independence, 10, 20, 29, 35, 80
War of the League of Augsburg, or King William's War, 6
War of Secession (the Civil War), 51, 54
War of the Spanish Succession, or Queen Anne's War, 6
Washington, D.C., 51, 55–56, 59, 61, 65, 69, 80, 86, 91, 97, 102, 127–28, 131, 150–51, 162, 164, 190, 192, 195–96, 202, 204–5, 207–9, 214, 218, 220, 230, 233, 244
Washington, George, 8, 11, 13, 16–19, 21–22, 27–28, 35–37, 39, 48, 63, 138, 183, 246
Washington Post (newspaper), 240
Watergate, 242
Waterloo, Battle of, 45–46
Weimar Republic, 121
Welles, Sumner, 139
Wehrmacht, the, 137, 147
Werth, Alexander, 223
Weygand, General Maxime, 153
Weygand-Murphy agreement, 153
Whigs, 24
White, Elizabeth Brett, 79
White House, 140, 175
William II, 59, 104
Wilson, Harold, 237
Wilson, Woodrow: and the First World War, 84–93, 96–97; French opinion of, 83; and the peace, 73, 102, 104–7, 109, 111–21, 130, 141, 246; and the war debts, 123, 125
Woëvre, plain of, 101
Wolfe, General James, 9
World Bank. *See* International Bank
World Economic Conference, 139
World Peace Foundation, 130
World Trade Conference, 231
World War, First, 150, 244
World War Foreign Debts Committee, 127

World War, Second, 62, 95, 98, 144, 147, 166, 245
Wright, Gordon, 251
Wylie, Lawrence, 251

Yalta, 156, 169-72

Yom Kippur War, 242
Yorktown, 22-24, 80
Young Plan, 128

Zimmermann telegram, 90

'F